The Story of the
Tour de France

*How a Newspaper Promotion Became
the Greatest Sporting Event in the World*

Volume 1: 1903–1964

By Bill and Carol McGann

Picture credit: All pictures are from the collection of and copyright Fotoreporter Sirotti and are reprinted with his permission.

First published by Dog Ear Publishing
4010 W. 86th Street, Ste H
Indianapolis, IN 46268
www.dogearpublishing.net

ISBN: 1-59858-180-5
Library of Congress Control Number: 2006930198

This book is printed on acid-free paper.

Printed in the United States of America

Table of Contents

Acknowledgements and an explanation

If this history has any merit it is because of the generous help I have had from so many kind people.

Two men stand out, Owen Mulholland and Les Woodland. You will probably recognize their names because they have been prolific and valuable contributors to the literature of cycling for decades. Both men possess a depth of knowledge not only of bike racing but also of history and general culture that is nothing short of astonishing. They have put this vast storehouse of personal accomplishment at my service time and time again. When I grew shy about asking for so much help they both made it clear that I was not to hold back. I took them at their word and was rewarded with endless valuable insights and countless little-known facts, nearly all of which I quite happily included in this work. They have searched for answers when I could not find them, they allowed me to quote from their books, they have given me priceless advice and they have been kind and good friends.

A case in point. When I had trouble identifying riders in an old photograph, the erudite Mr. Woodland posted it on a Flemish chat room with my question translated into Flemish. Within minutes the zealous bike-mad Flemings had the answers I needed. This was a solution that was utterly beyond me.

In addition to fielding my countless inquiries Mr. Mulholland reviewed the text of this book and made numerous valuable suggestions, saving me from committing several crimes against the English language.

I should try to be like them.

Scott Gibb and Mary Lou Roberts also scrutinized the text along the way, making sure that people with varying levels of familiarity with the subject and jargon of cycling would understand the story. I ended up incorporating almost all of their suggestions.

Podofdonny of www.dailypeloton.com graciously let me use his telling of the 1951 Tour as the basis of my own history of Hugo Koblet's beautiful win.

Francesca Paoletti drew the map of France at the beginning of the book. I needed a map that was drawn specifically for a Tour de France history and Francesca has done a wonderful job.

Antonio and Mauro Mondonico and Valeria Paoletti also lent invaluable help. Peter Joffre Nye caught an error that few scholars in the world would have had the knowledge to see. My gratitude to them and the many others, listed in the bibliography, is profound.

Special thanks are due to Joël Godaert, Robert Janssens and Guido Cammaert, authors of the Tour Encyclopedie. In their words, they researched the results of each and every Tour like archeologists. I depended heavily upon their work, which is now largely posted on www.memoire-du-cyclisme.net. The *Memoire* site is a wonderful store-house of information that was an essential tool in completing this story. The prodigious work the contributors to the site performed is a valuable service that has earned my deep gratitude.

Any errors are my own.

An explanation

As Tolkien wrote, this was a tale that grew in the telling. It started out as a short history of the Tour for my website to guide many of the people who, because of Lance Armstrong's Tour success, were brought into an appreciation of the greatest sporting event in the world. Sports writers, enthusiasts and even one poet often displayed a ferocious enthusiasm for the event but didn't understand the history and culture of the Tour that guided the organizers and the European fans. I set out to do my part to try to bring some light to the subject.

As I drafted the first short history, old Henri Desgrange fascinated me with how he turned another cheap newspaper promotion into an event that now paralyzes much of the sporting world for 3 weeks. That fascination drove me to expand my history of the Tour to what you now have.

Originally envisioned as a single volume, the history of the Tour was too rich and the story too big for 1 book. It escaped it original confines and will be issued in 2 volumes. The first, which the reader holds, is the story from the Tour's origins to 1964, the year of Jacques Anquetil's fifth and final win. This seemed to be a good place to divide the work. The second volume, scheduled to be completed in the late fall of 2006, will take the story of the Tour from the 1965 to 2006.

I have done no original research for this first volume. The stories have been told over and over. What I tried to do was to explain each year's edition and how a particular rider came to win it. Along the way, there was almost always a good tale to tell. Some years are more interesting than others and that is reflected in the amount of space devoted to a given year.

Any writer delving into the history of the Tour finds himself in a morass of errors and self-serving propaganda. Since some of these fables are now part of the lore of the Tour, I have retold them anyway, pointing out where I believe they depart from fact.

A note on names. Many racers' names, especially early Flemish ones, either have several possible spellings, or their names were changed by French reporters. Often this French rendition is the way we know them. Jozef becomes Joseph. Ferdy Kübler becomes Ferdi Kübler. I have tried to use the names that the racers were either born with or at least as they were used by their countrymen. When following this rule would create more confusion, I have ignored it. For example the Buysse brothers (Lucien was the winner of the 1926 Tour) were officially surnamed Buyze. Nowhere in the literature of the Tour have I found them so referenced, so Buysse they shall remain.

There is nothing like the Tour. Come along and join me in the story of how stubborn, willful, brilliant, dictatorial Henri Desgrange created the most exciting, important and spectacular sporting event in the world.

FRANCE

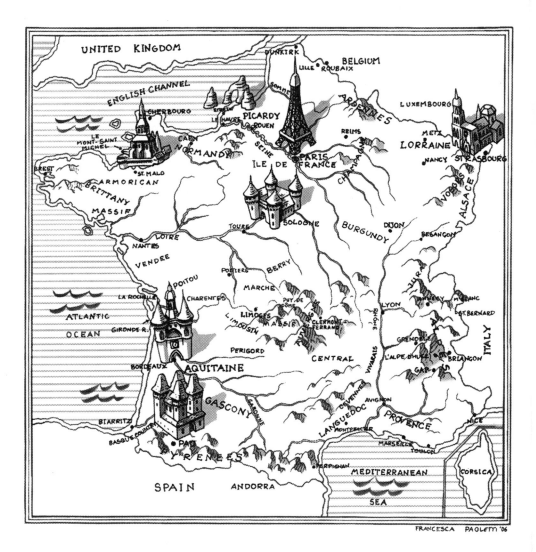

FRANCESCA PAOLETTI '06

Preface by Owen Mulholland

After forty years of study on the subject, I can with some confidence say Bill and Carol McGann's *The Story of the Tour de France* is the finest such work ever produced in the English language, and perhaps in any. Most of my preferred references are in French, one runs to over 800 pages, yet the McGanns' opus revealed information new to me in almost every paragraph. His research has been not only impeccable, but insightful. After all, it is a huge subject, one that can overwhelm the reader with details on top of details on top of details.

The great asset here is the choice of significant details. Where else could I have discovered the 1927 Tour was the first since 1903 to start without a former winner in its ranks? Anger of some sort formed a portion of Lance Armstrong's amazing drive to win, but he never matched Henri Pélissier's ability to offend. Once Pélissier stopped to respond to a "call of nature" and the whole peloton attacked just to get even. McGann lavishes an entire paragraph on a stage sprint in the 1925 Tour because it was such a Who's Who of the time. What better way to remember the Armstrongs and Ullrichs and Bassos of 80 years ago?

Patterns within patterns—personalities, capabilities, technologies, route changes, loyalties, jealousies and feuds, financial interests, even political influences—all are masterfully weaved here into a giant fugue that points past itself to even larger portents. For much of human history most people have struggled to satisfy the minimum necessities of food, clothing, and shelter. In the centuries B.C. the Greeks managed to satisfy those necessities sufficiently well they were able to turn their attention to what it means to be truly human. Among other things this meant activity with no ulterior purpose, i.e. play.

A 2,000 year hiatus had to be endured before humanity could

find itself on this level again. In the late nineteenth century many forms of play were invented, but for us bike fans none were as interesting as those on two wheels. The Tour de France is an ultimate expression of the will to play. The Tour's current popularity is no accident. This book reveals the endless experimentation the Tour endured before arriving at the modern synthesis of flat, mountain, and time trial stages necessary to provide the kind of contest we've come to expect, and of course it's a process that will never end.

Nor should it be forgotten what a debt we owe to France and its culture for this amazing invention. Nowhere else did the necessary synthesis emerge. The U.S. may beat the world to the moon, but when it comes to how to make life on earth worth living one could do worse than emulate the French. The recent Tours of Georgia and California imply as much.

This is a book you will want to read and read. This is a book you will take to bed at night, and after you've turned out the light your dreams will be filled with the images conjured here. We can hardly thank Mr. McGann enough for his combination of clear prose revealing careful research about our favorite subject.

Introduction

The Tour de France started as nothing more than a publicity stunt to sell some newspapers. At its heart, the Tour remains just that, a vehicle to sell tires, shoes, bikes, telephones and countless other items that the eager sponsors of the teams and the race want to promote. To this day, it is a combination of the tawdry, the magnificent, the base, the noble, the crassly commercial and the spectacular. Others have noted that its roots are in the lowest and the highest motivations of human endeavor. That is why it is so fascinating.

Over the passing years, the Tour has grown into something much more than a sales tool. It is, simply, the greatest athletic test in the world. A 3-week bike race, called a "Grand Tour", is much like a Bach Concerto. It is dense, complex and difficult for a newcomer to really understand. It is also impossible for a newcomer to the sport to win. Even so-called "phenoms" in cycling have been racing and preparing for many years before their eventual breakout victory. In 2004, Damiano Cunego was only 22 years old when he won the Italian equivalent of the Tour de France, the Giro d'Italia. He was no newcomer to racing. He had been racing for over 7 years when he won the Giro.

Some sports, such as basketball, are straightforward enough that a man right out of high school, if he has enough talent, can perform at the highest professional level. You will not see that happen in the Tour de France. It's impossible. And the athletic challenge is greater than requiring a long, difficult preparation in order to toughen the body and sharpen the mind. The window of time in which a racer can effectively compete for victory in the Tour is cruelly short. In the last 50 years, only 4 men over 32 years old have been able to win. Only 1 of the 5 men who have won the Tour 5 times have been able to win upon reaching their thirty-second birthday. The ever-so-slightly-older body cannot recuperate from the daily blows the Tour delivers to the system. For just a brief, beautiful time, when the body is at its glorious best and after a lifetime of work an unusually talented man can try for the greatest palmare in cycling. And then it's over.

In America, we watch the Tour and marvel at the tenacity, strength and endurance of the competitors. To us it is a fascinating but purely athletic event. Europeans see the great bike races such as the Tour in a slightly different light. They often view the confrontations of the athletes in metaphorical terms. Their sports writing is laced with terms such as "redemption", "confirmation", and "torment". To an American, Jan Ullrich is a racer who couldn't quite measure up to Lance Armstrong. In Europe he can be a Hector, who, knowing he will lose, still dons his armor and goes out to battle. A French friend once told me that one cannot understand France without understanding the Middle Ages. Almost all Medieval French literature is simile and metaphor. That tradition carries on in cycling literature. When you come across European press reports of a bike race or a translation of a French book on cycling, the verbiage may seem overblown and Wagnerian. It's the difference in cultures and history. Beholding an athletic event such as the Tour as a confrontation symbolizing higher themes gives greater interest and depth to the sport. Owen Mulholland, America's finest Tour historian, tells the following story:

"Just read the columns written by Henri Desgrange, Jacques Goddet, and Pierre Chany and you will soon be swept into analyses of mere mortal cyclists struggling against the infinite and measuring those struggles in terms of European religious and historical metaphors.

"*L'Equipe* was kind enough to give me a perfect example one day. Throughout the 1997 Tour the French hero, Richard Virenque, had thrown himself against the German 'übermensch', Jan Ullrich. It was obvious Virenque was not going to bring down his adversary, but all France loved how he never gave up trying. One day, *L'Equipe's* headline blared, *'Richard Virenque, le coureur sans peur et sans raproche!'* (Richard Virenque, the racer without fear and beyond reproach). Although unexplained in the article, it was just assumed every reader would recognize the reference to France's most famous medieval knight, the Chevalier Bayard.

"There is no end of Bayard stories about his heroism, loyalty, generosity, and indefatigable capabilities when once engaged on the field of battle. My favorite tells of his death while fighting in the rear guard as the French army retreated. He received a mortal wound, was lifted from his horse, and set against a tree. The king, seeing his favorite knight in distress, rushed to Bayard's side and inquired as to what he could do. Bayard's reply was, "Fear not for me, my lord. I die with my face toward the enemy" (unlike the king, who was retreating).

"Now look at the attitude of Virenque through the spectacles of Bayard. How Virenque's actions are elevated and filled with insight and deeper appreciation!"

Chapter 1

Origins and the first 2 Tours. How a culture war in turn of the century France spawned the greatest sporting event in the world

Almost from the dawn of the invention of the bicycle, newspapers used bicycle road racing to increase their circulation. They would sponsor a race, drumming up publicity for the paper. They ended up creating their own news for which they were the only suppliers in the age before television and radio. Very early on, brutally long races of epic difficulty became the norm. In 1869, *Le Vélocipède Illustré*, seeking to promote itself and the bicycle, sponsored the 130-kilometer long Paris–Rouen. That doesn't seem so far today, but this was before paved roads and the modern safety (chain drive to the rear wheel) bicycle. It took the winner, James Moore, over 10 hours to cover the distance. The races got longer. *Le Vélo* ran Bordeaux–Paris and *Le Petit Journal* organized Paris–Brest–Paris, races that were stupefyingly hard. The newspapers thrived on them as people all along the route bought papers to learn about the progress and the final victors of the race. Bicycle manufacturers helped sponsor professional riders who promoted the bikes with their superhuman efforts.

At the turn of the twentieth century, the French magazine *Le Vélo* had upset its advertisers with its high rates. To make matters worse, one rich industrialist was very unhappy that its editor, Pierre Giffard, was on the wrong side of the Dreyfus affair. Alfred Dreyfus was an Alsatian Jew who was railroaded with manufactured evidence into a life sentence on Devil's Island for supposedly passing secrets to the Germans. After 3 trials he was pardoned and eventually exonerated. France split along conservative and progressive fault lines with a fury that is hard to understand today. The greatest writers and thinkers of the time, including Émile Zola and Anatole France, lined up against the government in favor of Dreyfus.

An aside: there is a lesson for us today. The Dreyfus affair was a terrible case of ethnic profiling in which an innocent man, fitting an ignorant set of prejudices, was wrongly convicted of a crime. The government, the military and the church, trying to protect themselves, their neatly preconceived notions and institutions, were willing to let Dreyfus rot on Devil's Island. Today, as we let a fearful and aggressive government set aside our precious and cherished constitutional rights, let us remember Alfred Dreyfus and that nothing is more important than justice. If we don't, our children will view us with the same contempt as we view Dreyfus' jailers.

The 2 sides, Pro-Dreyfus and Anti-Dreyfus, were more interested in the cultural war he symbolized than in Dreyfus himself. For this reason, the affair consumed France almost as powerfully as the French revolution a century before. Today, the effects of this affair still resonate in France. It is a more secular and civilian country because of the reforms enacted in its aftermath. The Tour de France is just one unexpected consequence.

To continue:

The Compte Dion was an engine manufacturer who had recently been jailed for participating in a violent anti-Dreyfus demonstration. Dion, who was a substantial advertiser in the green pages of *Le Vélo*, received a visit from Giffard while he was in jail. Nothing is terribly clear about what happened during that jailhouse meeting, accounts differ. But the result was a complete breach between them. After the meeting Giffard, not worrying about the financial consequences, wrote a passionate pro-Dreyfus editorial.

Angered by high advertising prices and Giffard's politics, a group of *Le Vélo* advertisers, led by Dion and manufacturers Michelin and Clément, defected. They formed a new magazine, *L'Auto-Vélo*, with the express intention of driving *Le Vélo* out of business. Devoted to sports in general with an emphasis on cycling, it was to be printed on its now legendary yellow paper to contrast with the green of *Le Vélo*. They made Henri Desgrange, a cycling promoter and former racer, its editor. The founders were familiar with Desgrange because he had worked for Clément doing public relations work. A man of many hats, Desgrange had written a successful book about racing, *Head and Legs*. Over the years the importance of racing with the head as well as the legs (*la tête et les jambes*) would become a Desgrange mantra. He had also managed a velodrome that got little mention from Giffard, another sore point.

Henri Desgrange, the father of the Tour de France, in an undated photo, probably in the 1930s.

Desgrange had already earned cycling immortality by setting the first World Hour Record of 35.325 kilometers in 1893. His record wasn't even close to the limits of human endurance. A little over a year later

Jules Dubois added almost 3 kilometers to the record. But Desgrange was there first. His sense of promotion was clearly evident.

Le Vélo sued the upstart magazine for plagiarism, claiming that the new magazine's name infringed upon *Le Vélo's* name. *Le Vélo* won the lawsuit in January 1903. The new magazine was forced to change its name to *L'Auto*. To make the sporting emphasis clear, they added the subheading, *Motoring, Cycling, Athletics, Yachting, Aero-navigation, Skating, Weightlifting, Horse-racing, Alpinism. L'Auto* was hardly the right name for a magazine wanting to attract cycling fans.

From the beginning, the 2 magazines fought a ferocious war for circulation. *L'Auto* was in trouble. Its backers were restless over the lack of success. What to do? Or as Desgrange put it, speaking about Giffard, "What we need is something to nail his beak shut."

In November of 1902, there was a now-famous lunch in a Parisian restaurant called *Zimmer* (the same location has now become a *TGI Fridays* restaurant). Géo Lefèvre, a writer hired from *Le Vélo* to cover cycling, proposed the idea of a race on roads all around France to Desgrange.

Les Woodland, in *The Yellow Jersey Companion to the Tour de France,* recounts the following conversation between Lefèvre and Desgrange:

"Géo Lefèvre said, Let's organize a race that lasts several days longer than anything else. Like the 6-days on the track, but on the road. The big towns will welcome the riders.'

"Desgrange replied: 'If I understand you, petit Géo, you're proposing a Tour de France?'"

As will happen repeatedly with Desgrange, he was initially cold to the idea. But as he and Lefèvre discussed it, Desgrange understood the genius of the idea. He seized it and made it his own. It would entail 6 days of racing with rest days in between each stage. Desgrange apparently took credit for the idea when he proposed the race to the financial controller of *L'Auto,* Victor Goddet. Goddet, to the surprise of Desgrange, approved the idea, understanding the huge promotional value of the epic proposal.

The loss of the plagiarism suit gave *L'Auto* fresh reason to proceed with all due speed with the race in order to promote the magazine to cycling fans. *L'Auto* had already been losing the circulation war before the name change and they needed to act. The other sports magazines had their own races, but Lefèvre's idea would completely leapfrog these others in scope and appeal.

1903. Just days after it lost the lawsuit, on Jan 19, 1903, *L'Auto* announced the first Tour de France. It was to be "the greatest cycling trial in the entire world. A race more than a month long: Paris to Lyon to Marseille to Toulouse to Bordeaux to Nantes to Paris." The original schedule was for a 5-week race with a May 31 start and a finish in Paris on July 5. The winner would be the racer with the lowest elapsed time racing after the 6 stages. This total time was and still is called the "General Classification".

With a week to go before the start only 15 riders were signed up. As a sign of the adaptability and willingness to change that has always characterized the Tour, Desgrange shortened and re-scheduled the race to a July 1 start and July 18 finish. There would be 2 to 4 rest days between each of the stages except for stage 4, which would be held the day after the 268-kilometer third stage. To attract more riders, expense money of 5 francs a day was promised to the first 50 racers who signed up and a 20,000 franc purse of prize money was dangled.

Desgrange got his first peloton. 60 riders departed from the now famous Cafe au Réveil-Matin in Montgeron on the southern outskirts of Paris at 3:16 p.m., July 1. Of these, 21 were sponsored or professional racers. There were a few racers in the pack who competed under pseudonyms. Racing was a sketchy business and not always held in high repute. Julien Lootens raced the 1903 Tour as *Samson*. Later Lucien Mazan would compete in the Tour as *Petit-Breton*.

Lefèvre, only 26 at the time, traveled with the race while Desgrange remained in Paris. Desgrange stationed men along the way, sometimes hidden, to make sure that the riders rode the entire route. They rode 6 stages totaling a staggering 2,428 kilometers.

Desgrange, from the very beginning, wanted his race to be a superhuman test of an individual's endurance and strength. He banned pacers from his race except for the final stage. At the time, racers employed lines of pacers to lead them, much as a protected professional rider uses his team today. At the time this was quite a change from the norm and many, including eventual winner Maurice Garin, doubted that it would work.

Maurice Garin, riding the red, white and blue tricolor bike of his sponsor, La Française, won the first stage of the first Tour, beating Émile Pagie by 55 seconds. The first stage, from Paris to Lyon was 467 kilometers long, and it took a cruel 17 hours, 45 minutes, riding both day and night, for Garin to finish. Only 37 riders were able to complete the day's racing. The 37th rider took more than 20 hours longer than Garin to get to Lyon. Hippolyte Aucouturier, one of the favorites, had to drop out with stomach cramps.

Today, that abandonment would put an end to his Tour. Back then, a racer was allowed to race for stage wins even if he had failed to finish a previous stage, which Aucouturier did. A racer who failed to finish a stage was out of contention for the overall lead. Pagie, the victim of a crash in the second stage had to abandon the Tour. He never rode the Tour again.

On the first stage, a racer was caught cheating. Jean Fischer was seen pacing behind a car. I haven't found any particular record of a sanction for this breach of the rules. If Desgrange could have known what 1904 was to bring, perhaps he would have made an example of Fischer.

Aucouturier, who was quite revived after dropping out of the first stage, won the second and third stages, from Lyon to Marseilles and Marseilles to Toulouse. Garin maintained his lead, by this time almost 2 hours over second place Léon Georget who would drop out of the race in stage 5. Garin won the penultimate stage, still in the lead.

On July 19, 21 of the 60 starters finished. The 20,000 spectators at Paris' *Parc des Princes* velodrome saw Maurice Garin win the final stage and win the Tour. The final finisher came in over 2 days later. While the famed "Yellow Jersey" worn by the man leading the Tour would not be adopted until 1919, Garin was given a green armband to signify his lead during the 1903 Tour, and the *Lanterne Rouge* or Red Lantern was used to designate the rider in last place. Arsène Millocheau has the dubious fame of being the first *Lanterne Rouge* by coming in at 64 hours, 57 minutes, 8 seconds behind Garin in total time.

Garin, riding for the powerful La Française team, was nicknamed "the Chimney-Sweep" for his occupation before he became an accomplished professional bicycle racer. He won the first stage and held the lead throughout the Tour. His win was no accident. He was by far the finest and strongest racer in the Tour. He was already a 2-time winner of Paris–Roubaix as well as a victor of Bordeaux–Paris and Paris–Brest–Paris.

Garin pocketed 6,125 francs for his exploit, enough to buy a gas station where he worked the rest of his life after retiring from racing. To this day, a gas station still stands on the spot of Garin's old station. But as Les Woodland noted in *The Unknown Tour de France*, no one working there has any idea about the importance of the former owner of the site. Garin is quite forgotten.

Adjusting for currency and inflation across a century is highly inaccurate, but those 6,000 francs Garin won should be something like $40,000 in today's U.S. dollars. Garin's winning margin of 2 hours and 49 minutes remains the largest in Tour history. The first Tour at 2,428 kilometers remains the second shortest ever. The 1904 Tour was shorter than the 1903 version by 8 kilometers. The average speed for this first Tour was 25.679 kilometers per hour. The 50th Anniversary Tour in 1953 averaged 34.593 kilometers per hour and the speed of the Centennial 2003 Tour was 40.94 kilometers per hour. There were dramatic changes in equipment, training, roads, diet, Tour rules and sometimes even doping over the next 100 years that made this increase possible.

The Tour was a fantastic success. Circulation of *L'Auto* boomed. 130,000 copies were printed for the final stage (an increase of 100,000). *Le Vélo* went out of business and the Tour de France was born. Desgrange, knowing talent when he saw it, hired Giffard to write for *L'Auto*.

Final 1903 Tour de France General Classification:

1. Maurice Garin: 94 hours 33 minutes 14 seconds
2. Lucien Pothier @ 2 hours 59 minutes 2 seconds
3. Fernand Augereau @ 4 hours 29 minutes 24 seconds
4. Rodolphe Muller @ 4 hours 39 minutes 30 seconds
5. Jean Fischer @ 4 hours 58 minutes 44 seconds

1904. Desgrange and Lefèvre had a tiger by the tail. Their race was immensely popular. The 1904 version followed the same 6-stage clockwise route again, and took about 3 weeks in July. There was no shortage of racers this year. 88 took off from Paris on Saturday, July 2. The best riders from the first Tour, Garin, Pothier (both riding for La Française) and Aucouturier were considered the favorites.

It was a strange Tour and no one is sure exactly what happened. Because the stages were so long, the riders were required to ride at night. Even with Desgrange's men doing what they could to watch the race, cheating was easy. Some riders were accused of hopping in a car. Others took trains. Moreover, Desgrange's race had lit fires of passion among racing fans that would almost be the ruin of the race. Partisan mobs hindered and helped various riders.

Early in the first stage, Hippolyte Aucouturier, riding for Peugeot, suffered a substantial time loss because of numerous flat tires and crashes. The inexplicable bad luck seemed to be the result of sabotage. Before the stage even ended he was out of contention. He ended up finishing the stage 2 $1/2$ hours behind the winner and the other favorite, Maurice Garin.

Garin had his own troubles. Towards the end of the first stage, coming into Lyons, Garin and Lucien Pothier were riding away from the others when a carload of thugs tried to run them off the road. Garin was able to get by them and win the stage.

It was thought that Garin was getting illegal feeds from race officials. It turns out that Garin was pressuring Lefèvre to help him. Lefèvre, even though he was a race official, did not want to endanger the participation of the Tour's genuine star by having Garin drop out from hunger. Lefèvre succumbed to the pressure to break the rules. As we'll see, this bit of official corruption is very unusual in the Tour. This rarity is one of the reasons the Tour is the most important race in the world.

The news of Garin's cheating further inflamed the fanatical crowds. During the second stage, on the Col de la Républic, a group of hoodlums waited in hiding for the racers. They planned on beating or knifing the leaders to help their local favorite, Antoine Faure. After first being warned by angry race fans driving in a car alongside Garin and Italian Giovanni Gerbi, this mob attacked the pair. Gerbi suffered broken fingers and was forced to return to Italy. After race officials intervened to break up the mob, Garin pressed on. Eventually Aucouturier, Pothier, and César and Maurice Garin made it just about together to the finish, with Faure only a couple of seconds behind.

The hooliganism continued into the third stage. Ferdinand Payan was disqualified for taking pace from riders not entered in the race. When the race went through Nîmes, near Payan's home town of

Ales there was another riot. The racers fought with the crowd that had traveled from Ales to obstruct the race. Barricades were set up and some of the riders had to defend themselves against armed spectators. Tour officials had to fire a revolver to disperse the crowd. All along the 1904 Tour route, partisans continually threw nails on the roads.

Aucouturier won the last 2 stages but had lost too much time in the first stage to make up the difference to the very powerful Maurice Garin.

At the end of the race, Maurice Garin was ahead by a far smaller margin than in 1903, probably because of all the crashes and flats caused by the saboteurs. At first, his victory of a little over 3 minutes seemed to stand. Then an inquiry was initiated into the abuses of the race. The UVF (*Union Vélocipédique Française*) carefully waited until December to announce its judgment, well aware of the passions aroused by the race. The UVF disqualified the first 4 riders, disciplined a total of 29 riders and awarded the Tour victory to the youngest winner in Tour history, 20 year old Henri Cornet. To the end of his life, even though he probably cheated by taking a train and getting illegal feeds, Garin publicly maintained that he was robbed and that he was the rightful winner of the 1904 Tour.

But wait…it's not quite that simple. Garin maintained a public face but in his old age was a bit more honest to his friends. Again I refer to Les Woodland and his *Unknown Tour de France*. Woodland tracked down an aging friend of Garin's and asked him about the scandalous Tour and the accusations against Garin. "He admitted it. He was amused about it, certainly not embarrassed, not after all those years. There wasn't the same significance to the Tour then, of course, and he used to laugh and say, 'well I was young, quoi…' Maybe at the time he said he didn't, but when he got older and it no longer mattered so much."

The man who was awarded the victory, young Henri Cornet, was also guilty of cheating. He had been warned not to take further liberties with the rules after he got a lift in a car. The race was just completely out of the control of the organizers.

At first Desgrange despaired. "The Tour de France is over. Its second edition, I very much fear will have been its last. It will have died of its success."

After he was finished moaning and the sanctions were administered by the UVF, he set about planning the 1905 Tour.

The 1904 General classification as of July 23:

1. Maurice Garin, 93 hours 6 minutes 24 seconds
2. Lucien Pothier @ 3 minutes 28 seconds
3. César Garin @ 1 hour 51 minutes 13 seconds
4. Hippolyte Aucouturier @ 2 hours 52 minutes 26 seconds
5. Henri Cornet @ 2 hours 59 minutes 31 seconds

The final 1904 Tour de France General Classification after the UVF judgment on December 2, 1904:

1. Henri Cornet, 96 hours 5 minutes 55 seconds
2. Jean-Baptiste Dortignacq @ 2 hours 16 minutes 14 seconds
3. Aloïs Catteau @ 9 hours 1 minute 25 seconds
4. Jean Dargassies @ 13 hours 4 minutes 30 seconds
5. Julien Maitron @ 19 hours 6 minutes 15 seconds

Chapter 2

1905–1913. From an unruly race that was almost ruined by the passions of its fans, the Tour grows to an early maturity

1905. Desgrange understood that he had to make the race easier to supervise, in order to reduce cheating. The 1903 and 1904 versions of the Tour had been decided on elapsed time, but for 1905 Desgrange changed to points to determine the winner. The rider with the lowest total when his placings were added up won the race. If a racer won all 11 stages he would have a points total of 11. This method continued until 1913. Today, this system is used, with some refinements and adjustments, to determine the winner of the sprinter's competition for the Tour's Green Jersey.

Desgrange also shortened the stages and increased their number. The 1905 edition had 11 stages, reducing the amount of riding in the dark. The longest stage of 1905 was the fourth stage, 348 kilometers. It was still terribly long by modern standards but nothing like the stages of the earlier Tours that could approach 500 kilometers. The 1905 Tour was substantially longer, being 2,994 kilometers, compared to the roughly 2,400 kilometers of the first 2 editions.

The 1905 Tour is notable for another big change. One of Desgrange's staffers, Alphonse Steinès, had a vision of how to make the Tour even more heroic. He wanted to include mountains. Up until now the Tour had been raced almost entirely on flat roads. So far the 1,145 meter high Col de la République was the only lump the racers had to climb. At Steinès' urging, Desgrange had the Tour take a trip through the Vosges Mountains in Eastern France with the Ballon d'Alsace (12.5 km of a 5.2% average gradient, with a patch of 10%) and the Col Bayard climbs. Desgrange was terribly afraid of a failure. He reluctantly buckled under Steinès' advocacy, telling him if the racers could not get over the mountains, the blame would belong to Steinès. Yet Desgrange, true to form, took the credit when it was a roaring success.

Fans still scattered nails to hinder the riders. It was estimated that 125 kilograms of nails were used on the roads of the first stage. Since only 15 riders were able to make it to the finish of that first stage on their bikes, Desgrange let riders who arrived by car or train start the next day without disqualification. Yet, for all that, the 1905 edition was more civilized than the year before. Louis Trousselier, riding for Peugeot, won the first stage and the lead.

The second stage, from Nancy to Besançon, had the feared climb up the Ballon d'Alsace. The riders were allowed to change to bikes with lower gears. On the climb, it came down to a contest among 4 riders: Trousselier, René Pottier, Hippolyte Aucouturier and the winner of the 1904 Tour, Henri Cornet. Trousselier succumbed first, then Aucouturier couldn't take the pace. It was left to the young Cornet and Pottier in the final kilometers. Finally Cornet had to yield and let Pottier ride away. At the top of the mountain Pottier changed bikes. To make that defeat more painful, Cornet had to wait at the top of the mountain for 20 minutes for his replacement bike with a higher gear for the descent and run-in to Besançon. His support car with the bike had broken down. Aucouturier caught and dropped Pottier, the first "King of the Mountains" and won the stage by 10 minutes. At the end of the stage, Pottier had the lead in the General Classification with 7 points to the 9 held by both Aucouturier and Louis Trousselier.

Pottier, having suffered a crash during the stage, was unable to start stage 3.

The next day, stage 4 from Grenoble to Toulon included the Bayard and Laffrey climbs. Aucouturier and Trousselier dueled in the mountains with Aucouturier the winner. He rode into Toulon 24 minutes in front of Trousselier. While the time differences are a good tool to understand the relative strengths of the riders, they in no way affect the standings. A win by a second is as good as a win by an hour.

The General Classification after stage 4:

1. Louis Trousselier: 16 points

2. Hippolyte Aucouturier: 16 points

3. Jean-Baptiste Dortignacq: 44 points

Trousselier won 2 more stages and made sure that he had high placings in the others. His consistent riding earned him a clean victory. He ended up with only 35 points to Aucouturier's 61. Remember, the lowest points total won. Trousselier, nicknamed "Trou-Trou" by the public, had a tough edge. At one checkpoint where the riders were required to sign in, he broke the inkstands so that following riders could not sign in.

The night after he won the final stage, Trousselier spent the entire evening gambling and drinking with his friends. When the night was over, Trousselier had lost every bit of his Tour winnings, 6,950 Francs. Since he had taken an unofficial leave from the army to ride the Tour, the next day, broke, he rejoined his regiment.

Final 1905 Tour de France General Classification:

1. Louis Trousselier: 35 points

2. Hippolyte Aucouturier: 61 points

3. Jean-Baptiste Dortignacq: 64 points

4. Émile Georget: 123 points

5. Lucien Petit-Breton: 155 points

1906. Desgrange was really getting a feel for what would make the Tour de France "click". The larger number of shorter stages was a success. The inclusion of tough climbs was a clear winner, adding excitement and a new element of contention to the mixture. The 1906 Tour was even longer, 4,543 kilometers broken into 13 stages. This time the Tour made a real circumnavigation of the perimeter of France.

The riders begin the 1906 Tour de France

René Pottier, who in the previous year became the first man to abandon the Tour while holding the lead, had his eyes set on the victory from the start. In the second stage, even though he was the victim of several flat tires and had been forced to ride on the rim for a while, he fought his way back to the front. He then broke away and soloed to victory taking the lead in the General Classification. He held the lead for the rest of the Tour.

The climbing ability that he had shown on the Ballon d'Alsace in 1905 was a taste of what was to come. When the 1906 Tour hit the mountains in the third stage Pottier took off and stayed away, riding alone for 200 kilometers for the win. The next rider, Georges Passerieu, came in over 47 minutes after Pottier. Pottier's mastery of the sport was complete. Not everyone was happy with the Tour's inclusion of mountains. At the stage's end in Dijon, 4 racers were disqualified for taking the train. Desgrange had brought the cheating under control but did not eradicate it.

Pottier, who wore a strange, floppy white hat, won the next 2 stages, making it 4 in a row. Georges Passerieu did well winning 2 stages and placing highly in the others, but Pottier was not to be denied that year. To finish things off properly, he won the final stage.

It was this 1906 Tour that saw the *Flamme Rouge* (Red Flag) placed at the 1 kilometer to go mark on each stage.

Pottier's joy in his wonderful victory was short-lived. In January of 1907, René Pottier hanged himself in the clubhouse of his Peugeot team. He despaired after learning that he wife had engaged in an affair while he was riding the Tour.

Final 1906 Tour de France General Classification. Only 14 of the 75 starters made it to Paris.

1. René Pottier: 31 points
2. Georges Passerieu: 39 points
3. Louis Trousselier: 59 points
4. Lucien Petit-Breton: 65 points
5. Émile Georget: 80 points

Before continuing, it would be useful to understand the bikes and the roads of these early days. Today's athletes race up the Tour's monster climbs on modern, reliable 20-speed lightweight machines. The equipment then was quite different. The first Tour bikes had single-speed fixed gears, as on a track bike. With but the one exception of Arsène Millocheau, the first riders could not freewheel (coast without the pedals turning) even though freewheels had been commercially available since 1898. It wasn't until 1906 that the freewheel again showed up in the Tour and made a difference. Once mountains had to be descended, a fixed gear was a real impediment because it forced the riders' legs to turn as the rear wheel forced the cranks to turn. A rider could either remove his feet from the pedals or limit his downhill speed. One racer had footpegs welded onto his forks for descending so that he could take his feet off the pedals.

Both Garin's 1903 bike and Trousselier's 1905 bike had toe clips, but no straps. Petit-Breton's 1908 bike did have straps. Exactly when straps were adopted is very hard to pin down because the pictures are grainy. It looks like sometime around 1907 to 1908.

The gearing on early Tour competitor Jean Alavoine's bike was 22 x 11 (with a modern half-inch chain, the gearing would be equal to 44 x 22). For the mountains, lower gears were mounted and the riders were allowed to change bikes. Looking at the gearing one is surprised at how low the ratio is. In his wonderful book, *Hearts of Lions*, Peter Nye showed that early racers were capable of and did race at very high cadences. Sometime between 1910 and 1913, dual sided rear hubs became the norm. With 2 different sized freewheels, one on either side of the hub, a racer could climb a mountain in one gear, dismount and flip his wheel around to use a smaller sprocket and descend in a higher gear.

The rims were of wood with tubular tires glued onto the rims. Brakes were incredibly primitive. At first they were pads that rubbed the tops of the tires. Around 1910, caliper brakes seem to have become common. The calipers were steel and had very low mechanical advantage. They just didn't stop the way modern brakes stop. The bars and stem were both of steel. The frames were generally lugged steel.

Modern bikes have a wheelbase (the distance from axle to axle) of about 1 meter. The early bikes had wheelbases of about 1.2 meters. The fork rake was generous for 2 reasons. First, the roads were usually unpaved and the spring of the extra rake was needed to soften the impact of the appalling roads. Also, with the slacker angles of the early bikes, more rake was needed to keep the trail correct for good handling.

Several sources hold that Garin's 1903 bike was about 20 kilograms (42 pounds). The eminent British cycle historian Derek Roberts told me that at the turn of the century, bikes were available to the public that weighed about 28 pounds. It seems unlikely that an accomplished, sponsored professional cyclist would have anything less. Jacques Seray's meticulously researched *1904, the Tour de France which was to be the last* says Garin's bike and that of the other top pros weighed 11.5 kilograms (25.5 pounds). In light of Mr. Roberts' information, this makes sense to me. This is what I would expect a mild-steel track bike with steel cranks to weigh.

The roads were usually unpaved. Dust, mud, cobbles, rocks, even cattle and sheep were the normal conditions. This is why you always see pictures of early racers with goggles. In the mountains, the riders would often ride on tracks that were little more than footpaths.

1907. The Tour became international in 1907. For the first time, the route went into Germany. Not just anywhere into Germany, but through Alsace-Lorraine, territory taken from France in the Franco-Prussian war. Remember the Dreyfus affair? That Dreyfus was from Alsace was one of the reasons he was suspected of spying. The sensitivities surrounding the subject were still very close to the surface of the French consciousness. Desgrange got permission from the German government to have his Tour go to Metz. The German authorities treated the riders better than the French did. When the Tour re-entered France, 2 French customs officers held up the riders so long with their intrusive examinations that the stage had to be re-started. After World War One, Alsace and Lorraine were returned to France.

René Pottier would have been the favorite, expected to repeat his dominating win. With his tragic suicide taking him out of the picture, others could again dream of winning the Tour de France.

Louis Trousselier won the first stage, from Paris to Roubaix. Then Émile Georget won 5 out of the next 7 stages including both mountain stages. At the end of stage 8, Georget had a commanding lead, 13 points to Trousselier's 29 points.

Since Desgrange found that the mountains really made his Tour a better competition, he decided that a little more would be a lot better. He included a taste of the western Alps by sending the riders up the Col de Porte in the Chartreuse Massif in the fifth stage. This was a much harder climb than the Ballon d'Alsace that had given him palpitations 2 years before. Émile Georget came in almost a half-hour ahead of eventual winner Petit-Breton, but with the points system, he might as well have been ahead by 5 hours.

It was on stage 9, from Toulouse to Bayonne, that things went wrong for Georget. He crashed at a checkpoint. His Peugeot teammate Gonzague Privat gave Georget his bike. This bike change was against Desgrange's strict rules that the rider start and finish with the same bike. While this was going on, Petit-Breton was scooting down the road and winning the stage, beating the field to the finish by 23 minutes.

After Garrigou won stage 10, here were the standings:

1. Lucien Petit-Breton: 39 points
2. Gustave Garrigou: 54 points
3. Émile Georget 64.5 points

The Tour organization was hard on Georget but not cruelly so by the standards of the Tour and the time. Not wanting to eliminate a star rider whose adventures sold papers, they added enough points to put him in third place in the General Classification. Petit-Breton, also a

Peugeot rider, by virtue of his masterly stage win and the penalties heaped upon Georget, was now in the lead.

Petit-Breton is the name usually used when writing about this fine racer, Lucien Mazan. He is sometimes called "The Argentine" because his father had emigrated to Buenos Aires. The father didn't want his son to race bicycles, so a pseudonym was taken to keep the occupation secret from the family. In 1905 Petit-Breton set a new World Hour Record of 41.11 kilometers. At the start of the 1907 season he won the first Milan–San Remo. He was an accomplished track racer with a very good sprint. In all of those early 20th century photographs, he looks lean, quick and always perfectly groomed with a carefully upturned "Hercule Poirot" waxed mustache.

Reflecting the hardness of the rivalry between Peugeot and Alcyon, Trousselier's Alcyon team wasn't happy with the penalty given to Georget. They didn't want him to receive a mere points penalty, they wanted him out of the race. Not getting their way, they withdrew completely from the Tour. This would not be the last time an angry team pulled out of the Tour, but it was the first.

Georget went on to win 2 more stages. He surely would have won the Tour if that unfortunate bike change had not occurred.

Petit-Breton was the winner, finishing with 47 points to Gustave Garrigou's 66 and Georget's 74.

Final 1907 Tour de France General Classification:

1. Lucien Petit-Breton: 47 points
2. Gustave Garrigou: 66 points
3. Émile Georget: 74 points
4. Georges Passerieu: 85 points
5. François Beaugendre: 123 points

No discussion of the 1907 Tour is complete without mentioning Henri Pépin who styled himself Baron Henri Pépin de Gontaud. The title wasn't valid, being an expired relic of pre-revolution days that the family continued to affect. Yet the man was a gentleman. Perhaps inspired by Baron de Coubertin, the originator of the modern Olympics, this sporting amateur nobleman was determined to take part in the Tour de France. The participation, not the victory, was to be the reward.

Pépin hired 2 professional riders, Jean Dargassies and Henri Gauban, to ride with him and assist him through the Tour. Because they were professional riders who would forfeit a lot of money by riding for the "Baron", Pépin generously promised to pay them more for helping him than they would earn even if they won the Tour. Who could resist that proposition?

The trio set off. They ate in nice restaurants and took their time completing the stages. They would interrupt a stage and have a delicious gourmet meal before getting on their bikes to complete the stage. The angry timekeepers had to wait long hours until the 3 gentlemen arrived at the finish. This was before the Tour instituted cutoff times that eliminated the slower riders. They took more than 12 hours longer to complete the second stage than the winner, Georget. They sang songs and waved to the crowds. They became famous as they ambled across France.

One day they came across an exhausted, famished rider in a ditch. This was before Desgrange instituted the broom wagon in 1910 to carry abandons to the finish. They got him up, got him to a restaurant, fed him and were now a quartet.

Pépin was wearied by the fifth stage and abandoned. Honorable man that he was, he paid the full wages to Dargassies and Gauban and took the train home. He tried to ride the Tour again in 1914, but again could not finish. He died shortly thereafter.

1908. Henri Desgrange hated teams, sponsors, combines and anything that would make his Tour less than the supreme test of the individual. He wrote eloquently about the beauty of the athlete's endurance and will. It was always the greatness of the individual athlete that moved him. He spent his remaining years fighting technical innovation as well as the natural tendency of men to form alliances to further their mutual goals. For 1908 he required the racers to ride on frames the Tour organization provided. They could be built with some components of the racer's choice. The bikes were then stamped and sealed. Desgrange thought this would at least lessen the influence of the hated sponsors.

The 1908 Peugeot team had some of the greatest riders of the time on its roster: Petit-Breton, Émile Georget, François Faber, Hippolyte Aucouturier and Henri Cornet. Both Petit-Breton and Cornet were former Tour winners. The individual Peugeot team members had already accumulated over 20 stage wins during the short life of the Tour de France. There was no team to compare with the 1908 Peugeot squad. Alcyon, another powerhouse, would begin its fabled days of dominance next year.

114 riders started in Paris, riding the same route as the 1907 edition. Petit-Breton was the favorite given his dual talents of riding long stages with power and endurance as well as his quick sprinting. The points format of this era favored a sprinter. Winning by a second or by an hour counted the same in the General Classification. Petit-Breton raced with his head, keeping himself at or near the front of those stages he couldn't win. Racing under rules in which the rider had to perform his own repairs, being a good mechanic could be as important as being a strong racer. Petit-Breton was a skilled bicycle mechanic.

The first stage, from Paris to Roubaix, went to Georges Passerieu with Petit-Breton 5 minutes slower. The other major contender, François Faber, was another 4 minutes back. Already, the competition started to take shape. Petit-Breton took the second stage with Passerieu right behind him. Passerieu still had the overall lead, even though they were tied at 3 points each.

Stage 3 with its climb up the Ballon d'Alsace broke the deadlock. Petit-Breton took the lead in the General Classification when he came in second to Faber. To get an idea of the riding conditions and bikes of the time, only Georges Passerieu was able to climb what is now considered a modest ascent without getting off his bike and pushing it up the hill.

The General Classification after stage 3:

1. Petit Breton: 5 points

2. Luigi Ganna: 20 points

3. Gustave Garrigou: 24 points

Big François Faber won again in stage 4, but his teammate Petit-Breton was right with him.

Stage 5 included the 1,326 meter high Col de Porte. Passerieu won by 19 minutes. The big time gap meant little with Petit-Breton finishing in third place, tightening his grip on the race.

Faber and Petit-Breton virtually traded stage wins throughout the balance of the Tour, demonstrating the power of the Peugeot team. By my count, Peugeot won all 14 stages.

Petit-Breton won 5 stages and finished out of the top 4 only once. Faber won 4. Peugeot captured the top 4 places in the General Classification.

Final 1908 General Classification:

1. Lucien Petit-Breton: 36 points

2. François Faber: 68 points

3. Georges Passerieu: 75 points

4. Gustave Garrigou: 91 points

5. Luigi Ganna: 120 Points

   36 out of the 114 starters finished the 1908 Tour.

In World War One, Petit-Breton, the first racer to win the Tour twice, was a driver in the French army, and was killed in a head-on collision.

1909. Always the adaptable opportunist, Desgrange abandoned his 1908 requirement that all the riders compete on Tour-supplied frames. The teams went back to riding their own bikes. Still, the bikes of all riders were stamped by the Tour organization to make sure that the riders started and finished with the same machine. Desgrange never let go of this plan to take the riders off their own factory produced and sponsored bikes. In 20 years we'll see this idea come back with a vengeance.

Petit-Breton said that he was passing the baton to his teammate François Faber. The 1909 Tour would be a worthy test for the big man from Luxembourg. Faber was nicknamed "The Giant of Colombes" for the suburb of Paris that he then called home. For the time, he was truly a large man, being about 6 feet (1.86 meters) tall and weighing 200 pounds (91 kilos). Even today, that is huge for a man in the business of winning Grand Tours.

Alcyon had finally put together a first-class team, hiring Faber away from Peugeot. The Alcyon manager, Alphonse Baugé, who earlier had been an inexperienced neophyte, was now a knowledgeable and wily veteran.

The peloton for the start of the 1909 edition was big. 150 riders decided to take their chances. If they had known what they were in for, they might have reconsidered. The riders were forced to compete, even by the standards of the time, under appalling conditions.

Cyrille Van Houwaert won the first of the 14 stages. Then Faber went on a tear. He performed the unequaled feat of winning 5 stages in a row.

The second stage, 398 kilometers from Roubaix to Metz, was ridden entirely in freezing rain. Faber, all power and strength, rode the second half of that stage solo in a magnificent breakaway. He was now leading in the General Classification.

Stage 3 went over the Ballon d'Alsace. Faber took the snow- and ice-covered mountain by himself and finished a half hour in front of Gustave Garrigou. The next rider, Eugéne Christophe, came in an hour later.

Stage 4 was another epic Faber adventure. Coming into Lyon, the finish town, he broke his chain. The most famous picture of Faber shows him pushing his bike at a full run on the wet streets of Lyon, his right hand holding his bike by the bars, no chain to be seen. The crowd is thick and deep, all bundled up against the strange cold weather of that July. Even with all this trouble, he still beat the next rider by 10 minutes.

The man was unbelievable. The next stage, which took in the Col de Porte, was held in wind so strong that Faber was twice knocked off his bike. He even had a horse knock him down and kick his bike away. Still Faber remounted and pressed on and again won alone.

He wasn't done. Stage 6, with the Col Bayard and Côte de Laffrey didn't slow down the huge Faber. Yet again he won alone.

The General Classification after stage 6:

1. François Faber: 7 points
2. Gustave Garrigou: 24 points
3. Cyrille Van Houwaert: 32 points

Faber had some bad luck in the next few stages, but won again in stage 10. The weather during that first week had been so bad that after 7 stages 77 riders abandoned.

The final stage saw another rider with a broken chain run with his bike for a victory. Jean Alavoine got his crippled bike across the line first for the 13th Alcyon stage victory out of a possible 14. Alcyon took the first 5 places in the final stage and the first 5 places in the final General Classification. Their dominance was more complete than Peugeot's in the 1908 Tour. Faber's victory is also notable in that the stages he won were the hardest and run in the worst weather.

The Final 1909 Tour de France General Classification:

1. François Faber (Alcyon): 37 points
2. Gustave Garrigou (Alcyon): 57 points
3. Jean Alavoine (Alcyon): 66 points
4. Paul Duboc (Alcyon): 70 points
5. Cyrille Van Houwaert (Alcyon): 92 points
6. Ernest Paul (*isolé* or independent, and Faber's half-brother): 95 points

A few postscripts to the 1909 Tour:

It is thought that the 1909 Tour was raced in the coldest weather ever.

François Faber, being a citizen of Luxembourg, was the first foreigner to win the Tour.

François Faber was every bit the hero his race fans thought he was. In World War One the powerful giant died, shot in the back while carrying a wounded comrade back to the French lines through no man's land.

1910. Alphonse Steinès desperately wanted to expand the Tour and make it even more monumental, so for the 1910 edition he badgered Desgrange into including the first modern high mountain stage. Steinès knew that the story of the assault on the high mountains would be great for the race and fantastic for *L'Auto's* circulation. It would be an exciting exploit, seizing the attention of the public.

Desgrange, ever the fearful boss of the Tour, was reluctant to include a challenge that might be beyond the racers. Even though that first climb in 1905 had been successful, and tougher climbs than the Ballon d'Alsace had been included in subsequent editions, the Pyrenees were another matter again. These were mountains!

With 2 months to go to the start of the 1910 Tour, Desgrange sent Steinès to the Pyrenees to see if indeed, it was practical for the riders to climb the mountains in the Tour de France. His reconnaissance trip was very eventful. Ascending the Tourmalet his car was stopped on the mountain by a snowdrift. Abandoning the car, he set off on foot and lost his way on the snowy mountain at night. He finally fell off a ledge of snow into a ravine. The locals who set out to find the missing scout found him at 3:00 a.m. Steinès sent the following famous telegram to Desgrange: "No trouble crossing Tourmalet. Roads satisfactory. No problem for cyclists. Steinès"

Desgrange was sucked in. He announced in *L'Auto* that the 1910 Tour route would include ascents of the Peyresourde, Aspin, Tourmalet and Aubisque mountains. It would be 4,737 kilometers long and divided into 15 stages. The penultimate stage from Brest to Caen would be the longest, at 424 kilometers. Stages 9 and 10 would feature climbing in the Pyrenees with the tenth stage the promised colossus.

In modern times teams bulging with talent have come under terrible stress as the best riders vie for the honor of being the team's protected man. The most famous recent example is probably the 1986 Tour with the tension in the La Vie Claire team. Bernard Hinault reneged on his promise to help Greg Lemond win, and both men fought hard for victory. Hinault insists, it must be noted, that he did help Lemond, but that story must wait. The rivalry between Hinault and Lemond tore the team into 2 separate camps. The past is prologue. Alcyon had assembled a magnificent stable of superb athletes allowing them to take the first 5 places in the 1909 Tour. For 1910, it was assumed that their man François Faber would be the man to win the Tour. But the addition of the Pyreneen stages tipped the balance a bit towards another rider on the Alcyon team, Octave Lapize, setting up the intra-team competition.

With a victory in stage 2, Faber was on track to repeat Petit-Breton's 2 consecutive Tour wins. Faber was riding just as he had the year before. His second stage win was a solo victory with Garrigou 7 minutes back and third place Octave Lapize a stunning 17 minutes slower. Eleventh place Trousselier was almost an hour behind.

By stage 4, Faber had won half the stages and was assembling a substantial lead. He had 8 points while second place Garrigou had 23. Faber flagged a bit on the fifth stage, which went over the Col de Porte. Octave Lapize showed that he had his climbing legs on for this Tour, winning the stage with Faber sixth, 22 minutes back.

Faber struck back, winning stage 7 despite a crash that would leave him injured for the rest of the Tour. At the end of stage 8, before the Tour's first day in the Pyrenees, here was the General Classification:

1. François Faber: 33 points

2. Octave Lapize: 48 points

3. Cyrille Van Houwaert: 56 points

All 3 were riding on the Alcyon team. This was not turning out to be the Faber runaway that 1909 was.

Stage 9 was 289 kilometers from Perpignan to Luchon. The riders were to climb the Portel, the Col de Port, the Aspet and the Ares. This was not the epic day that Desgrange had promised. This was only the lead-in. Octave Lapize won by 18 minutes over Émile Georget and was 22 minutes ahead of third-place Faber. Now Faber's Achilles heel was showing. The massive man had trouble getting his giant body over the bigger mountains. Yet because the race was determined by points, not by time, Lapize had only slightly closed the gap to Faber.

The tenth stage of the 1910 Tour was a 326-kilometer brute that included the 4 monster mountains, the Peyresourde, the Aspin, the Tourmalet and the Aubisque. Desgrange didn't have the heart to watch and had his assistants supervise the stage. If the stage were a debacle, at least he wouldn't have to witness it. Fearing the worst, he made another addition to the 1910 Tour, the Broom Wagon. It followed the last rider to pick up those who could not finish the stage. Desgrange had ruled that a rider unable to finish the mountain stage could ride to the finish in the Broom Wagon and start again the next day.

The riders departed at 3:30 a.m. in order to finish the titanic stage. Lapize took off and was first over the Peyresourde and the Aspin. On the Tourmalet, Lapize's teammate Garrigou caught him. The 2 riders dueled up the mountain with Lapize getting a 500 meter lead over the top.

On the Aubisque, the last of the big climbs, Steinès and an assistant, Victor Breyer, stationed themselves well up the mountain at a point in the stage with 150 kilometers to go. They waited for the first rider. Breyer wrote of the moment when they saw the first man coming up the mountain:

> And suddenly I saw him, a rider, but one I didn't know.
> His body heaved at the pedals, like an automaton on 2 wheels.
> He wasn't going fast, but he was at least moving. I trotted
> alongside him and asked, "Who are you? What's going on?

Where are the others?" Bent over his handlebars, his eyes riveted on the road, the man never turned his head nor uttered one sole word. He continued and disappeared around a turn. Steinès had read his number and consulted the riders' list. Steinès was dumbfounded. "The man is François Lafourcade, a nobody. He has caught and passed all the 'cracks'. This is something prodigious, almost unbelievable!"

Still the minutes passed. Another quarter-hour passed before the second rider appeared, whom we immediately recognized as Lapize. Unlike Lafourcade, Lapize was walking, half leaning on, half pushing his machine. His eyes revealed an intense distress. But unlike his predecessor, Lapize spoke, and in abundance. "You are assassins, yes, assassins [*Vous êtes des assassins!*]" To discuss matters with a man in this condition would have been cruel and stupid. I walked at his side, attentive to all he said. After more imprecations, he finished by saying, "Don't worry, at Eaux-Bonnes [the town at the bottom of the mountain] I'm going to quit"

—from *Uphill Battle*, by Owen Mulholland

Lapize didn't quit. He tore down the Aubisque, riding dangerously on the unpaved rutted paths. He caught Lafourcade and won the stage with Pierino Albini, beating third-place Faber by 10 minutes.

At the end of this historic stage, Faber still had 36 points in the General Classification to Lapize's 46.

With the mountain stages finished, it was a fratricidal war between the 2 Alcyons to the end of the Tour with Lapize slowly closing the gap on Faber. Faber had an unexpected string of misfortunes, crashing and getting many flat tires. On stage 13, Lapize took the lead and put it on ice when he won the penultimate stage to Caen.

The closeness of the final General Classification showed how worthy both Faber and Lapize were.

1. Octave Lapize (Alcyon): 63 points

2. François Faber (Alcyon): 67 points

3. Gustave Garrigou (Alcyon): 86 points

4. Cyrille Van Houwaert (Alcyon): 97 points

5. Charles Cruchon (independent or *isolé*): 119 points

Lapize was by no means a shock winner. By the time the 1910 Tour came around, he had already won Paris–Roubaix twice as well coming in second in Paris–Brussels. He went on to win a third Paris–Roubaix as well as 3 Paris–Brussels and 3 Championships of France. Lapize never again finished the Tour de France although he tried 4 more times. In World War One he was a fighter pilot and was shot down near Verdun and died. He was only 29.

1911. The Pyreneen stage was such a success that in 1911 the Tour added the Alps with the Col du Galibier. This addition made the 1911 edition the first modern Tour de France. The Tour has a certain feel and rhythm as it circumnavigates the hexagon of France. It's an undependable rule that it goes clockwise in even-numbered years, counter-clockwise in the odd ones. It starts with several flat stages, then it heads into the Alps or the Pyrenees. After the first dose of hard climbing there are a few transition days before assaulting the other mountain range. To seal the General Classification there is usually a time trial and then the ride into Paris. In 1911 a time-trial stage had yet to be adopted, but otherwise the 1911 edition was a modern Tour. It was also a complicated Tour, with 15 stages covering a then-record 5,344 kilometers going clockwise with the new Alpine stage preceding the Pyrenees.

Alcyon fielded a terrific team with Trousselier, Faber, Garrigou, Eugène Christophe and René Vandenberghe. La Française countered with Petit-Breton, Georget, Lapize and Passerieu. Note that after the intra-team fight for the 1910 victory between Faber and Lapize they were no longer on the same team. The depth of the field for the 1911 Tour de France was as great as at any time in the Tour's history and promised a good, hard battle for victory.

Misfortune struck during the first stage. La Française rider and former winner Lucien Petit-Breton was forced to abandon after a bad crash. 1 contender gone.

Garrigou, an excellent climber, signaled his superb overall form when he won the first stage, which was a flat one. His teammate Masselis took the second stage and the overall lead.

François Faber, ever the great strongman, used one of his favorite launching pads, the Ballon d'Alsace to do one of his long, powerful breakaways. Unfortunately, he chose to flout the rules to do it. And the rules he broke were those of Henri "this-is-my-Tour" Desgrange. He blew by one of the sign-in controls and had to wait almost $2 \frac{1}{2}$ minutes to make up for his transgression. Faber had so much strength that when his blood was up and he was on the attack even a penalty that big meant little. He won the stage by 17 minutes. We were still in the era when the General Classification was calculated by points, so 1 minute or 17 minutes or 3 hours, it was all the same. Faber took over the lead of the Tour after his stage 3 victory. Octave Lapize had his hopes crushed that day. He came in 10th, 49 minutes after Faber. His name doesn't appear in the list of finishers for the next day, so he must have dropped out after that stage.

The fourth stage, from Belfort to Chamonix (won by Crupelandt with Garrigou third and Faber fifth) put Gustave Garrigou in the lead at 10 points with Faber at 11. The first Alpine stage in Tour history was next, putting Faber in an insecure position. He would like to have been ahead at this point. Garrigou was an excellent climber and François Faber was a big man who struggled in the high mountains.

The fifth stage, 366 kilometers from Chamonix to Grenoble crossed the Aravis, the Télégraphe and the monster Galibier. Émile Georget won the stage with Garrigou in third, 26 minutes behind. Georget's ride was notable for a couple of reasons. He had crashed 2 days before on the descent of the Ballon d'Alsace while avoiding a motorcycle coming the other way. Yet, he was the only rider to conquer the Galibier without getting off his bike and walking. François Faber was 12th, an hour more behind Garrigou. Garrigou's lead was much firmer with Faber still in second place.

Here's the General Classification after stage 5:

1. Gustave Garrigou: 13 points
2. François Faber: 23 points
3. Paul Duboc: 27 points

The next day was still hilly, but the hills were not what we now call "first" and "hors" category climbs. They covered the Laffrey, the Bayard and the Allos. They were the sort of climb Faber could handle and handle them he did, winning the stage by 10 minutes over Garrigou who came in second.

The General Classification after stage 6:

1. Gustave Garrigou: 15 points

2. François Faber: 24 points

3. Paul Duboc: 31 points

Duboc could not be ignored. In the 3 following stages leading up to the big day in the Pyrenees Duboc got a fourth and 2 firsts.

The General Classification after stage 9 had changed a bit.

1. Gustave Garrigou: 27 points

2. Paul Duboc: 37 points

3. François Faber: 59 points

Faber was struggling, coming in twentieth on that ninth stage leading to the Pyrenees. Duboc was getting better with every stage.

Stage 10 was the queen stage in the Pyrenees with enough drama for a book. First let's look at the actual racing. The stage went from Luchon to Bayonne, 326 kilometers that covered the Peyresourde, the Aspin, the Tourmalet and finally the giant Aubisque. Duboc attacked at the first opportunity and carved himself a significant lead. At the summit of the Tourmalet Duboc was 8 minutes ahead of his nearest chaser. At the base of the Tourmalet, still well ahead, he took on food. At a sign-in control he accepted a drink from a spectator. He seemed poised to further close the General Classification gap on Garrigou with a near-sure victory in this stage. He rode up the Aubisque, turned pale, and fell off his bike. He lay on the road, vomiting. Because of the strict rules against helping riders in the Tour, no one came to his aid. The other riders just rode past him. He was finally able to remount his bike and finish the stage over an hour after the winner had crossed the line.

Maurice Brocco pounded to the finish, winning the stage with Garrigou a distant second at 34 minutes.

So, here's how the main protagonists finished the stage:

1. Maurice Brocco: 13 hours 26 minutes

2. Gustave Garrigou @ 34 minutes

8. François Faber @ 1hour 15 minutes

21. Paul Duboc @ 3 hours 47 minutes

But the story of this stage isn't nearly over.

It was assumed that Duboc had been poisoned. At first, the suspicions fell on Garrigou because he had the most to lose from a Duboc victory. It is now thought that perhaps the bottle given to Duboc at the sign-in contained the poison and that François Lafourcade, who had done so well in the mountains in the 1910 Tour, may have concocted it. It is universally accepted now that Garrigou was innocent. That didn't keep partisans of Duboc from threatening Garrigou. In later stages, as the Tour went through Duboc's home area of Rouen, someone put up signs along the road.

"Citizens of Rouen! If I had not been poisoned, I would be leading the Tour de France today. You know what to do when the Tour passes through Rouen tomorrow."

People in the crowds watching the Tour pass by threatened Garrigou. Desgrange had given Garrigou a bodyguard. But from previous experience with the partisanship of the race fans for their local heroes Desgrange knew his Tour leader was in real danger. For the stage through Rouen, Desgrange had Garrigou ride a bike painted a different color. Garrigou was also given different clothes and new goggles with blue lenses. One writer says that Desgrange glued a mustache on Garrigou's upper lip, but all the pictures I see of Garrigou before and after the Tour show him with an abundant, full mustache. In any case, the transformation was good enough for Garrigou to ride safely and finish the Tour without harm.

And now we get to the story of Maurice Brocco.

First remember that Desgrange wanted his Tour to be a supreme test of the individual athlete. He detested anything that subverted this goal. Teams, drafting, tactics: it was all the work of the devil.

Brocco had a bad day on the fourth stage, coming in fourteenth and ruining his chances at winning the Tour. He then offered to assist other contenders in return, we must assume, for money. Faber took him up on it on a day he was having trouble, the eighth stage (Faber was unable to finish the 1911 Tour). Brocco helped him and thus infuriated Desgrange. Desgrange, if he had had his way, would have tossed Brocco out of the Tour on the spot. But he needed more than the appearance of impropriety to disqualify Brocco. He did invent a new term, however. Dripping with contempt as he wrote about Brocco in his newspaper *L'Auto*, he said Brocco was unworthy, no more than a *domestique* (servant).

And thus a term was invented for a rider who sacrifices his own chances to assist another. Bicycle racing was still evolving. The racers, writers, promoters and fans were not only inventing a whole new vocabulary; in stage racing, the Tour de France was really creating an entirely new sport.

The next day was that big day in the Pyrenees that saw Duboc poisoned. Brocco rode masterfully, finally passing the vomiting Duboc on the Aubisque, beating Garrigou and dropping Émile Georget who was thought to be the finest climber in the Tour.

Furious at the treatment he had been receiving from Tour officials and *L'Auto* over his actions as a *domestique*, Brocco had been goading Desgrange the entire day. When confronted with Brocco's stage win Desgrange's reaction was not to praise him or think that Brocco had somehow redeemed himself. Instead, he finally did what he had wanted to do for a while. He tossed him out of the race. If he could ride that well against the finest riders of the world, Desgrange reasoned, he had clearly been holding back in the earlier stages and using his energies to help others. The penalty for that was removal from the Tour.

That gave Garrigou the Pyreneen stage victory. Paul Duboc wasn't done fighting for victory, however. The next day he took the eleventh stage into La Rochelle and then went on to win fourteenth stage into La Havre.

It wasn't enough. That disastrous day in the Pyrenees put an end to Duboc's 1911 Tour hopes. Garrigou rode consistently, avoiding the bad fortune that seemed to dog the other fine riders that year. Alcyon's manager Alphonse Baugé had engineered another brilliant win. La Française managed to put 3 riders in the top 5, but missed the big one again.

Final 1911 Tour de France General Classification:

1. Gustave Garrigou (Alcyon): 43 points
2. Paul Duboc (La Française) 61 points
3. Émile Georget (La Française) 84 points
4. Charles Crupelandt (La Française) 119 points
5. Louis Heusghem (Alcyon) 135 points

Before leaving 1911, we should note that Garrigou was a superb, experienced and accomplished rider. Here are a few of the notable palmares leading up to his Tour victory:

1907: French Champion, Tour of Lombardy, second in the Tour de France

1908: French Champion, fourth in the Tour de France

1909: second in the Tour de France

1911: Winner of the Tour with 2 stage wins, Milano–San Remo

He went on to get a second, a third and a fifth in the Tour before the First World War ended his career as a professional rider.

1912. Desgrange's headline in the July 1, 1912 *L'Auto*: "*Le X Tour De France Cycliste. Le Vainqueur de Paris–Roubaix Triomphe a Dunkerque*". Desgrange had made it to his tenth Tour and the winner of the 1912 Paris–Roubaix, Charles Crupelandt, had won the first stage of the Tour.

Desgrange stuck with his 1911 formula: a Tour of 15 stages and 14 rest days. It was only a little shorter at 5,319 kilometers. Like 1911, it went clockwise, Alps first.

This year the Tour lifted its ban on freewheels. I can't find when this ban was put in place. Early Tour riders had them. At some point the riders were required to ride fixed gears. Desgrange constantly tinkered with his race with the ever-growing complexity of the rules a constantly changing minefield for any Tour history buff. Finding the threads and links can be a real challenge. Often the connections are just lost.

There were some shifts in the team lineups. The sponsored riders rode in squads of 5. François Faber now rode for Automoto. La Française included Crupelandt, Lapize and Brocco. Alcyon, ever the wizards of the Tour in the late pre-war years had Garrigou, Duboc, Heusghem and Belgian Odile Defraye. Peugeot had Petit-Breton and some important names for the future: Philippe Thys and Marcel Buysse. Armor's team had Eugène Christophe and Jean Alavoine. There were 10 teams on the line at the start who, along with the *isolés* (independent riders), made up a field of 131.

The second stage, a 388-kilometer run from Dunkirk to Longwy saw Lucien Petit-Breton again crash out of the Tour. This time he hit a cow. Alcyon's Odile Defraye won the stage, putting him in second place in the General Classification, 1 point behind JB Louvet's Vincenzo Borgarello. Defraye's win came at the expense of the Alcyon team's designated leader, Gustave Garrigou.

The climbing started in stage 3 with the Ballon d'Alsace. Defraye attacked on the climb but Eugène Christophe and Gustave Garrigou were able to join him. Christophe nailed the sprint for the stage win and Defraye took over the lead with a 2-point gap on Borgarello.

Christophe was riding in a state of grace. He won the next 2 stages, including the great day in the Alps. The 1912 Alpine stage, 366 kilometers, covered the Aravis, the Télégraphe and the Galibier. Christophe won the stage, coming in alone after a huge solo break. I believe his 315 kilometers alone on the road is the Tour's longest individual breakaway. Defraye was ninth, a half-hour behind. Now, both Christophe and Defraye were tied in the General Classification at 29 points apiece. Octave Lapize was right on their heels at 30.

The next day, stage 6, had more climbing and Lapize showed he could ride. With a victory in this stage—Defraye was right behind in second place—Lapize and Defraye were tied for first at 31 points. Christophe was third with 33. Partisans of various teams, regions and racers were still spreading nails on the road, an occupation that had made the 1904 Tour such a disgrace. Garrigou fell victim to nails spread on the road on this stage. Defraye waited for him and the 2 chased together until it became obvious that Defraye was by far the stronger of the 2. At Garrigou's insistence, Defraye took off and regained contact with the leaders, making his second place possible.

The next day, stage 7, Defraye won the sprint into Marseille and with that win, took over the lead.

The standings at this point:

1. Odile Defraye: 32 points

2. Octave Lapize 35 points

3. Eugène Christophe 38 points

There were 2 Pyreneen stages that year. Stage 9 from Perpignan to Luchon with the Port, Portet d'Aspet and the Ares climbs was a tough warm-up to the very hard tenth stage. Defraye tightened his grip on the Tour by winning stage 9. Christophe was only a couple of minutes behind, taking second. Lapize, disheartened by the authoritative way he was dropped and the collusion between the Belgian racers helping Defraye, abandoned the Tour midway into the stage. This collusion was strictly against the rules. But Defraye profited greatly from help from the other Belgians, no matter what their trade team affiliation was.

"How can I fight in conditions like these? Everybody is working for Alcyon. The Belgians are all helping Defraye whether they belong to his team or not. I've had enough of it and I'm pulling out", Lapize said when he talked to reporters on quitting the Tour. That evening the rest of Lapize's La Française team, angry at the wholesale breach of the rules by the Belgians, also quit the Tour. The French riders continued to ride individually and suffered accordingly.

Stage 10, the great Pyreneen stage, involved crossing the Peyresourde, the Aspin, the Tourmalet, the Soulor and the Aubisque: 326 kilometers from Luchon to Bayonne. A stage this monstrous took over 14 hours to complete. Today, we would never consider asking racers, even with their higher level of fitness compared to racers of a century past, to tackle such an inhuman agenda. In fact modern rules prohibit such distances. To make matters worse, it rained hard that day. Louis Mottiat of the Thomann squad won the stage with Eugène Christophe right with him. Defraye, keeping a firm hold on his lead, finished third.

Jean Alavoine, riding with an early gear-changing device, won 3 of the remaining 5 stages. From stage 7 when he took the unshared lead in the General Classification, Defraye was never in any danger. He rode vigilantly. It is interesting that he won this Tour so masterfully and easily. Yet, when Defraye rode the 1909 Tour the year before, he didn't finish. He rode the Tour 5 more times and was unable to finish or win a stage again. 1912 was his year. It was also the first time a Belgian had won the Tour. While the French reviled him for his victory based on collusion with other Belgian riders, he received a hero's welcome when he returned to his home country.

The final 1912 Tour de France General Classification:

1. Odile Defraye (Alcyon) 49 points
2. Eugène Christophe (Armor) 108 points
3. Gustave Garrigou (Alcyon) 140 points
4. Marcel Buysse (Peugeot) 147 points
5. Jean Alavoine (Armor) 148 points

The point spread between Defraye and Christophe is very large, but if the 1912 Tour had been calculated on time, it would have been very close with Christophe winning.

1913. Desgrange had a problem. Calculating the winner of the Tour on a points-based system instead of elapsed time created rather flat racing. Since a gap of 1 second had the same effect on the overall lead as a deficit of 3 hours, riders could let a break get a big lead without worrying about its having a serious effect on the standings. Defraye's 1912 victory showed how a racer, riding economically, could win without worrying about these time gaps.

Nothing has changed. Watch the sprinters racing for the Green Points' Jersey in a modern Tour. When they get to the mountains they know they can't win the stage, but they also know the other contenders for the Green Jersey can't win in the mountains either. They go just fast enough so that they can finish the day's stage without being eliminated by the time cutoff. Dull racing indeed. And on those stages where they are fighting for a stage win, it's also usually negative, controlled rolling across the flats with a final furious minute at the end.

But it wasn't really as simple as just changing to calculating time instead of points and being done with it. The points system grew out of 2 needs. After the 1904 cheating scandal points were much easier to monitor and reduced cheating. This was the basic reason for instituting the points system in the first place.

The other reason was a consequence of Desgrange's stern rules regarding cycle repairs. A rider had to fix his own bike without assistance. Just fixing a tire could be a big job in those days. As we shall see, if a rider had to spend the better part of an hour performing a repair it would be devastating to his standings in a time-based system. In a points based system, it might mean the loss of only a few places in a single stage.

The basic unfairness of the points system was really brought home when Christophe was a distant second in points to Defraye in 1912, but he beat Defraye on time. Desgrange had no good solution. As Les Woodland put it, "I think Desgrange was tied up between 2 ideals: the wish for a proper race in which the fastest rider won and the need for that race not to be influenced by what he saw as an unfortunately unavoidable adjunct: the bicycle." Well said. Desgrange wanted his Tour to be a pure test of the individual's strength, endurance and fortitude. A bicycle complicated Desgrange's quest with the advantage it gave to drafting riders and the misfortune mechanical problems could bring to worthy athletes.

Pictures of Tour boss Henri Desgrange are hard to come by because at the time no one thought pictures of the Tour's organizer to be interesting or newsworthy. Here he is in the 1913 Tour smoking and watching a suffering rider.

Desgrange has been accused of making the switch to time to keep Defraye the Belgian from winning again. Desgrange had his strong nationalistic streak, but again, it was not that simple. There were important economic considerations. When Belgians did well, his *L'Auto* magazine with its French circulation sold poorly. To make matters worse, Belgian makers didn't advertise in Desgrange's French paper. In those days, each national market was insular, protected by high tariffs. Belgian manufacturers sold in Belgium, French makers sold mostly in France. There was no point in a Belgian maker advertising his product in France, a market where he didn't sell. If it were indeed Desgrange's intention to protect French riders by going to a time-based system, he was going to get a rude reward. Belgian riders dominated his Tour for years to come.

So in 1913 the Tour de France went back to calculating the winner by using his elapsed time. The 1913 Tour was, for the first time, counter-clockwise: Pyrenees first with 15 stages and 14 rest days. At 5,388 kilometers, it was the longest Tour yet. Wanting to make the Tour harder for the riders, freewheels were banned on most stages. I know they were allowed on stage 4. These arcane and now seemingly arbitrary rule changes sometimes seem to make no sense. Yet at the time, each had its purpose in Desgrange's mind. He wanted his race to be the greatest race in the world.

Over the winter the best Tour racers played musical chairs with their team affiliations. With the race now one for the shortest elapsed time, the tactics a team employed were different. A good team was essential for success.

La Française had Émile Georget, Octave Lapize, Paul Duboc and Maurice Brocco. On paper this was a formidable team. Yet, for all the strength of this team, none of the 8 men on the La Française team made it to the fifth stage.

Peugeot looked very good, sporting 2 former Tour winners in François Faber and Gustave Garrigou, plus Jean Alavoine, Eugène Christophe, Marcel Buysse and Philippe Thys. They also had induced Alcyon's brilliant manager, Alphonse Baugé, to come over. This more than made up for the loss of Trousselier (to JB Louvet), and Petit-Breton (to Automoto). The odds-on favorite to win the 1913 Tour was Eugène Christophe, nicknamed "Cri-Cri" by his fans. He rode in an aggressive manner, willing to break away. He was 28 years old, the age at which most stage racers reach their peak. And in Baugé, he had the best manager in the business.

Alcyon came back with last year's victor Odile Defraye and had a new rider, the brilliant but troublesome Henri Pélissier. None of the Alcyons would finish the 1913 tour either. Counting the *isolés* 140 riders rolled out of Paris on Sunday, June 29.

The first 5 stages were relatively uneventful. Octave Lapize, the winner of the 1910 Tour, quit during stage 3. He felt his La Française team could not compete against the well organized opposition. Several of his teammates quit that same day and the rest of the team abandoned the following day. That made it 2 years in a row that all of the La Française riders had abandoned the Tour.

Alcyon's Odile Defraye was never out of the top 7 and usually in the top 3 in the first 5 stages. That put him in the lead after stage 5 with Eugène Christophe second. Defraye rode his usual tactical, careful race, not winning any stages, but staying right up at the front, never losing time or place. Philippe Thys, Christophe's Peugeot teammate, was sitting in fifth place. 85 riders had already abandoned the Tour.

After stage 5, the standings were thus:

1. Odile Defraye
2. Eugène Christophe @ 4 minutes 55 seconds
3. Marcel Buysse @ 10 minutes 5 seconds

Stage 6, with crossings (in order) of the Aubisque, Tourmalet, Aspin and Peyresourde is one of the most famous, iconic days in cycle history. We should pause a bit and closely examine those terrible 326 kilometers from Bayonne to Luchon that took the winner 14 hours to complete. Bayonne is just inland from Biarritz, near the Spanish border on the western coast. The stage headed inland along the Pyrenees in an east-southeast direction.

Early in the stage most of the important men, less 1, broke away: Christophe, Buysse, Alavoine, Rossius, Thys, Garrigou, Spiessens and Engel. After crashing, Defraye was in trouble early on. By the time he got to Barèges at the foot of the Tourmalet he was slightly over 2 hours behind the leaders. Making up that kind of time on the gifted climbers up the road was impossible and Defraye abandoned. By the next day, the rest of his Alcyon team also quit the Tour.

On the Aubisque, the road deteriorated. The riders were forced to ride, dismount and push their bikes and then remount as they forced the pace. Marcel Buysse and Christophe led over the top with Thys just behind. Christophe said that had the road been in better condition he could have ridden the entire length of the climb. After the descent of the Aubisque, at the checkpoint in Argelès—the riders must have gone over the Col du Soulor as well—Thys, Christophe and Buysse, all Peugeot, were together. The nearest chasing rider, Jean Rossius of Alcyon, was 10 minutes back.

The city of Barèges is the start of the Tourmalet. At that point, Thys and Christophe were still together with Buysse a few minutes behind. Gustave Garrigou had managed to close a lot of the gap and was now between Buysse and Rossius.

On the Tourmalet Thys started to pull away from Christophe. At the top, Thys was still ahead with Christophe chasing, about 5 minutes behind. Could Christophe have caught Thys on the Aspin or was Thys the truly superior rider? Christophe fans argue that this was a temporary lapse and that their man would have won the stage. I remain unconvinced that this is true given the formidable form that Thys continued to display not only during this Tour but in Tours to come.

Partway down the descent, Christophe recalls, "All of a sudden, about 10 kilometers from St.-Marie-de-Campan down in the valley, I feel that something is wrong with my handlebars. I pull on my brake and stop. I see that my fork was broken." At this point, accounts differ. Some writers say that on the descent Christophe hit a car. I have found no mention of a car in Christophe's own retelling of the story. Broken forks were not unusual. I am sure that the poor state of 1913 metallurgy and bad mountain roads caused the disaster. When the incident was finished, Peugeot took the fork from Christophe for examination. It was never seen again. My own theory, based on little information, is that the car story is probably a piece of Peugeot disinformation. It must have been awful for Peugeot to have their famous rider celebrated for having broken a fork. A car crash makes this all easy to explain. The final nail in the coffin of this story is that Christophe said, "I wouldn't have told you [about the fork failure] then because it was bad publicity for my firm." If it had been a car crash, there would have been no bad publicity because no one expects a bike to withstand a car crash.

In those days, remember, there were no follow cars with bikes ready at a moment's notice to be handed to a racer with a mechanical problem. A racer had to perform his own repairs on his own bike.

Again, accounts differ. *L'Auto* says that Christophe was 14 kilometers from the next town; Christophe puts it at 10 kilometers. At this point, in order to complete the Tour, Christophe had no choice. He put his bike over his shoulder and carried his fork with the front wheel in the other hand and hiked down the rest of the valley to the little town of St.-Marie-de-Campan. With Defraye's departure Christophe had been the leader in the General Classification. It took him over an hour to get off the mountain and get to the town. Riders he had long ago dropped passed him. Christophe, realizing the size of the tragedy, cried as his bravely ran and walked to town.

Upon arriving in the town he met a little girl who took him to the blacksmith, a Monsieur Lecomte. Christophe explained his situation to Lecomte. Lecomte let Christophe use his forge to repair his fork. Christophe was not only a good bicycle mechanic, he had been a locksmith and had metalworking skills. He knew enough to ask for a 22 millimeter diameter tube to make the repair. The blacksmith gave Christophe some verbal guidance. Under the rules, that was all that could be allowed.

Christophe ran out of hands. He not only needed both hands to repair the fork, someone had to work the bellows to keep the flames high and hot. Realizing that he had no choice, and working under the watchful eye of Desgrange's commissars and representatives of competing teams who wanted to make sure that this dangerman followed the rules, he allowed a boy named Corni to work the bellows.

He must have been exhausted. He had been racing the finest riders in the world over some of the toughest terrain in Europe for hours when his fork broke. Then carrying his broken bike, he had to hike down a steep mountain on roads that were little more than treacherous paths. For about 3 hours Christophe worked at the forge.

One of the Tour's monitors, tired and hungry, asked permission to step out and get a bite to eat. Christophe growled back at him, "Eat coal! I am your prisoner and you will remain my jailer."

Finally the bike was finished. He got some bread and before riding off asked the time, wanting to get to the checkpoints before they closed. Knowing he still had 4 hours to finish the stage, the man the French now call *Le Vieux Gaulois*, the Old Gaul, resolutely took off for Luchon with the Aspin and the Peyresourde climbs still before him. Some men are made of steel.

As he left the blacksmith's shop one of Desgrange's officials stopped him. Christophe was given a 10-minute penalty because the little 7-year old boy had helped him with his repair by working the bellows. The penalty was later reduced to 3 minutes.

Christophe came in twenty-ninth that day, 3 hours, 50 minutes, 14 seconds behind the winner, Philippe Thys. Christophe still managed to beat 15 other riders.

Second that day was Buysse at 17 minutes, 57 seconds and Garrigou was third, almost a half-hour behind Thys. Christophe's Tour hopes were crushed for that year. If the Tour had still been calculating the standings by counting points, Christophe's Tour might have been salvageable.

By the end of that sixth stage many of the best riders had abandoned the 1913 Tour, among them Lapize, Georget, Crupelandt, Defraye and Rossius. Thys was now the leader of the Tour.

The new General Classification:

1. Philippe Thys
2. Marcel Buysse @ 5 minutes 58 seconds
3. Gustave Garrigou @ 31 minutes 36 seconds

The building where Christophe repaired his fork still stands. It had a brass plaque on the outside, proclaiming the structure's place in history. With his sharp eye for irony, Les Woodland has noted that Christophe's name was misspelled: "Cristophe". As we visit other Tours, we'll see that this plaque is a sad metaphor for a man who had unbelievably bad luck. And by not bending to the force of misfortune he earned a place in the heart of the French, reserved for those who lose the battle against fate without knuckling under. In 2003, the old plaque was replaced with Christophe's name spelled properly.

Stage 7, the second Pyreneen stage, was not nearly as brutal as stage 6. The riders still had to cover 323 kilometers, but the climbs included the Portet d'Aspet, Port and the Puymorens. These weren't the monsters that the riders had faced the stage before, but they were formidable nonetheless. Buysse won the stage and took the overall lead.

That's the way things stood until stage 9 to Nice. Marcel Buysse, leading the Tour, crashed. Like Christophe, he was forced to carry his bike for several kilometers and then perform his own repairs. He accepted help with the repair and suffered a nearly half-hour penalty. On that day he lost 3 hours, the lead, and any chance of winning the Tour de France.

In the Alps, Buysse won 2 more stages with Thys always only minutes behind him. Thys, who was not only very fit but also a superb tactical rider, might have ridden differently if Buysse were not so far behind in the General Classification after his crash. He would have been forced to ride more aggressively and one wonders if he could have sustained such a pace. In any case, one cannot escape the feeling that Desgrange's tough rule requiring riders to make their own repairs probably

Thys, Christophe, Buysse and Garrigou suffer the appalling roads of the time, here pictured in a Pyreneen stage.

cheated 2 worthy contenders of a fair shot at winning the Tour in 1913.

Through the Alps, Lucien Petit-Breton became ever more competitive. Using the Sturmey-Archer internal hub gear system, Petit-Breton was able to shift gears on the fly while the others had to flip their rear wheels with their 2-sided rear hubs to change gears. Even with this technical advantage, Thys and Buysse were able to out climb Petit-Breton. I am sure that the large energy losses that are part of any planetary gear system more than erased any advantage in time the gear system gave a racer. The internal hub experiment was not abandoned quickly, though. In 1914, most of the Tour riders used 2-speed Eadie hubs.

By the end of the 13th stage, with all the climbing behind them, Petit-Breton had moved up to second place, 1 hour, 3 minutes behind

Thys. And then, on stage 14, Petit-Breton crashed out of the Tour. Buysse won the last 2 stages, but Thys was in control. The Tour was his.

The first Yellow Jersey? A tired-looking Philippe Thys savors his 1913 Tour victory.

Before leaving the 1913 Tour, let's examine a vague bit of Tour history. The official history says that Eugène Christophe was awarded the first Yellow Jersey in 1919 after stage 10. Philippe Thys says that in 1913 Desgrange asked him to wear a unique distinguishing jersey as the

Tour's leader. Thys, ever the tactician, declined, not wanting to have a big target on his back. However, Peugeot saw the marketing advantage of having their rider, the race leader, easy to spot. Thys relented and agreed to the plan. A yellow jersey was purchased for him. The head hole had to be enlarged for the Belgian. Scholars and Tour officials have gone back to try to verify or discredit Thys' claim to being the first Yellow Jersey. While they can find no mention in any newspaper account, and the Tour's own records from this era were largely lost in the Second World War, it is generally believed that Thys is telling the truth. This is mostly because of Thys' character. He was a man not given to boasting. He brought so many details to the story that Tour scholars believe Thys was really the first *Maillot Jaune*.

Final 1913 Tour de France General Classification:

1. Philippe Thys (Peugeot) 197 hours 54 minutes
2. Gustave Garrigou (Peugeot) @ 8 minutes 37 seconds
3. Marcel Buysse (Peugeot) @ 3 hours 30 minutes 55 seconds
4. Firmin Lambot (Griffon) @ 4 hours 12 minutes 45 seconds
5. François Faber (Peugeot) @ 6 hours 26 minutes 4 seconds
6. Alfons Spiessens (JB Louvet) @ 7 hours 57 minutes 52 seconds
7. Eugène Christophe (Peugeot) @ 14 hours 6 minutes 35 seconds

Peugeot took 5 of the top 7 places and won 10 of the 15 stages. 25 riders finished.

1914. For the 1914 Tour, the only notable change in Tour protocol was the addition of race numbers being affixed to the rider's bikes.

Peugeot's team was as mighty as any in the history of the Tour. It was still under the management of Alphonse Baugé, generally considered the best in the business at the time. Peugeot brought back a squad whose names resonate through cycling history: Philippe Thys, Gustave Garrigou, Émile Georget, Oscar Egg, Eugène Christophe, Jean Alavoine, Firmin Lambot, Louis Heusghem, Marcel Baumler, Émile Engel and Henri Pélissier. I count 4 past and future Tour winners (Thys, Garrigou, Lambot, Pélissier) and 4 Tour podium occupants (Alavoine, Christophe, Heusghem, Georget). Has any team in history had that kind of horsepower?

Alcyon had Marcel Buysse who moved from Peugeot, Odile Defraye and Jean Rossius. Of the 8 men in their team, only Rossius made it to Paris.

Automoto's team had several great names including one from the past, 1905 Tour winner Louis Trousselier. 2-time Tour winner Lucien Petit-Breton and Paul Duboc were also on the Automoto squad. The great Costante Girardengo, perhaps the first truly great Italian champion or *campionissimo* decided to try his luck in the Tour, also riding for Automoto. Girardengo was just beginning his mastery of bicycle racing, having won the Italian Championship in 1913. He didn't really start to dominate Italian racing until 1919, and by then he was almost unstoppable. For now, he was not the team leader and he was allowed the freedom to race for his own victories only if a great opportunity presented itself.

La Française tried again with Octave Lapize and Charles Crupelandt. Again, no La Française rider made it to Paris. La Française's time had passed.

The 2 favorites were the 1913 winner Philippe Thys and his teammate, the talented but volatile Henri Pélissier. The 1914 Tour was again counter-clockwise, Pyrenees first, covering 5,405 kilometers over 15 stages.

At 3:00 a.m., 147 riders took off from the St. Cloud suburb of Paris. The first stage, to Le Havre, was a monstrous 388 kilometers and took stage winner Philippe Thys 13 hours, 18 minutes to complete. Jean Rossius was second and given the same time. The next day Jean Rossius won the stage with Thys second. With both having the same time and points total, the lead in the General Classification was awarded as a tie to Thys and Rossius. It stayed that way until stage 6. At this point, Henri Pélissier, showing more than just a promise of what he could do, was sitting in third place in the General Classification at $5\,^1/_2$ minutes behind the tied duo.

Stage 6 was the big Pyreneen stage. As in 1912, it crossed the Aubisque, Tourmalet, Aspin and the Peyresourde. It blew the 1914 Tour wide open. Firmin Lambot won the stage with Thys 7 minutes, 40 seconds behind. Pélissier took over 38 minutes to reach the finish after Lambot's win. Rossius' hopes for a Tour victory, which started out so well, were finished. He lost over an hour that day.

The General Classification stood thus:

1. Philippe Thys

2. Henri Pélissier @ 34 minutes 27 seconds

3. Jean Alavoine @ 46 minutes 23 seconds

Girardengo crashed several times in stage 5, losing over an hour. In the mountains of stage 6 he crashed again and abandoned. He never again returned to ride the Tour. He was the first of a long line of great Italians who never really found that racing in the Tour de France suited them. Italy would have to wait until 1925 to have one of her sons win the Tour.

The next day, still in the Pyrenees with crossings of the Aspet and Puymorens, saw Thys, Alavoine and Pélissier finish together in the front group, so there was no change to the standings.

Across southern France Thys stayed glued to Pélissier, finishing at the same time with him each stage. Even in the Alps with the mighty Galibier, Thys and Pélissier finished with the same time. Thys had the advantage. He had the lead and was strong. Tactically, he was in the enviable position of being able to ride defensively and economically.

It wasn't until stage 12 with the Ballon d'Alsace that Pélissier was able to drop Thys. Even then, Pélissier was only able to gain 2 minutes, 37 seconds. Thys had a nice time pad and if everything went reasonably well, he could afford to give up small amounts of time this late in the race. That is, if everything went well.

Big, powerful François Faber won stages 13 and 14. Those would be the last bike races the mighty Faber would win. Thys almost came to grief chasing Faber in stage 14. Ruining a wheel, he decided to gamble on the time penalty for getting assistance by buying one from a shop. He figured that this was preferable to surely losing the Tour by messing with the broken wheel and risking the huge time loss he would face trying to repair it. Christophe's lesson was burned into the psyche of the peloton. Thys was hit with a 30-minute penalty that left him with a very close 1 minute, 50 second lead over Pélissier. Thys held this slim lead all the rest of the way to Paris. Pélissier did win the final stage, but Thys wasn't letting Henri get away from him. They finished with the same time that day.

Thys had now matched Petit-Breton's 2 Tour wins.

Another context can be used to judge the magnitude of Thys' 1914 accomplishment. All Tour winners from 1905 (Trousselier) to

1923 (Pélissier) started the 1914 Tour except René Pottier, who was dead. In addition, Lucien Buysse, the 1926 winner also started. That made 11 men at the line who were either past or future Tour winners. Thys emerged supreme.

Final 1914 Tour de France General Classification:

1. Philippe Thys (Peugeot) 200 hours 28 minutes 48 seconds.
2. Henri Pélissier (Peugeot) @ 1 minute 50 seconds
3. Jean Alavoine (Peugeot) @ 36 minutes 53 seconds
4. Jean Rossius (Alcyon) @ 1 hour 57 minutes 5 seconds
5. Gustave Garrigou (Peugeot) @ 3 hours 21 seconds

Peugeot took 4 of the top 5 places.

And what of Eugène Christophe who had come so close to winning in 1913 before he was brought down by his broken fork? On stage 6, the first Pyreneen stage, he lost 2 hours. The next day with the Port d'Aspet, he lost another half-hour. In stage 11, the Alpine stage, he lost 1 hour, 14 minutes. By the time he arrived in Paris, he was sitting in 11th place in the General Classification, 8 hours, 31 minutes, 58 seconds behind Thys.

The 1914 Tour was completed under the gathering clouds of war. The day the Tour started, June 28, was the same day Serbian secret agent Gavrilo Princip assassinated Austro-Hungary's Archduke Ferdinand. This event started the tragic series of ultimatums between the great powers of Europe and catapulted the world into the first of the 20th Century's monumental tragedies. The 1914 Tour ended on July 26. On August 3, Germany declared war on France and invaded Belgium. The Tour de France and almost every other normal activity in Europe came to a terrible halt.

Chapter 3

1919–1929. Amid growing popularity for his event Desgrange relentlessly experiments with the design of the Tour but fails to find the perfection he seeks

1919. The hostilities of World War One ended November 11, 1918 ("the eleventh hour of the eleventh day of the eleventh month"). France, like the rest of Europe, was shattered. Out of her population of roughly 40 million, 8.4 million had been mobilized. And of those 8.4 million, 6.1 million were killed or wounded. The roads of Northern France were ruined. Shortages were everywhere. Parts of Germany were suffering near-famine. Symbolic of life everywhere in Europe, after the war there were many who could not sign in to start the Tour. Several notable Tour veterans died during the war: Henri Alavoine, Lucien Petit-Breton, Octave Lapize, François Faber, Edouard Wattelier, Émile Engel, among others.

Desgrange insisted on going ahead with promoting the 1919 Tour despite the profound problems France was suffering. He scheduled 15 stages over 5,560 kilometers of the war-torn roads of France. The riders lacked any sort of racing form, not having trained or raced for years. The Tour started only 7 months after the armistice. The result was the slowest Tour ever, 24.056 kph. Of the 67 starters, 10 finished.

Given the terrible conditions and rampant shortages in France, the bicycle manufacturers were unable individually to sponsor teams as they had before the war. They banded together to equip about half of the peloton under the name "La Sportive". William Fotheringham says that this consortium gave the bike companies an added benefit. They could, through their newfound sponsorship monopoly, control the rider's salaries.

Stage 1 did not start well for Henri Pélissier's brother, Francis. A broken fork at the start forced him to find a shop and perform the repair before continuing. He lost almost 4 hours the first day of the Tour.

The poor level of fitness that the peloton brought to the 1919 Tour showed that first day. Only 41 riders completed the 388 kilometers to the stage finish at La Havre. Conditions may have been tough and the riders were suffering, but that did not mean that Tour boss Henri Desgrange would let up in enforcing his harsh rules. Stage 1 winner Jean Rossius was penalized 30 minutes for giving Philippe Thys a drink. Assistance to other riders was absolutely forbidden. Desgrange envisioned his Tour as a test of individuals and wrote the rules accordingly. Thys hadn't come to the 1919 Tour with the same sharp fitness that he displayed in 1913 and 1914. He was fat and out of shape. Even after Rossius' sacrifice and penalty, Thys wasn't able to finish the first stage. Some accounts say that he had stomach problems. I don't know if his stomach troubled him because of its size or its infirmity. I lean towards the former given the tough criticism Desgrange gave Thys in *L'Auto* that following autumn. Desgrange called Thys a *petit bourgeois* who no longer loved the bike. We'll see next year the effect those hard words had on Thys.

1914's third place Jean Alavoine had a rough start. His first stage was marred with several flat tires. At one point he ended up in a ditch and stayed there for a half-hour before continuing. Some days it hardly seems worth going to work.

With Rossius' first stage penalty, Henri Pélissier became the leader in the General Classification.

Henri Pélissier won the next stage. His brother Francis, whose misfortune with a broken fork at the start of the first stage cost him any hope of a high placing overall, won stage 3. Brother Henri was right with him that third day, finishing at the same time. After stage 3, Henri Pélissier was firmly in the lead. Eugène Christophe was second, a big 23 minutes behind.

Stage 3 shows how the Tours of that time took place in an entirely different world than the one we know today. Léon Scieur had a troublesome ride as he tried to make it to Brest. He flatted at least 4 times that day. At one point, to get some shelter from the cold rain, Scieur huddled in a doorway and repaired his tires. He had 2 people for company. One was the woman who lived in the house. The other? One of Desgrange's race commissars who watched Scieur to make sure that the woman did not give the racer even a piece of thread in violation of the rules forbidding assistance to riders making repairs. Eventually Scieur's fingers became too cold to thread the needle he used to re-sew the tubulars. Scieur asked the lady to thread the needle. The commissaire forbade even that small help on pain of a time penalty.

Although magnificently talented, Henri Pélissier's self-destructiveness would regularly manifest itself. We'll see more instances of this as our history progresses. After the clean Pélissier win in stage 3—Jean Alavoine was third, over 3 minutes behind—Henri Pélissier ungraciously said that he was a thoroughbred and the rest of the pack were work horses. I think it is possible that Henri was obliquely referring to the nature of bicycle racing at the time. The huge, long stages were stultifying and made for poor racing. He believed shorter stages at higher speeds would vastly improve the quality of the competition. In fact, Pélissier was one of the first roadmen to train with speed in mind. Time has shown Pélissier to be right, but his remarks deeply offended the rest of the peloton. On stage 4 he flatted—or stopped to remove a jacket, accounts differ—and the peloton attacked. In no time he had lost his 20 minutes' lead over Eugène Christophe. He chased and was closing in on the pack when Desgrange ordered Pélissier to stop working with other riders in his pursuit. The result was that he came in 35 minutes after stage winner Alavoine. Eugène Christophe was third, finishing in the same time as Alavoine. Francis Pélissier lost almost 4 hours that day.

So the General Classification was turned upside down:

1. Eugène Christophe
2. Henri Pélissier @ 11 minutes 42 seconds
3. Émile Masson @ 15 minutes 51 seconds

Christophe was now in the lead. Henri Pélissier displayed his red-hot temper. He was furious at race manager Desgrange and wasn't afraid to make his feelings known. Desgrange belittled Pélissier in print (I think he said Pélissier had a "tiny brain", but I can't find the specific reference). And so started the war between the 2 strongest personalities in the Tour. This fight would rage with unabated fury for years to come.

Full of anger at both their situation in the race and the poor quality of the food the Tour was providing, the Pélissier brothers pulled out of the Tour. This would not be the first time they would storm out in a fit of anger.

At the start of stage 6, the first day in the Pyrenees, there were only 17 riders left in the Tour. As the Tour progressed, poor physical form and tough conditions continued to plague the peloton. The stage 6 mountains—the Aubisque, Tourmalet, Aspin and Peyresourde—were kinder to Christophe than they had been in 1913. Christophe came in fifth that day and comfortably kept his lead in the General Classification. Stage 7 was also a tough mountain stage and Christophe, coming in second, increased his lead.

After stage 7, the General Classification:

1. Eugène Christophe
2. Firmin Lambot @ 30 minutes 23 seconds
3. Jean Alavoine @ 47 minutes 34 seconds

During the rest day between stages 10 and 11, Henri Desgrange's promotional genius showed itself again. He had been asked by the journalists for some way to pick out the Tour leader. He presented the Tour leader, Eugène Christophe, with a yellow jersey. In contrast to the current practice, this first presentation was done without any particular ceremony.

Yellow was the color of the paper Tour sponsor *L'Auto* was printed on. Perhaps that's why the leader's jersey is yellow. But perhaps not. It has also been said that when it was decided to give the leader a distinctive jersey, because of post-war shortages, unpopular yellow was the only color that could be had in the variety of sizes needed so that different riders could be accommodated.

Accidentally or on purpose, the *Maillot Jaune* was born. This way, Desgrange said, one could always spot the current leader in the pack. At that moment in 1919 the peloton was 11 men. Officially, this was the first Yellow Jersey. Christophe wasn't happy about wearing it and received much ridicule from the other riders who called him a canary. For another side to this story, see the 1913 Tour history for Philippe Thys' claim to be the first man in Yellow.

Christophe kept the lead in the Tour as well as his Yellow Jersey through stages 12 and 13, extending his lead. It looked as if Christophe would wipe away the disaster of the 1913 when he lost the lead because of a broken fork.

Here was the General Classification with only 2 stages to go:

1. Eugène Christophe
2. Firmin Lambot @ 28 minutes 5 seconds
3. Jean Alavoine @ 49 minutes 29 seconds

During the penultimate stage, stage 14 from Metz to Dunkirk, fortune was again cruel to Eugène Christophe. Earlier in the Tour, I think it likely stage 9, Christophe had crashed in Nice. It is now thought that this crash weakened his forks. The 1919 Tour was counter-clockwise, so now the Tour was headed to the worst of the war-torn roads of northeastern France. This had to have further stressed those now-fragile tubes. To make things worse, this fourteenth stage had over 100 miles of cobbles, torture to any bike. In the suburbs of Valenciennes unbelievable disaster struck Christophe. His fork broke. Again, as in 1913, he had to walk his bike with a broken fork to a forge and repair his bike. This time there was a bicycle factory with a forge a kilometer away. Still, the rules said he had to perform his own repair. He lost over 70 minutes doing the actual repair. His total time loss for this broken fork was 2 hours and 28 minutes. He lost not only the time, he lost the Tour de France. The Tour was surely to have been his.

Firmin Lambot took over the lead.

To make matters even worse, on the final stage to Paris Christophe had several punctures, further delaying him another 35 minutes.

The final 1919 Tour de France General Classification:

1. Firmin Lambot (La Sportive) 231 hours 7 minutes 15 seconds
2. Jean Alavoine (La Sportive) @ 1 hour 42 minutes 54 seconds
3. Eugène Christophe (La Sportive) @ 2 hours 26 minutes 31 seconds

4. Léon Scieur (La Sportive) @ 2 hours 52 minutes 15 seconds

5. Honoré Barthélemy (La Sportive) @ 4 hours 14 minutes 22 seconds

11 riders finished the Tour. Paul Duboc was disqualified 2 weeks later when it was ruled that he had used a car to go get his pedal repaired. That left 10 official classified finishers.

The Tour took up a collection for Christophe, calling him the moral victor. Eventually over 13,000 Francs were awarded to Christophe, far more than the 5,000 awarded to Lambot.

Jean Alavoine was able to finish second even with his half-hour penalty on the first stage. He was a worthy second-place, having won 5 stages.

1920. Desgrange stuck to the basic formula he had used since 1910: 15 stages over about 5,000 kilometers, going counter-clockwise around the perimeter of France. In 1920, it was 5,519 kilometers to be exact, from Sunday, June 27 to Sunday, July 25. He kept this configuration through 1924. 113 riders started that Sunday in June 1920.

Philippe Thys had attempted the 1919 Tour in poor physical condition, being unable to finish even the first stage. Humiliated by the verbal caning Desgrange gave him in the pages of *L'Auto*, Thys resumed his habits of hard work and trained assiduously over the winter. By the start of the 1920 season he was ready to begin racing at his former high level. It almost all came to naught when he broke his collarbone in a crash in Milan–San Remo in March. Made of steel, Thys finished the remaining 50 kilometers of that race. He was able to recover his form in time to start the Tour. He rode for the manufacturer's consortium, La Sportive and had as manager Alphonse Baugé, who had been the architect of many of both Peugeot's and Alcyon's pre-war victories.

The first stage ended in a sprint won by Louis Mottiat. Since 5 riders finished with the same time that day, they shared the lead: Louis Mottiat, Thys, Jean Rossius, Félix Goethals and Émile Masson. Of these, only Goethals was French. The other 4 were Belgian. This was only the beginning of the Belgian lock on the 1920 Tour. As the race progressed, the Belgians would tighten their grip.

With his win in the second stage from La Havre to Cherbourg, Thys became first among the 5 who were still tied on time for first place in the General Classification. He was now the Yellow Jersey and never relinquished the lead from then on.

The first 5 stages ended in big sprints. Desgrange hated that. He wanted his riders suffering and straggling in one by one. Henri Pélissier showed his wonderful class by winning 2 of those stages, numbers 3 and 4. He would have been leading the Tour at that point if he hadn't lost almost 17 minutes in the first stage.

Again, Henri Pélissier's stubborn, angry side came out. On stage 5 Henri threw away a spent tire. Desgrange assessed him a 2-minute penalty. Tour rules were strict. A rider must end a stage with everything he had at the start: clothing, tires, etc. Henri did the predictable thing. He quit. Desgrange also did the predictable. He used his newspaper, *L'Auto*, to make fun of Pélissier. Desgrange said Pélissier didn't know how to suffer and that he would never win the Tour.

Stages 6 and 7 went over the Pyrenees. Thys rode economically, avoiding any bravado or useless displays. He kept within range the riders who might be threats to his lead, and rode no harder than necessary. He might have been able to win one of the stages, but he seems content to have let others (Lambot and Rossius) take the wins while he kept both his time and physical energy intact. The result was a 28-minute lead over his fellow Belgian, Louis Heusghem. Eugène Christophe, continuing his bad fortune, had to abandon with back pains. The Pyrenees had so far managed to ruin 2 Tours for Christophe.

Thys really iced his victory in stage 9, with some tough climbing on the way to Nice, by winning the stage. Hector Heusghem, who was in second place in the General Classification, came in over 30 minutes later. That day Thys increased his lead over Heusghem from 28 minutes to almost exactly 1 hour. Heusghem won the next day, but Thys finished right with him, coming in third with the same time.

In that same stage 9 the epic suffering of Honoré Barthélemy started when he had a hard crash. His back was so badly hurt he had to turn his handlebars up so that he didn't have to bend over as far. Yet that wasn't the worst of the crash. A road flint had pierced and ruined one eye. He was not only bleeding and beat up, he was now half blind. Unstoppable, he removed the flint, re-mounted his bike and finished the stage. We're not done with Honoré yet.

The Tour did have imperfections in its organization. The Yellow Jersey hadn't been awarded to the Tour's leader that year so far. After Thys' victory in stage 9, he was belatedly given the *Maillot Jaune*.

There was only 1 Alpine stage, stage 11. It went over the Galibier and the Aravis. Thys' worst performance of the 1920 Tour was this day, fifth place, showing how tightly he controlled the race. After the Alps, Thys won 2 more stages, 12 and 13.

When the Tour concluded at the *Parc des Princes* in Paris the crowds were so large that the racers had to walk their bikes to get to the finish line. There were only 22 finishers of the 1920 Tour, still over twice the number who had completed the Tour the year before. Even though Thys was Belgian, the 20,000 cycling-crazed fans who were there to greet the brave finishers generously acclaimed the winner. The band played the Belgian anthem, *La Brabançonne*.

Honoré Barthélemy (who lost his eye on stage 9) finished the Tour. His eighth place made him the best-placed Frenchman in a sea of Belgians. He crashed several more times after his terrible fall in stage 9. In addition to losing an eye and ruining his back and being cut, bruised and bleeding, the later falls added a broken wrist and a dislocated shoulder to his suffering. The fans, moved by his courage, carried him after he crossed the finish line. He later replaced the blinded eye with a glass eye, which he would occasionally lose during bikes races.

Philippe Thys had done what no other racer had been able to accomplish. By winning the 1920 Tour de France, he was the first to win 3 Tours. This feat would not be matched again until the 1953, '54, and '55 triple victories of Louison Bobet. Thys' completion of the hat-trick came 7 years after his first win. He surely would have won more if the war had not interrupted his career. *L'Auto* thought that without the Great War's interruption Thys might have been winning his sixth or seventh Tour.

L'Auto went on to say that Thys was the most complete racer since Gustave Garrigou. His record-breaking third Tour victory was the result of a tough regimen of training and clear-headed, thoughtful riding. He took his trade, bike racing, seriously. His results (let us charitably ignore 1919) prove it. *L'Auto* also wrote that when a rider finished a Tour at the same weight he started, it was a sign of his good form and ample preparation. In 1919 Eugène Christophe started and finished at 67 kilograms. In 1920 Thys started and finished at 69 kilograms.

Thys' 1920 victory continued the domination of the Tour by Belgian riders. Belgians won in 1912, '13, '14, '19, '20, '21, '22, '26, and '29.

Let's look at how the small nation of Belgium mastered the 1920 Tour de France.

1. Victory in the General Classification
2. Belgians took the top 7 places overall
3. Belgians won 12 of the 15 stages
4. The Yellow Jersey was always worn by a Belgian, from Mottiat after stage 1 until Thys' final victory in stage 15

1920 Tour de France final General Classification (all rode for the La Sportive manufacturer's consortium):

1. Philippe Thys: 228 hours 36 minutes 13 seconds
2. Hector Heusghem @ 57 minutes 21 seconds
3. Firmin Lambot @ 1 hour 39 minutes 35 seconds
4. Léon Scieur @ 1 hour 44 minutes 58 seconds
5. Émile Masson @ 2 hours 56 minutes 52 seconds

1921. The 1921 Tour de France started out much the same way the 1920 edition did. Louis Mottiat again won the first stage, with 138 starters going from Paris to Le Havre. This time it wasn't a bunch sprint, with 1920's hard-luck man Honoré Barthélemy coming in second, 2 minutes, 37 seconds behind. 11 punctures ruined Barthélemy's chances of grabbing the year's first Yellow Jersey. Philippe Thys, the dominant stage racer of the time, could not defend his 1920 win. Recovering from an illness contracted at the Brussels 6-Day, he and consistent Tour high finisher Jean Rossius lost contact with the leaders and both abandoned the race. With Firmin Lambot also weakened by sickness, the Tour was looking rather open.

Stage 2 from Le Havre to Cherbourg saw the wide-open Tour get shut tight, although it didn't look that way at the time. A rare French stage win by Romain Bellenger hid the fact that Léon Scieur finished with Hector Heusghem only about 3 minutes behind Bellenger. The rest of the field was strung out behind with large gaps. Sixth place Jean Alavoine finished almost 20 minutes after Bellenger.

The General Classification after stage 2 with the big gaps already showing:

1. Léon Scieur

2. Hector Heusghem @ 3 minutes 26 seconds

3. Albert Dejonghe @ 26 minutes

Léon Scieur was a discovery of 1919 Tour winner Firmin Lambot. They both came from the same village in Wallonia (French speaking Belgium), the town of Florennes. Lambot encouraged Scieur to become a professional cyclist. Scieur had started racing late, at 22 years of age; he was now 33.

With the Yellow Jersey on his back, Scieur became a determined, driven racer, defending his lead with tenacity and toughness. The press nicknamed him "The Locomotive" as he extended his lead over the others. By the time the Tour reached the Pyrenees before stage 6, Scieur's lead over fellow Belgian Heusghem was in excess of 29 minutes.

Over the Pyrenees the low-gear spinning Scieur faltered a bit. Heusghem was first over the Tourmalet, the Aspin and the Peyresourde and won the stage, beating Scieur by 25 minutes, 17 seconds. Things had tightened up.

The General Classification after stage 6:

1. Léon Scieur

2. Hector Heusghem @ 4 minutes 6 seconds

3. Albert Dejonghe @ 50 minutes 4 seconds

Scieur and Heusghem stayed together over the second Pyreneen stage. There was no time change between the 2 leaders. Eugène Christophe's sore back again gave way during stage 8, forcing him once more to abandon the Tour.

On stage 9 the 1921 Tour got really interesting. Going from Toulon to Nice, the 272-kilometer stage had 2 tough climbs. Firmin Lambot won the stage with Scieur a little over 3 minutes behind. Heusghem missed the boat, losing 10 minutes, 32 seconds to Scieur. He was now 15 minutes, 38 seconds back. He started to become desperate.

Stage 10, the day leading to the Alpine stage, went from Nice to Grenoble. It was tough going with the 2,247-meter Allos and the 1,248-meter Bayard in the way. Scieur punctured on the Allos climb. Heusghem, breaking the unwritten rule, attacked the leader while he was repairing his bike. Scieur was furious. He completed his repair and went after Heusghem with a vengeance. After catching him, he then less than politely explained the way professionals should behave under these circumstances. Scieur went on to decisively drop Heusghem and win the stage. Heusghem finished 6 minutes behind Scieur. He was now 21 minutes, 47 seconds behind "The Locomotive".

Stage 11 was the Alpine stage with the Lautaret, Galibier, Télégraphe and Aravis climbs. There was no change in the standing between the 2 leaders as they went over the mountains together and finished together.

Fireworks erupted again on stage 12, but not the usual kind. Honoré Barthélemy, Heusghem and Scieur broke away. The pack's chase was listless. The peloton came in a half-hour after the trio. Desgrange was furious. He relegated Lambot and Mottiat to last place in the stage placings for failing to ride the day's stage competitively.

At that time, the race was divided into Group 1 and Group 2. Group 1 contained the superior, sponsored riders. Desgrange was so angry with the Group 1 riders for not racing hard that he let Group 2 start early. With a truce now declared between Heusghem and Scieur, the racing became even duller. Félix Sellier, a Group 2 rider, won the stage. The first Group 1 riders came in over a half-hour later. After stage 13 and Desgrange's failed attempt to use time sanctions and staggered starts to get his race going, the General Classification stood thus:

1. Léon Scieur
2. Hector Heusghem @ 21 minutes 47 seconds
3. Honoré Barthélemy @ 1 hour 58 minutes 35 seconds

Stage 14, the penultimate stage, put Scieur to the test. Well into the day's 433 kilometers, Scieur's rear wheel failed with 11 broken spokes. Tour rules of that time said that if the mechanical failure is real and no repair possible a rider may replace the broken item. When Scieur's wheel broke there were no Tour monitors around to verify his problem. After replacing the wheel he strapped the broken wheel to his back and carried it for 300 kilometers to show the officials at the finish that his need was real. Scars left on his back by the sprocket remained with him for years.

Scieur kept his lead through the final stage to Paris. His hometown of Florennes is still the only small town to produce 2 Tour winners. Lucien Pothier, who placed second in the 1903 Tour (not to be confused with René Pottier who won in 1906), rode his last Tour in

1921. He finished thirty-second out of the 38 finishers: 41 hours, 45 minutes, 11 seconds behind Scieur. Fourth place Lucotti was the highest placed Italian to date in Tour competition.

The final 1921 Tour de France General Classification:

1. Léon Scieur (La Sportive): 221 hours 50 minutes 26 seconds

2. Hector Heusghem (La Sportive) @ 18 minutes 36 seconds

3. Honoré Barthélemy (La Sportive) @ 2 hours 1 minute

4. Luigi Lucotti (Ancora) @ 2 hours 39 minutes 18 seconds

5. Hector Tiberghien (La Sportive) @ 4 hours 33 minutes 19 seconds

1922. The start of the sixteenth Tour de France must have heartened French cycling fans. A Frenchman instead of a Belgian won the first stage. In his fourth Tour start, Robert Jacquinot won stage 1 to Le Havre, beating second-place Eugène Christophe by over 8 minutes. Yes, that Eugène Christophe of the 1913 and 1919 tragically broken forks. Now 37 years old, Christophe was still tough as nails and was riding the Tour to win. The sentimental favorite of the French, he had been forced to retire from the previous 2 Tours with back pains.

Stage 2 was the scene of yet another French win. Romain Bellenger beat Philippe Thys, Jacquinot, Victor Lenaers, Jean Alavoine and Émile Masson in a sprint win. Christophe and most of the other contenders came in 47 seconds later.

Stage 3 was another bunch sprint. Jacquinot edged out toughguy Honoré Barthélemy and 22 other riders. Desgrange must have been fuming to have had such a large mass romp to the line. He felt that unless the racers straggled in exhausted, by ones and twos, they must have dosed their efforts and raced without real aggression. After stage 3 Jacquinot was still in the Yellow Jersey.

Stage 4, 412 kilometers from Brest to Les Sables d'Olonne, saw fortune get a chance to make up for all the misery she had caused Eugène Christophe. Overall leader Jacquinot lost 1 hour, 41 minutes that day. At the end of the stage, Eugène Christophe, the Tour's first official Yellow Jersey back in 1919, again donned the leader's garment. This Tour was turning out the way the French wanted it. The fact that Belgian Philippe Thys won the stage was unimportant in this new, improved big picture. At last, a Frenchman who could win the Tour de

France had assumed the mantle of leadership.

After stage 5 and before the Pyrenees, here was the General Classification. Christophe had a good, solid lead:

1. Eugène Christophe
2. Philippe Thys @ 8 minutes 15 seconds
3. Félix Sellier @ 34 minutes 49 seconds

Over the Aubisque, the Aspin and the Peyresourde in stage 6, perennial runner-up Jean Alavoine sprouted wings. He led over all the climbs and won the stage. Although Christophe finished 38 minutes behind the soaring Alavoine, Christophe kept his lead. Alavoine was now in second place, 27 minutes behind Christophe. 3-time winner Thys lost 3 1/2 hours because of a broken wheel. His chances for a fourth Tour win were about finished. Stage 7, the second Pyreneen stage, covered 323 rugged kilometers over the Portet d'Aspet, the Port and the Puymorens. This time, defending and keeping the Yellow Jersey was more than Christophe could do. "The Old Gaul" lost over 46 minutes. The time loss cost him the Yellow Jersey.

After the Pyrenees, this was how things stood:

1. Jean Alavoine
2. Firmin Lambot (1919 Tour winner) @ 14 minutes 19 seconds
3. Eugène Christophe @ 19 minutes 34 seconds

Jean Alavoine had been knocking on the door of Tour success for a decade. Pictures of him show a barrel-chested man with thick, muscular legs that make his climbing success seem unlikely. Twice Champion of France, Alavoine had been second, twice third, and fifth in the Tour. It looked as if his time to win had finally come. To earn the Yellow Jersey this year, he had won 3 stages in a row: stages 5, 6 and 7. Now he had the lead and had it by a healthy margin.

Stage 9, 281 kilometers from Toulon to Nice, had some tough climbing. Philippe Thys, who had won the day before, romped away with Alavoine to beat third place Émile Masson by almost 5 minutes. Several superb racers had their hopes for a top placing shattered that day. Jean Rossius and Eugène Christophe lost over 22 minutes. Hector Heusghem lost over 24 minutes. Stage 9's time loss knocked Christophe off the podium. He was now over 40 minutes behind Alavoine in the

General Classification.

Stage 10 was the first of 2 Alpine stages. The riders faced the Allos, Vars and the mighty Izoard. This was the first time for the Tour to assault the Vars and Izoard climbs. Thys' victory in this stage made 3 stage wins in a row for the Belgian. Thys also goes down as the first man in Tour history to lead the pack over both the Vars and the Izoard. Alavoine was only 32 seconds behind Thys that day with Firmin Lambot yet another 3 minutes back.

So, after the first Alpine stage the General Classification started to look pretty solid:

1. Jean Alavoine
2. Firmin Lambot @ 22 minutes 18 seconds
3. Victor Lenaers @ 39 minutes 34 seconds

France still had a man in Yellow. The Belgians (Lambot and Lenears) looked to be far off the back.

Riders pause at the top of a hill to flip their wheels to get a bigger gear for the downhill. This was over a decade before Tour riders were allowed to use derailleurs.

Stage 11 was another tough day in the Alps. That Saturday the riders had to climb the Galibier, the Télégraphe and the Aravis. The weather was bad with a rainstorm hitting them as the leaders were on the Galibier. Honoré Barthélemy, who had suffered so terribly in the 1920 Tour, was having no better luck this year. After several crashes, perhaps the toughest man to have ever ridden the Tour had to abandon.

More bad luck was in store for the other riders. On the Galibier Eugène Christophe broke his forks for an unbelievable third time. The same Christophe who broke his forks at crucial moments in the 1913 and 1919 Tours again had to walk his bike down a mountain and make his own repairs. At least Christophe was out of contention when his forks broke this time. Alavoine had his own mechanical troubles in the bad weather and lost 38 minutes.

Émile Masson won the stage. The perennially high placing Hector Heusghem was close by at 4 minutes, 47 seconds back. Lambot had a tough day in the bad weather, coming in over 22 minutes behind Masson.

After all this tumult, here was the General Classification podium:

1. Jean Alavoine

2. Firmin Lambot @ 6 minutes 53 seconds

3. Hector Heusghem @ 15 minutes 49 seconds

More action was coming to roil this incredible Tour. Stage 12, from Geneva to Strasbourg, was Masson's second win in a row. Lambot lost 22 minutes and Alavoine had an even worse day, losing 37 minutes.

So here were the new standings. Belgians had moved back into the first 2 places. *Ma Foi!*

1. Hector Heusghem

2. Firmin Lambot @ 3 minutes 13 seconds

3. Jean Alavoine @ 10 minutes 24 seconds

We're not done. On stage 13 Heusghem wrecked his bike on a pothole. He took a new machine from a teammate to finish the stage. Today we would understand that as the proper course. In 1922 when riders had to repair their own bikes, trading bikes under the complex rules of the Tour was usually forbidden. The judges slapped Heusghem with a 1-hour penalty. Heusghem had gotten permission for the swap from a race judge, making the whole situation even sadder—the decision to impose the penalty came later after reviewing the rules. Without this penalty, he surely would have won the Tour.

So:

1. Firmin Lambot
2. Jean Alavoine @ 33 minutes 16 seconds
3. Victor Lenaers @ 47 minutes 10 seconds

Sad-faced yet very lucky Firmin Lambot, 37 years old, had stayed out of trouble. As his competitors suffered one misfortune after another, Lambot slowly rose in the standings.

There were 2 stages left and Fortune, who seems to have had a grudge against Christophe, loved Lambot. His victory at 37 years of age makes him the oldest man to have won the Tour. In addition, he is the first man to win the Tour de France without winning a single stage. Thys won a total of 5 stages in the 1922 Tour, including the final stage into Paris. With better luck with his wheels in the Pyrenees 1922 would surely have been his fourth Tour win.

Alphonse Baugé, still managing the Peugeot team, crafted another win. Second place Alavoine was also a Baugé-coached Peugeot rider. Peugeot's ownership of the Tour was almost total, having won 12 of the 15 stages.

Final 1922 Tour de France General Classification:

1. Firmin Lambot (Peugeot): 222 hours 8 minutes 6 seconds
2. Jean Alavoine (Peugeot) @ 41 minutes 15 seconds
3. Félix Sellier (Alcyon) @ 42 minutes 2 seconds
4. Hector Heusghem (Thomann) @ 43 minutes 56 seconds
5. Victor Lenaers (Peugeot) @ 45 minutes 32 seconds

1923. Desgrange had established a large, complex set of rules with the intention of making the Tour a test of the individual rider and his machine. 1922's problems caused him to reconsider one rule. Up until 1923 a rider had to perform his own repairs. Think back to the tragedy of Eugène Christophe and his multiple broken forks. In 1922 Thys won 5 stages yet finished in fourteenth place because of a broken wheel in the Pyrenees. Heusghem was leading the Tour when he hit a pothole, relegating him to fourth place. In 1923 the rules were changed to allow riders to swap parts instead of repairing them. This is a monumental change in the character of the Tour de France. Before, bad luck reigned as the supreme arbiter of the race. Now, perhaps the race might be more of a test of the athletic prowess of the riders.

That didn't mean the other regulatory burdens were relaxed. A rider still had to finish with everything he had at the start. That included clothes and spare tires. A flatted tubular had to be transported to the end of the stage. The rider had to carry the warm clothing he needed for the early morning starts on the terribly long stages of those early days to the end of the stage and not discard it. These rules set the stage for a series of disputes with one of the Tour's most headstrong riders. The immovable object, Desgrange, again met Henri Pélissier, the unstoppable force. Before proceeding with the story of the 1923 Tour let's pause a moment and learn a little bit about the Pélissiers.

There were 3 remarkable cycling Pélissier brothers: Charles, Francis and Henri. All were superb riders. Charles, the youngest, won stages in 4 different Tours. Francis won Paris–Tours, the French Championship, Bordeaux–Paris and stages in 2 different Tours, but finished only 1 Tour, 1923. He went on to have a wonderful career as a team manager, discovering a 19-year old racer named Jacques Anquetil, the first man to win the Tour 5 times. But it was Henri, the oldest of the surviving brothers, who had the real cycling talent.

A look at Henri Pélissier's palmares reveals an astonishing ability. And speaking of discoveries, it was 2 time Tour winner Lucien Petit-Breton who discovered the thin, young Henri. Starting in 1911 Henri won Milan–Turin, going on to win Milan–San Remo, Tour of Lombardy, Paris–Roubaix, Paris–Brussels, Paris–Tours, Tour of the Basque Country and after much agony, the Tour de France.

Let's list his Tour de France history. If he hadn't fought Desgrange tooth and nail, his Tour palmares would have been quite different:

1912: Did not finish (DNF)

1913: DNF

1914: 2nd in General Classification and 3 stage wins

1919: DNF, 1 stage win

1920: DNF, 2 stage wins

1923: 1st in General Classification with victories in stages 3, 10, and 11

1924: DNF

1925: DNF

As we saw earlier, Henri Pélissier started his feud with Desgrange when Desgrange penalized him 2 minutes in the 1920 Tour for throwing away a flatted tire. Pélissier quit the Tour in protest. Desgrange wrote of Henri, "This Pélissier knows nothing about suffering, he'll never win the Tour."

Yet, for all the fireworks between the 2 of them, Desgrange respected Pélissier. A famous interchange between the 2 of them before a Paris–Roubaix:

"Never forget, *L'Auto* made you what you are."

"Never," replied Pélissier. "I'm the one who made *L'Auto*. Next Sunday you will print: 'First, Henri Pélissier', then you will see the difference in your sales between this name and the others."

After being so bold, Pélissier did have the good legs and good fortune to win Paris–Roubaix. For the 1923 Tour, Henri decided to stick it out and suffer the million petty rules of the tyrannical Desgrange, no matter how outraged he might be.

This was the year that Desgrange introduced time bonuses for stage wins. To make the racers dig more deeply for the win, 2 minutes were removed from the elapsed time of the winner of each stage. Today (2005), the time bonus is 20 seconds for the winner, 12 seconds for second and 8 seconds for third.

In 1923 Pélissier's team, Automoto, hired Alphonse Baugé to manage the team. He had engineered many Tour wins for teams Peugeot and Alcyon in previous years. The Automoto team had real depth. Henri's strong brother Francis was on the team and was determined to do everything possible to help Henri make it to Paris in Yellow. In addition, Automoto had Honoré Barthélemy, Hector Heusghem, Victor Lenaers and future Tour winner Lucien Buysse.

Automoto had another rider of note. Because it had commercial interests in Italy, Automoto wanted some quality Italian riders on its team. Several Italians were hired and were supposed to have journeyed to Paris to ride the Tour for Automoto. But the only Italian who made the trip was a young man who had just turned pro the previous year, Ottavio Bottecchia. Only 2 weeks before, Bottecchia had finished riding the 1923 Giro to a fine fifth place. With that excellent result quiet

Bottecchia ended up at the side of the fiery Henri Pélissier. Les Woodland writes that at the time of his arrival in France Bottecchia's only French was the sentence, "No bananas, lots of coffee, thank you". Because Bottecchia was the only Italian hired by the team who actually made the journey to France, Automoto decided that its marketing plan to use Italians wasn't worth the trouble. They were ready to send the skinny Italian back. In the end good sense prevailed and Bottecchia stayed on the team.

Robert Jacquinot started the 1923 Tour the same way he started the 1922 edition, by winning the first stage. It was good for Automoto that they put Bottecchia on the start line in Paris. He came in second in the first stage. Bottecchia wasn't finished. He won the second stage, from Le Havre to Cherbourg. That put him in the overall lead, becoming the first Italian ever to wear the Yellow Jersey. Automoto's team leader Henri Pélissier lost over 13 minutes the first stage and almost 2 minutes on the second stage.

The Pélissier brothers came alive on stage 3, 405 kilometers from Cherbourg to Brest. Henri won the stage with Francis coming in second with the same time. Bottecchia was third, only 37 seconds back. That left Bottecchia still in Yellow with Peugeot's Romain Bellenger in second, only 2 minutes adrift.

Bottecchia lost the lead on stage 4, which went from Brest to Les Sables d'Olonne. He came in ninth that day, 15 minutes behind the stage winner Albert Dejonghe and 6 minutes after Bellenger. Robert Jacquinot won stage 5, but that didn't change the podium of the General Classification. Here were the standings after stage 5 and just before the Pyrenees:

1. Romain Bellenger
2. Hector Tiberghien @ 3 minutes 15 seconds
3. Ottavio Bottecchia @ 3 minutes 54 seconds

The 326 kilometers of stage 6 crossed the Aubisque, the Tourmalet, the Aspin and the Peyresourde. Jacquinot, who so far had ridden the Tour as a very fine sprinter, was first over the Aubisque, the Tourmalet and the Aspin. He looked like he would be the new Yellow Jersey at the end of the day, but he ran out of gas before he ran out of mountains. There was still the 1,569 meter Peyresourde to pass and it was one mountain too many for the Frenchman. He was so exhausted that he fell off his bike on the Peyresourde. Jean Alavoine rode past him and took the stage win. Jacquinot was able to get back on his bike and finish the stage, coming in second, but he was a huge 16 minutes behind Alavoine. Henri Pélissier came in at 23 minutes and Bottecchia a little over 27 minutes after Alavoine.

So, Bottecchia reclaimed the Yellow Jersey and Alavoine was in his usual position as a runner-up. Here were the standings in the General Classification after the first day in the Pyrenees:

1. Ottavio Bottecchia
2. Jean Alavoine @ 8 minutes 28 seconds
3. Romain Bellenger @ 21 minutes 50 seconds

Stage 7 was also a Pyrenean stage. Alavoine won the stage but Bellenger, Bottecchia and the Pélissier brothers were right there with him, finishing with the same time. No change to the General Classification.

Stage 8 from Perpignan to Toulon was a terrible day for Bellenger. He lost 20 minutes to leader Bottecchia and 12 to Alavoine. That pushed Henri Pélissier on to the podium of the General Classification:

1. Ottavio Bottecchia
2. Jean Alavoine @ 14 minutes 19 seconds
3. Henri Pélissier @ 22 minutes 8 seconds

Pélissier lost some time on the next stage, but their relative positions remained unchanged before the first of the big Alpine stages. Philippe Thys abandoned the Tour at this point.

Stage 10, from Nice to Briançon, would cross the Allos, the Vars and the gigantic Izoard. It was on this stage that the ambitious Henri Pélissier planned to attack his own teammate, the Yellow Jersey'd Bottecchia, in a gamble to take the lead. Brother Francis and teammate Lucien Buysse had been working hard to keep Henri close to the lead. Francis Pélissier was riding with an injured knee but he was determined to see his brother in Yellow. Now they would try to make Francis' pain pay off.

A break with Buysse, Alancourt, Alavoine and Bottecchia went clear on the Allos. Henri Pélissier, initially missing the move, joined them. Apparently Bottecchia was in too big a gear and was having trouble as the others forced a fast pace up the mountain. Changing gears in the days before derailleurs meant dismounting the bike, flipping the rear wheel and getting going again. Sensing the young, inexperienced Bottecchia's difficulty, Pélissier attacked and got clear.

On the descent Buysse and Alavoine joined Henri. The trio climbed the Vars together. Pélissier attacked Buysse and Alavoine on the Izoard and again easily broke away. Pélissier was riding in a state of grace as he pulled away from the entire field and won the stage.

The results for the day:

1. Henri Pélissier: 12 hours 45 minutes 29 seconds
2. Lucien Buysse @ 5 minutes 28 seconds
3. Arsène Alancourt @ 18 minutes 24 seconds
4. Hector Tiberghien same time
5. Jean Alavoine @ 26 minutes 58 seconds
12. Ottavio Bottecchia @ 41 minutes 8 seconds

So, the General Classification was turned upside down:

1. Henri Pélissier
2. Jean Alavoine @ 11 minutes 25 seconds
3. Ottavio Bottecchia @ 13 minutes 16 seconds

Henri Pélissier consolidated his gains in stage 11 as he was first over the 2,556-meter high Galibier and then the Aravis. He and brother Francis came in together with Henri taking the stage win. Bellenger was a plucky third, over 8 minutes back. Bottecchia was fifth at 13 minutes, 56 seconds. After an accident, Alavoine was forced to abandon. This left Pélissier in command in the General Classification:

1. Henri Pélissier
2. Ottavio Bottecchia @ 29 minutes 12 seconds
3. Romain Bellenger @ 1 hour 5 minutes 14 seconds

It seemed as if the Belgian hammerlock on the Tour had been released. Not only was a Frenchman in Yellow and riding with confident power, French racers won the last 4 stages: first Joseph Muller, then Romain Bellenger, then Félix Goethals won the last 2 stages.

Desgrange was thrilled. He had 2 reasons to be happy. First of all, a fellow countryman had won the Tour. Desgrange had a strong nationalistic streak. Pélissier was the first French victor since Gustave Garrigou in 1911. And, it was just as Pélissier had called it. Sales of *L'Auto* spiked when a Frenchman won the Tour. Desgrange was effusive in his praise of Pélissier saying that he "has put on a show for us that is the equal of the highest artistic performance."

Pélissier recognized the talent of his young Italian teammate. "Bottecchia will succeed me," he said.

The final 1923 Tour de France General Classification:

1. Henri Pélissier (Automoto): 222 hours 15 minutes 30 seconds
2. Ottavio Bottecchia (Automoto) @ 30 minutes 41 seconds
3. Romain Bellenger (Peugeot) @ 1 hour 4 minutes 43 seconds
4. Hector Tiberghien (Peugeot) @ 1 hour 29 minutes 16 seconds
5. Arsène Alancourt (Armor) @ 2 hours 6 minutes 40 seconds

1924. Desgrange was so happy with the 2-minute stage win time bonuses that he had introduced in 1923, he increased the bonus for a stage win to 3 minutes for 1924.

Ottavio Bottecchia returned to France to ride for Automoto and showed that he had arrived with truly fine form, winning the 2-man sprint for victory in the first stage. Henri and Francis Pélissier finished the stage with the same time as Bottecchia, but it was the quiet Italian, a stonemason before he took up racing, who put on the Yellow Jersey. Neither Bottecchia nor Pélissier distinguished themselves in the second stage. Both were placed high enough in the sprint to keep their General Classification positions with Bottecchia staying in Yellow. Already Henri Pélissier could sense that Bottecchia had improved over the previous year, publicly (and generously) noting that Bottecchia was head and shoulders above the rest.

But, while Henri Pélissier may not have had a particularly fine placing that day, he did manage to have another one of his fierce fights with Desgrange. This clash was one for the history books. Stage 2, being 371 kilometers long and needing over 14 hours to complete, started before sunrise. The day started out cool and Pélissier wore a couple of jerseys. As the day warmed, Pélissier removed and discarded one. The manager of the competing Legnano team, Eberado Pavesi, saw Pélissier toss the shirt and reported the infraction to Desgrange. Because this violated Tour Rule 48 that said a racer must finish the stage with everything he had at the start, Pélissier was penalized. "But, this is my shirt!" Henri protested to Desgrange. That the discarded jersey was Pélissier's property did not enter into the question. He had broken Rule 48. Pélissier had quit in 1920 when he received a 2-minute penalty for throwing away a tire. History seemed about to repeat itself. Still, he stayed in the race.

Stage 3, 405 kilometers from Cherbourg to Brest, showed that Philippe Thys (winner in 1913, 1914, 1920) still had it. He and Théophile Beeckman tied for the stage win. Beeckman was now tied with Bottecchia in the General Classification. But that wasn't the real story of the day.

A fuming Henri Pélissier started the day's stage. A couple of times a race commissaire actually stopped Henri and counted the jerseys he was wearing. This was too much for the volatile and proud Pélissier. He protested the treatment to Desgrange who refused to argue with the hotheaded racer during the race and promised to get it sorted out that evening in Brest. That wasn't good enough for Pélissier. Furious at the accumulated mistreatments and slights, Henri and his brother Francis along with Maurice Ville—who came in second in stage 2—withdrew from the race as it went through the town of Coutances.

When the Tour peloton passed through the city of Granville in the late afternoon journalist Albert Londres noticed that the Pélissier brothers were not in the peloton. Sensing something was up, he asked around and found that they had abandoned. Knowing that a good story was probably in play, he raced his Renault back to Coutances and found the Pélissiers and Ville having hot chocolate at a bar in the train station. There the racers poured out their angry grievances with Desgrange and the Tour: "…in the name of God, don't harass us. We accept the torment but we don't want vexations. My name is Pélissier, not Atlas," he said to the reporter.

Pélissier described the doping products the racers used to see them through the terrible, long stages. He showed Londres cocaine for his eyes, boxes of pills he took and the chloroform for the gums. "We run on dynamite," he said. Pélissier poured out his tale of the racers' suffering describing how even most of his toenails had fallen out.

Londres was a skilled and famous writer. He had just written about the conditions in the French penal colonies in French Guyana.

Searching for a new subject, Londres had decided to follow the Tour de France and write about it. His story of his meeting with the racers, *Les Forçats de la Route* (Prisoners of the Road) was a sensation.

Years later brother Francis Pélissier said that they were toying with Londres, saying that the reporter was not knowledgeable about cycle racing and that what they said to him was an exaggeration. At the time of the later comments Francis was the manager of a professional team. Might his redacting of the famous story be that of a man looking for respectability? The original tale has the sound and feel of truth.

Regarding the withdrawal of the Pélissiers and Ville: Ville was having trouble with his knees and was quite happy to quit when the Pélissiers invited him to abandon. Francis was having stomach problems. But Henri? Was he truly enraged or was it as *L'Equipe* describes it? *L'Equipe* says that the entire abandonment by Henri Pélissier was a giant set piece. He was well past his prime, sure to lose to Bottecchia and wanted out of the Tour. Seeking a fight with Desgrange gave him an out with honor.

While Pélissier did acknowledge that Bottecchia was the better rider, one could hardly think of Pélissier as the rider in decline that *L'Equipe* described. The year before, he had won the Tour by closing an enormous time deficit on the Izoard. This year he had stayed with Bottecchia for the first 2 stages and was about equal to him on time. And, he came back and rode the Tour in 1925. Given that Pélissier had been willing to quit over Desgrange's tyrannical dictates before, this abandonment has the feel of authentic Pélissier rage. Let's give his temper its due.

Stage 5, from Les Sables d'Olonne to Bayonne has the distinction of being the longest day by time in Tour history. The Tour had used this 482-kilometer stage since 1919. I believe it is the longest in distance of any Tour stage. This year the winner took a numbing 19 hours, 40 minutes to complete the distance. Seeing that it made for poor racing—Londres said it wasn't even cycling, the riders were moving so slowly—the huge stage was abandoned after 1924.

With Henri Pélissier out of the Tour there could be no worry about a fight within the Automoto team for leadership. Bottecchia was Automoto's man to win the Tour. When the Tour came to stage 6 with its 4 major mountain passes Bottecchia showed that he was a truly complete rider. The previous year he had been dropped on the tough Alpine climbs. This year he dominated. He was first over each of the day's climbs: the Aubisque, the Tourmalet, the Aspin, and the Peyresourde. He arrived at the finish in Luchon almost 19 minutes before the stage's second place finisher and later 1926 Tour winner Lucien Buysse. Bottecchia finished over 35 minutes ahead of 1927 Tour winner Nicolas Frantz.

The General Classification after stage 6:

1. Ottavio Bottecchia
2. Lucien Buysse @ 30 minutes 21 seconds
3. Nicolas Frantz @ 42 minutes 15 seconds

With such a commanding lead he was content to merely bury his General Classification contenders in the second Pyreneen stage rather than completely obliterate them. Philippe Thys and Arsène Alancourt were able to finish with Bottecchia. Frantz lost another 4 minutes. Buysse, who had been first over the first of the day's 4 major summits, the Ares, lost over a half-hour by the end of the day. Frantz was now in second place, but over 49 minutes behind Bottecchia.

Frantz seemed to shine once the Tour reached the Alps. Stage 10 required the racers to climb the Allos, Vars and Izoard. Frantz was first over all 3 but Italian Giovanni Brunero was able beat him to the finish by almost a minute. The stage did allow Frantz to gain about 9 minutes on the now-cruising Bottecchia. Frantz won the next 2 stages. All those fine efforts weren't nearly enough to take the lead from the speedy Italian. After all the major climbing was done, here was the General Classification after stage 12:

1. Ottavio Bottecchia
2. Nicolas Frantz @ 35 minutes 52 seconds
3. Giovanni Brunero @ 49 minutes 27 seconds

With a good lead in hand and no real trouble along the way in the final 3 stages, Bottecchia earned a beautiful Tour. To make sure the world knew that he was in charge and that he could almost win at will, he won the sprint in the final stage in Paris. Not only was Bottecchia the first Italian in Yellow the previous year, he was now the first Italian to win the Tour outright.

Brunero, who might have made it 2 Italians on the podium, had to abandon on the penultimate stage.

Final 1924 Tour de France General Classification:

1. Ottavio Bottecchia (Automoto): 226 hours 18 minutes 21 seconds

2. Nicolas Frantz (Alcyon) @ 35 minutes 36 seconds

3. Lucien Buysse (Automoto) @ 1 hour 32 minutes 13 seconds

4. Bartolomeo Aimo (Legnano) @ 1 hour 32 minutes 47 seconds

5. Théophile Beeckman (Griffon) @ 2 hours 11 minutes 12 seconds

1925. Since 1910, the year of Octave Lapize's victory, the Tour had used a 15-stage format. In 1925 the Tour went to 18 stages with roughly the same distance as in 1924, 5,430 kilometers. The average length of a stage in 1924 was 361 kilometers. It dropped to 321 kilometers in 1925. Henri Pélissier was winning one of his most important arguments. Pélissier believed that the numbingly long stages made for poor racing and fought for shorter stages ridden at higher speeds. In the end, history has validated Pélissier's argument. Desgrange also reduced the time bonus for stage wins.

Automoto brought a formidable team to the 1925 Tour. Its 6 men included Ottavio Bottecchia, Philippe Thys, Henri and Francis Pélissier, and Lucien and Jules Buysse. Among them, I count 7 Tour victories past, present and future.

Eugène Christophe, wearing the JB Louvet jersey was riding his last Tour. Also riding their last Tours were Jean Alavoine, Philippe Thys, Henri Pélissier and that eternal second, Hector Heusghem.

130 riders departed on Sunday, June 21 from Paris. 340 kilometers later Ottavio Bottecchia came in alone, 2 minutes, 59 seconds ahead of Francis Pélissier. Bottecchia started the 1925 Tour the same way he started the 1924 edition, in Yellow.

Bottecchia kept the Yellow Jersey until the end of stage 3 where he lost about 6 minutes to a front group that contained Belgian rider Adelin Benoit. Benoit took over the lead with Bottecchia only 8 seconds behind.

Future Tour winner Nicolas Frantz (1927, 1928) was getting better. He won stages 4 and 5 but Benoit kept the Yellow Jersey. Bottecchia shadowed him keeping the gap in the General Classification at 8 seconds.

Bottecchia won stage 6, still a long 293 kilometers from Les Sables d'Olonne to Bordeaux. The list of riders finishing at the same time with him reads almost like a *Who's Who* of the early Tour. Frantz was second. Not far behind him were Jean Alavoine, Philippe Thys, Francis Pélissier, Eugène Christophe, Émile Masson, Honoré Barthélemy and Romain Bellenger. In all 43 riders, many of them cycling immortals, galloped for the line that day. Oh, to have seen that finish! Bottecchia remained in second place, at 8 seconds behind Benoit.

Stage 7, 189 kilometers from Bordeaux to Bayonne, made a difference. Bottecchia was first in a 6-man lead group that beat the pack by 4 minutes, 30 seconds. Bottecchia took back the Yellow Jersey with Benoit over 4 minutes in arrears.

The next day, stage 8, was the first of the 2 days in the Pyrenees with the Aubisque, Tourmalet, Aspin and the Peyresourde. Bottecchia was first over Aubisque. Omer Huyse of the Armor team crested the Tourmalet and the Aspin in the lead. But Benoit was on fire. He led over the Peyresourde and came in alone, 9 minutes ahead of Huyse. Bottecchia trailed in almost 12 minutes later. The rest of the field was wrecked. Fourth place that day went to Frantz who was almost 22 minutes behind. Bottecchia's loyal Automoto teammate Lucien Buysse was 44 minutes down and he was only tenth! Hector Heusghem was over 2 hours slower and Philippe Thys was yet another hour behind. Bottecchia was back in second place in the General Classification, almost 7 minutes behind Benoit.

The General Classification:

1. Adelin Benoit
2. Ottavio Bottecchia @ 6 minutes 53 seconds
3. Omer Huyse @ 24 minutes 24 seconds

Benoit couldn't keep that pace up for long. In fact he couldn't keep it up for another day. Stage 9, which went from Luchon to Perpignan, had 4 major passes. Bottecchia was first over all of them, but by the time he and teammate Lucien Buysse came in to the finish they were 6 minutes behind Frantz and Albert Dejonghe. Benoit was an hour late in keeping his appointment with the Yellow Jersey, delayed by a sore knee. Bottecchia was back in Yellow. The General Classification after the Pyrenees:

1. Ottavio Bottecchia
2. Nicolas Frantz @ 13 minutes 20 seconds
3. Albert Dejonghe @ 26 minutes 25 seconds

Across Southern France, heading for the Alps, Lucien Buysse took care of Bottecchia, acting as a loyal, selfless *domestique*. In return, Bottecchia let Buysse take the stage wins in both stage 11 to Toulon and stage 12 to Nice.

In the Alps Bottecchia extended his lead without worrying about winning the stages. The Italian sports fans who had flocked to the Tour to see Bottecchia ride had the pleasure of seeing their compatriot Bartolomeo Aimo be the first over both the Vars and the Izoard as he rode to win stage 13. Bottecchia was 10 minutes back but General Classification second place Frantz was over 13 minutes slower.

Stage 14 took the riders over the 2,556-meter high Galibier and the 1,498-meter Aravis on their way from Briançon to Évian. Lucien Buysse led his team captain Bottecchia over the Galibier while Bottecchia took the point over the Aravis. JB Louvet rider Hector Martin won the stage but Bottecchia, Aimo, Buysse and Dejonghe finished with him with the same time.

After completion of the Alpine stages, Bottecchia was firmly in control:

1. Ottavio Bottecchia
2. Bartolomeo Aimo @ 55 minutes 49 seconds
3. Lucien Buysse @ 58 minutes 38 seconds

The gap between Aimo and Buysse was quite small. Buysse remedied what he surely thought was a curable deficiency in the standings by breaking away with Frantz, Dejonghe and Hector Martin in the sixteenth stage. Aimo missed the move and finished 5 minutes behind the fast-moving quartet. Buysse advanced to second place and Frantz was now third in the General Classification.

1. Ottavio Bottecchia
2. Lucien Buysse @ 55 minutes 36 seconds

3. Nicolas Frantz @ 55 minutes 39 seconds

For the last stage into Paris Bottecchia got into a break with his 2 teammates, brothers Jules and Lucien Buysse, as well as Aimo and Romain Bellenger. Bottecchia won the sprint, icing a perfectly run Tour. He rode economically and carefully, avoiding needless, energy-wasting display.

Both Francis and Henri Pélissier abandoned the 1925 Tour. Henri bailed out on stage 4 and Francis quit on stage 9 (the Luchon to Perpignan Pyreneen stage). Philippe Thys quit on stage 9 as well.

The French were shut out of the top 10 in the final General Classification. Alcyon rider Romain Bellenger's 4 hours, 26 minutes behind Bottecchia, eleventh in the General Classification, was the best the French could do. For the first time Italians took 2 of the 3 places on the podium. France would have to wait until 1930 before one of her sons would again wear Yellow in Paris.

The final 1925 Tour de France General Classification:

1. Ottavio Bottecchia (Automoto): 219 hours 10 minutes 18 seconds
2. Lucien Buysse (Automoto) @ 54 minutes 20 seconds
3. Bartolomeo Aimo (Alcyon) @ 56 minutes 37 seconds
4. Nicolas Frantz (Alcyon) @ 1 hour 11 minutes 24 seconds
5. Albert Dejonghe (JB Louvet) @ 1 hour 27 minutes 42 seconds

Since this was the last year Henri Pélissier rode the Tour, let's take a look at his post-Tour life. As we have noted, Henri Pélissier was a hothead, willing to get into an argument any time. One time his public comments describing his fellow racers as draft horses so offended the peloton that at an inopportune moment when he stopped to urinate the angry pack broke its unwritten rule and *en masse* attacked and permanently dropped him. He wasn't just a man who seemed to be at war with the outside world. His first wife, Léonie, finding life with Henri intolerable, killed herself in 1933.

Henri replaced her with a paramour, Camille Tharault. They argued ferociously. 2 years later in 1935 the warring pair had a terrible fight; Pélissier cut Tharault in the face with a knife. In return, Camille shot him dead with the same revolver Léonie had used to commit suicide.

She did the job correctly, putting 5 slugs into Pélissier. After pleading self-defense, the court gave her a year's suspended jail sentence. Les Woodland notes that this was as close to an acquittal as the courts could give her.

1926. Desgrange went back to longer stages. The 1926 Tour was the longest ever at 5,745 kilometers. He reduced the number of stages to 17 thereby raising the average length of a stage from 1925's 321 kilometers up to 338 kilometers per stage. This was still well below 1924's 361-kilometer average.

This was the first year the Tour did not start in Paris. Desgrange moved the start to a small city in the Alps, Évian. To get the riders to the little town on Lake Geneva the Tour shuttled the riders by chartered train. Desgrange wanted to spice up the racing in the early stages by starting in the mountains. Also, the stages that followed the Alps leading to Paris were always dull, anticlimactic promenades. His plan was to scoot to Paris after the Alps in only 2 stages and cut the tedious agony short. Overall the result was a Tour that was raced rather conservatively with sprint finishes in 10 stages. For all his efforts Desgrange ended up with a duller rather than a more aggressive Tour.

126 riders left Évian. There were 9 sponsored teams containing 44 pro riders. Several of the squads had as few as 2 riders. The other 82 racers were *touriste-routiers*, independent riders responsible for all of their travel and sleeping accommodations. In 1925 2 *touriste-routier* riders broke into the top 20. Usually the sponsored riders were the truly competitive ones who attained the superior placings.

On the Automoto team were Ottavio Bottecchia and the Buysse brothers, Lucien and Jules. The only other formidable team with a large squad of fine riders was Alcyon. They had Bartolomeo Aimo and Nicolas Frantz, third and fourth in the 1925 Tour. They also had Adelin Benoit, the Belgian who burned himself out challenging Bottecchia the year before. Tour boss Desgrange thought Benoit was the real challenger to Bottecchia's attempt at 3 Tour wins in a row.

Stage 1 didn't seem to put much hope into Desgrange's attempt to increase the racers' aggressivity in his race. Jules Buysse came in alone, 13 minutes clear of a 9-man chase group. Bottecchia, harassed by flat tires, finished sixteenth, 34 minutes behind Buysse. A poor start to a ride for the Yellow.

Stage 2, 334 kilometers from Mulhouse to Metz, ended in a 25-man romp to the finish with Automoto's Jules Buysse retaining the Yellow Jersey. The next day was a 433-kilometer stage. It took stage winner Gustave Van Slembrouck over 17 long hours to complete the distance. He and Albert Dejonghe beat the rest of the pack by almost 11 minutes. That gave Van Slembrouck the lead.

That day Lucien Buysse received the terrible news that his daughter had died, causing him to contemplate dropping out of the race. His family prevailed upon him to continue racing.

The General Classification after stage 3:

1. Gustave Van Slembrouck

2. Albert Dejonghe @ 1 minute 9 seconds

3. Jules Buysse @ 6 minutes 27 seconds

This is how the situation remained as each of the next 6 stages ended in a mass sprint. Stage 9, from Bordeaux to Bayonne, had 56 riders steam for the line together, unheard of for the Tour in those days.

Everything changed with stage 10. This was the first of the 2 days in the Pyrenees. The riders were to climb the usual passes: the Aubisque, the Tourmalet, the Aspin and the Peyresourde. This Tuesday, June 30, with 326 kilometers from Bayonne to Luchon is one of the great, memorable days in Tour history.

Lucien Buysse, who had been a selfless *domestique* to Bottecchia, especially in the 1925 Tour, set out to win the Tour this day. The Buysse brothers were still burning from what they thought was an unjust misfortune when their older brother Marcel, in Yellow, broke his handlebars on stage 8 of the 1913 Tour. That mishap cost him the lead. Marcel Buysse was able to finish third in the General Classification, but the Buysses considered all of this unfinished business that required rectification.

Although he was 22 minutes behind Van Slembrouck in the General Classification, Lucien Buysse was undeterred. He had predicted in Dunkirk (stage 5) that this stage would be the one where he would take the lead.

The weather conditions of the day have been described as apocalyptic, hellish and dantesque. It was certainly the worst in Tour history to that time. There was both torrential rain and nearly freezing fog. To make it worse, please remember that the passes in those days were not paved. In the rain the riders crossed the great mountains on roads of mud! These were indeed iron men on wooden rims.

The stage was so long the riders set off at 2:00 a.m. There was a cold rain falling. The riders knew that worse awaited them at the tops of some of the highest mountains in Europe.

Buysse signaled his intention by attacking on the Aubisque, the first climb. Van Slembrouck, a bigger man, was immediately shelled. 3 men went clear, Buysse, Albert Dejonghe and Omer Huyse. Bottecchia could not stay with them. Desgrange's pick for the Tour, Benoit, quit the race. At the tops of the mountains freezing sleet lashed the riders. At times the sticky mud forced the riders to dismount and walk their bikes.

On the Tourmalet, 3 riders made contact with the now lead duo (Huyse was dropped): Odile Taillieu, Léon Devos and Bartolomeo Aimo. Buysse was finally able to leave everyone and crest the Aspin and the Peyresourde first. He came into Luchon at 5:12 p.m., almost 26 minutes ahead of Aimo and almost 30 minutes ahead of Devos. Van Slembrouck? He was 1 hour and 50 minutes behind, his dreams of Yellow shattered.

The average speed for Lucien Buysse's day in hell was 18.9 kilometers per hour. Only 54 riders finished that day. Desgrange, recognizing the terrible circumstances of the stage, increased the cutoff time to 40% more than the winner's time. At midnight riders were still straggling into Luchon. Some sought shelter in bars. Others made it to Luchon by car. Rescue parties were sent out to find some of the riders who were cold, starving and shattered with exhaustion.

The day's results:

1. Lucien Buysse: 17 hours 12 minutes 4 seconds
2. Bartolomeo Aimo @ 25 minutes 48 seconds
3. Léon Devos @ 29 minutes 49 seconds
4. Théophile Beeckman @ 40 minutes
5. Nicolas Frantz @ 42 minutes 19 seconds

The General Classification after Stage 10:

1. Lucien Buysse
2. Odile Taillieu @ 36 minutes 14 seconds
3. Albert Dejonghe @ 46 minutes 50 seconds

Buysse had turned a deficit of 22 minutes into a lead of 36 minutes. This was a masterful, historic ride. Bottecchia, ill and suffering back pains, abandoned.

On Thursday, 2 days later, the riders had to face another tough stage. This time it was 323 kilometers from Luchon to Perpignan with the Ares, Portet d'Aspet, Port and Puymorens climbs in their way. At least the horrific weather conditions of the previous stage weren't present. Lucien Buysse proved he had staggering reserves of energy. He won again coming in alone after a 150-kilometer solo breakaway. His brother Jules was second, over 7 minutes back. Second place in the overall, Albert Dejonghe lost another 18 minutes to the speeding Belgian. Buysse now had a lead of over 1 hour. From here on Buysse rode to control his rivals. He worked to extend his lead without wasting energy. It was now a race for the other 2 places on the podium.

Here was the General Classification after the Pyrenees:

1. Lucien Buysse
2. Albert Dejonghe @ 1 hour 4 minutes 41 seconds
3. Odile Taillieu @ 1 hour 13 minutes 32 seconds

In the next stage Dejonghe missed the winning move and lost over 9 minutes. He was now in third place to Taillieu's second. Then the next day's stage, containing some preparatory climbing before the first alpine stage, both Taillieu and Dejonghe lost time and their positions on the General Classification podium. Nicolas Frantz moved up to second, but was a huge 1 hour, 19 minutes behind Buysse.

Stage 14 was the first day of the Alps. Buysse was first over the Allos, the initial climb of the day. Yet, not needing to waste energy, he finished with Frantz and Huyse 27 minutes behind Aimo. He had let Aimo, Félix Sellier and Marcel Bidot and 6 others ride away, since none was a threat to his lead. In the end Bartolomeo Aimo came in alone and moved up to third in the General Classification.

Even with the Galibier, Télégraphe and the Aravis, 27 riders finished stage 15 together. The racing was really over and the riders were exhausted. From here on Buysse just stayed out of trouble. The last 2 stages were also mass sprints. Buysse let others fight for stage glory. He had his Yellow Jersey.

1926 Tour de France final General Classification:

1. Lucien Buysse (Automoto): 238 hours 44 minutes 25 seconds

2. Nicolas Frantz (Alcyon) @ 1 hour 22 minutes 25 seconds

3. Bartolomeo Aimo (Alcyon) @ 1 hour 22 minutes 51 seconds

4. Théophile Beeckman (Armor) @ 1 hour 43 minutes 54 seconds

5. Félix Sellier (Alcyon) @ 1 hour 49 minutes 13 seconds

6. Albert Dejonghe (JB Louvet) @ 1 hour 56 minutes 15 seconds

Lucien Buysse's Tour victory was the culmination and high point of a long career. His first Tour was 1914, which he failed to finish. He tried again in 1919 and again abandoned. In 1923 he came in eighth. From then on it was a steady progression to third, then second and then his win in 1926. He never again finished the Tour de France.

And Ottavio Bottecchia? After his difficulties in the 1926 Tour he said that he would retire from professional cycling. On June 3, 1927 he was found murdered in the Italian countryside, his skull and several bones broken. He had been out riding his bike which was found parked safely a short distance from his broken body. Theories abound and we'll never know exactly what happened. One theory is that Bottecchia, an outspoken socialist and extremely popular, was proving to be an embarrassment to the Fascist government then ruling Italy. Murder might have been the simplest solution. Years later, an Italian lay dying in New York City. Before he expired, he said that he had murdered Bottecchia. Nothing was ever proved or disproved. It is a mystery to this day made deeper because Ottavio's brother was murdered near the same place 2 years later.

1927. Desgrange was convinced that the teams were combining to fix the outcome of the race. At the very best, even if they were honest, they helped a weaker rider do well. He also felt that on the flat stages the riders did not push themselves, saving their energy for the mountains. Like today, the flat stages were ridden in a controlled, slower pace with the final result decided in a sprint. There was more of this "economical" racing in 1926 than in any previous Tour.

To Tour boss Desgrange this went against everything he thought "his" Tour should stand for. He wanted the Tour de France to be a contest where unrelenting individual effort in the cauldron of intense competition resulted in the supreme test of both the body and will of the athlete.

He made the flat stages team time trials. Each team went off separately on these stages. An individual rider could ride ahead of his team to seek a better time. This made the Tour even harder as there could be no easy days of just sitting in. Every day required an almost supreme effort. This changed the way the Tour's outcome was decided. Until now, the mountain stages were the main arbiters of the Tour, where the real time was usually won or lost. Now, the flat stages were just as crucial as the hilly ones. 16 of the 24 stages (1 through 9, 14, and 18 through 23) would be run under this new format.

An unintended side effect was to give a still greater advantage to a rider on a strong team, an outcome Desgrange hated.

Desgrange wasn't done changing the Tour. He reduced the distance from 5,745 kilometers to 5,321 kilometers. He also dramatically increased the number of stages, going to 24. This reduced the number of rest days to 5. The average stage length fell to 221 kilometers from the previous year's 321 kilometers. But with the time-trial format the race was even more grueling and demanding because there was no time during a stage to rest. A team had to keep driving itself hard hour after hour, day after day. To relax would be to lose time to a rival.

The previous year's Tour winner, Lucien Buysse, chose not to ride the 1927 Tour. 1924 and 1925 winner Ottavio Bottecchia had been murdered 2 weeks before the start of the race. This is the first Tour since the initial one in 1903 to start without a previous winner in the peloton.

The race was a bit more open. Alcyon had Nicolas Frantz who was second the previous year and fourth in 1925. He had Adelin Benoit on his team. Benoit had tried for the win a couple of times but came up short each time. With the new format his formidable strength would be very valuable. Dilecta-Wolber had Francis Pélissier. None of the 8-man Dilecta team would endure past the ninth stage.

Desgrange also abandoned his Alpine start experiment of the previous year. 142 riders left Paris on Sunday, June 19. The teams departed at 15-minute intervals. The *touriste-routiers* went off after the sponsored pros were on the road.

4 Dilecta riders were first on stage 1 to Dieppe. Francis Pélissier put on the Yellow Jersey as his brother Henri had 4 years before. This was Francis's sixth Tour. He had only finished once, in 1923 when he suffered terrible knee pain while helping his brother win the Tour. Francis Pélissier kept the Yellow Jersey for the first 5 stages as the Tour crossed

the north of France with his Dilecta team winning stages 1 and 5.

Winning the Tour requires not only strength and fortitude, but also good fortune. Pélissier, ill, had to abandon on stage 6. That put his teammate Ferdinand Le Drogo in Yellow. Hector Martin of JB Louvet moved into second place. The JB Louvet team won stage 7 while Dilecta had a disastrous day losing over 20 minutes. Le Drogo lost the lead to Martin and was now behind him by over 17 minutes.

It got worse in stage 8. Dilecta lost over 1 hour, 21 minutes. Remember, these are team time trials, so the fortunes of the entire squad were affected by a good or bad team performance. Hector Martin (JB Louvet) was in the driver's seat for now with a lead of more than 34 minutes over Maurice De Waele of the Labor-Dunlop squad.

The Dilecta team, seeing nothing but humiliation in continuing, abandoned the race. At the end of stage 9, the last of the first round of team time trials, there were only 57 riders left in the Tour. Here was the General Classification:

1. Hector Martin

2. Nicolas Frantz @ 21 minutes 16 seconds

3. Gaston Rebry @ 30 minutes 59 seconds

Stage 11 was the traditional Pyreneen stage with the 4 major climbs: The Aubisque, Tourmalet, Aspin and Peyresourde. This was a mass-start stage, not a team time trial. Martin was starting his fourth day in Yellow.

Frantz, like Buysse the year before, saw this tough stage as the springboard to launch an assault on the Tour. By the end of the stage's 16 $1/_2$ hours of racing, Frantz was in Yellow. Martin came in 2 hours later, twenty-second.

The new General Classification:

1. Nicolas Frantz

2. Maurice De Waele @ 38 minutes 27 seconds

3. Hector Martin @ 1 hour 37 minutes 48 seconds

Martin lost almost another hour on the second Pyreneen stage. That put an end to his hope of a finish on the podium. Frantz and De Waele stayed up at the front and finished with the same time in the lead group. Julien Vervaecke moved up to third in the General Classification at 2 hours, 13 minutes. None of the men on the podium was French. Frantz was from Luxembourg and the other 2 were Belgians.

There was a faint ray of hope showing for the French. Antonin Magne, a young man who had just turned pro the year before, won stage 14 from Marseille to Toulon. He wouldn't win the Tour until 1931 when the great French teams of the 1930's dominated the Tour, but here was the first sign of Magne's promise.

Over the Alps the leading trio of Frantz, De Waele and Vervaecke kept their relative positions with small changes in their times. On the penultimate stage De Waele lost over a half-hour but the gap to third place Vervaecke was so big that De Waele's second place was still very safe.

The other great new hope of French cycling, André Leducq, won 3 stages including the final 2. It didn't matter to the General Classification. Frantz had things under complete control. He became the second Luxembourger—Francois Faber being the first—to win the Tour.

The final 1927 Tour de France General Classification:

1. Nicolas Frantz (Alcyon): 198 hours 16 minutes 42 seconds

2. Maurice De Waele (Labor) @ 1 hour 48 minutes 21 seconds

3. Julien Vervaecke (Armor) @ 2 hours 25 minutes 6 seconds

4. André Leducq (Thomann) @ 3 hours 2 minutes 5 seconds

5. Adelin Benoit (Alcyon) @ 4 hours 45 minutes 1 second

6. Antonin Magne (Alleluia) @ 4 hours 48 minutes 23 seconds

1928. Even though it confused the public and was generally unpopular, Tour boss Henri Desgrange retained his time-trial format. He continued to make things complicated, tinkering with and changing the rules. He saw that when teams lost riders under the team time-trial format they became non-competitive for the remainder of the Tour, so he allowed teams to replace a rider if necessary. 5 replacement riders entered the lists and rode the Tour when their teammates could not continue.

In addition to trade teams of sponsored professional riders and the independent *touriste-routiers* he added 9 French teams of *touriste-routiers* representing different regions of France such as Normandy, Alsace-Lorraine and the Île de France. 162 riders started the 1928 Tour, at the time a record peloton. The Ravat-Wonder-Dunlop team was made up of Australians and New Zealanders. Hubert Opperman, Harry Watson, Perry Osborne and Ernest Bainbridge were the first men from their countries to ride the Tour.

Opperman was the Australian cycling champion in 1924, 1926 and 1927. The *Melbourne Herald* newspaper believed "Oppy" should ride the Tour de France on a team made up of Australians and Europeans. The Herald's campaign to send a team of antipodeans to France was successful. Before the Tour, the team traveled to France with tickets paid for by the Dunlop tire company and attended a training camp. To help prepare for the Tour Opperman rode several French road races, even getting a third place in Paris–Brussels behind Nicolas Frantz and Georges Ronsse. While Opperman had the class to compete with the Europeans, his teammates were not close to being on that level. The plan to incorporate experienced Europeans into the team never happened.

Alcyon put together another powerful team. In addition to 1927 Tour winner Nicolas Frantz they had 2 future Tour winners, André Leducq and Maurice De Waele. Alcyon filled out their roster with strongmen Gaston Rebry, Ernest Neuhard and Désiré Louesse. Power was needed to assist in the relentless, punishing work of driving the squad across France in the time trials. Neuhard was the only Alcyon rider who failed to finish the Tour that year.

The 1928 Tour was 5,375 kilometers with 22 stages. 15 of the stages were team time trials: stages 1 through 8 and 15 through 21.

Alcyon showed that it was by far the strongest team on the very first stage: 4 of the top 6 finishers were Alcyon riders. 1927 winner Frantz was first across the line and became the leader of the 1928 Tour.

For the next 7 stages Alcyon crushed the competition. The fast moving pro teams hopelessly swamped the independent *touriste-routiers*. A single rider could not hope to compete with the elite teams. Opperman's Anzacs were left in tatters. They were utterly unprepared for the team time-trial format, with stages that could be 285 kilometers long. The team was more than once reduced to Opperman's dragging his teammates the entire length of the stage. Alcyon, who started 10 minutes behind Opperman's Ravat team would catch them and pick up Opperman in the process.

At the end of stage 8 and before the Pyrenees here was the General Classification. Frantz had worn the Yellow Jersey since the first stage:

1. Nicolas Frantz
2. Maurice De Waele @ 1 minute 39 seconds
3. Julien Vervaecke @ 2 minutes 15 seconds

Tour Boss Henri Desgrange changed the route of the first Pyreneen stage from the one he had used since 1913. Instead of the usual Bayonne to Luchon he started at Hendaye and crossed the Aubisque and the Tourmalet before arriving at Luchon. He left out the Aspin and the Peyresourde.

Frantz didn't destroy his competition on this stage this year as he had the year before. Victor Fontan of the weak Elvish team was almost 2 hours behind in the General Classification. The leaders allowed him to take off on a lone ride through the mountains, as he was not a threat to the General Classification. He was first to Luchon. Frantz was second, 7 minutes, 44 seconds behind. Frantz's Alcyons had put so much time between themselves and the rest of the riders that Frantz could afford the time loss.

Antonin Magne, one of the new, great French hopes, tried to get away from Frantz on the second Pyreneen stage. Magne was first over the Portet d'Aspet and the Port. He faded and Frantz was first over the Puymorens, the last of the day's major climbs. André Leducq won the stage with Frantz second and De Waele third, all 3 at the same time. Magne came in over 9 minutes later.

After the Pyrenees, the General Classification:

1. Nicolas Frantz
2. Maurice De Waele @ 41 minutes 5 seconds
3. André Leducq @ 1 hour 1 minute 59 seconds

And what about Opperman? He could climb with the best continental pros. But like Holland's Wim Van Est, a wearer of Yellow Jersey a little over 30 years later, he was incapable of descending with the good Tour men. He lost vast chunks of time getting down the mountains as weaker competitors flashed by him.

Through the Alps, Frantz increased his lead. Leducq was able to gain enough time on De Waele to get second place on the podium.

Even stage 15, from Évian in the Alps to Pontarlier didn't change the General Classification podium which stood thus:

1. Nicolas Frantz

2. André Leducq @ 1 hour 15 minutes 7 seconds

3. Maurice De Waele @ 1 hour 27 minutes 23 seconds

It looked as if the Tour were cast in concrete. Frantz even won stage 18, from Strasbourg to Metz. But to win the Tour, it takes more than a strong set of lungs and legs. Fortune must also smile on the winner.

On stage 19, from Metz to Charleville, about 100 kilometers from the finish Frantz went over a railroad track and broke his frame. The representative of the Alcyon bicycle company traveling with the team panicked over the bad publicity sure to follow the news of the failure of the Yellow Jersey's frame. He wanted Frantz to travel to an Alcyon bicycle dealer and get a replacement bike. The team manager, Ludovic Feuillet, feeling that first and foremost it was his job to win the Tour, vetoed the idea because of the huge time loss this would entail.

While this argument was going on, a woman with her classic lady's bike complete with wide saddle, fenders, and bell, was watching at the side of the road. That bike was good enough for Frantz. He jumped on the bike and tore down the road with his team. They did that final 100 kilometers at 27 kilometers per hour. Frantz ended up losing only 28 minutes. The old rule that riders had to start and finish on the same bike was fortunately no longer in force. Frantz kept his Yellow Jersey. He was still over 47 minutes ahead of Leducq after that fright.

From there on, there were no more threats to Frantz's leadership. His powerful Alcyon team had routed the competition and assisted the careful and thoughtful Frantz to his second Tour victory in a row. Alcyon took all 3 places on the podium.

Final 1928 Tour de France General Classification:

1. Nicolas Frantz (Alcyon): 192 hours 48 minutes 58 seconds

2. André Leducq (Alcyon) @ 50 minutes 7 seconds

3. Maurice De Waele (Alcyon) @ 56 minutes 16 seconds

4. Jan Mertens (Thomann) @ 1 hour 19 minutes 18 seconds

5. Julien Vervaecke (Armor) @ 1 hour 53 minutes 32 seconds

18. Hubert Opperman (Ravat-Wonder-Dunlap) @ 8 hours 34 minutes 25 seconds

Of the 162 starters, only 41 survived the relentless pressure that the time trial format placed on the resources of the riders.

1929. In addition to being a fascinating race with unpredictable twists and turns, the 1929 Tour transformed the great race for decades to come.

Tour boss Henri Desgrange didn't completely abandon his confusing and unpopular team time trial format for the flat stages. He left in 3 of them, stages 12, 19 and 20, with staggered departures by team. These were the stages deemed to be slower than 30 kilometers an hour. Desgrange went with a 22-stage, 5,276-kilometer Tour, just a little shorter than the year before.

Desgrange went back to requiring the riders to fix their own flat tires.

We should make a special mention here regarding distances given in the early Tours. They were not exact. Many stages had the distance estimated. From about 1928 on the distances given are pretty accurate. For that reason also, average speeds in the early Tours given to the thousandths of a kilometer per hour would rate an "F" from any math teacher because the underlying data is not accurate to that many digits.

Alcyon returned with nearly the same squad that they had used with such success the previous year, headed by 1927 and 1928 Tour winner Nicolas Frantz. 1926 Tour winner Lucien Buysse was now on the Lucifer team that sported some rather capable riders as well, including Gustave Van Slembrouck, Joseph Demuysére and Pé Verhaegen. Capable though they may have been, almost all of them, notably excepting Demuysére, abandoned the Tour by stage 9.

Belgian Aimé Dossche won the first stage with the sprint into Caen. He kept the Yellow Jersey over the next 2 stages with pack sprints deciding the winners.

Maurice De Waele and Louis Delannoy slipped away on the fourth stage, beating the group by 3 minutes. That put De Waele in Yellow. He had been second in the 1927 Tour and third in 1928. De Waele was able to keep the lead until stage 7, which went from Les Sables d'Olonne to Bordeaux. De Waele was delayed with 2 flats that day.

Under the 1929 rules, he had to fix them himself. The time loss cost him the lead. A 5-man break led in by Nicolas Frantz won the stage.

A new situation confronted the timekeepers. Frantz, André Leducq and Victor Fontan, who were in that winning stage 7 break, were exactly tied in time. Today the judges would go back to the time trials and look at the fractions-of-a-second differences. If that doesn't resolve the tie, then a look at placings solves the problem. The Tour didn't have rules to take care of ties, so 3 Yellow Jerseys were awarded.

The 3 Yellow Jersey problem resolved itself the next day when Gaston Rebry got in a 3-man break and took over the lead. Leducq, Frantz and Fontan were now tied for second.

The God of the Flat Tire wasn't done with De Waele. On the crucial stage 9 with the Pyreneen climbs of the Aubisque and Tour- malet, De Waele got into a break with Salvador Cardona and Victor Fontan. De Waele flatted while his companions continued on and won the stage. De Waele finished third, over 8 minutes later. Fontan was now in Yellow and De Waele almost 10 minutes behind.

Life should have been good to Fontan. He was a strong rider with a good lead. Although he was 37 years old, he had prepared for this moment with care and was riding in the Pyrenees, his home turf. But life takes strange turns. On the next stage, from Luchon to Perpignan, Fontan crashed badly after either falling into a gutter by the side of the road or hitting a dog; accounts differ. He was unhurt but his forks were broken. Starting with Eugène Christophe in 1913, the Pyrenees seem to have a long history of being hard on bicycle forks.

Being 323 kilometers, the stage started before sunrise. Fontan, the General Classification leader of the Tour de France and the wearer of the Yellow Jersey was reduced to knocking on the doors of the vil- lagers in the dark of the early morning looking for another bike that he might borrow. At last he found a bike to resume the race, but he didn't just ride off. He couldn't: he had his broken bike strapped to his back. That year a rider had to finish with the bike he used to start the stage.

Fontan rode for 145 kilometers in the high Pyrenees with a bike strapped to his back trying to catch the greatest riders in the world.

It was too much for him and in tears he quit, still wearing the Yel- low Jersey. Desgrange, realizing the arbitrariness and unfairness of the rule, changed it for 1930 to allow riders to get new bikes from follow vehicles. Fontan, by the way, was a bit of a miracle rider. In World War

One he was twice hit by bullets in the leg. He didn't ride the Tour until 1924 when he was 36, an age when most other racers have already retired. He was one of the oldest Yellow Jerseys in Tour history. It's a shame fate was not kinder to him.

With Fontan's retirement De Waele was back in Yellow with a nearly 15 minute lead on Joseph Demuysére of the Lucifer team. Again, this looked like a secure lead.

Stage 14 finished in Grenoble. De Waele became very ill. He was so sick that he could not eat solid food. The next day was the Queen Stage in the Alps with the Lautaret, the Galibier and the Aravis climbs. This would be a challenging stage for even the strongest rider in good health. In terrible misery, helped and pushed by his teammates, De Waele made it to the end of the stage in Évian and kept his lead. That was Saturday.

On Monday, at the start of the next stage, the Alcyon team asked for and was granted an hour's delay before starting the stage because De Waele was still asleep, exhausted by the efforts 2 days before. From then on until the last day in Paris, the Alcyon team did everything in their power to drag, help and push their Yellow Jersey'd leader to the end of the race.

De Waele won the 1929 Tour but Desgrange was furious. "A corpse has won my race!" Not only was Desgrange upset with the help given to De Waele by his teammates, some of it against the rules, he felt that there had been collusion from the other teams since the sub-par De Waele never received a serious challenge from the other teams.

As we will see in 1930, Desgrange's solution was a radical gamble that entirely changed the nature and style of racing in the Tour de France.

Final 1929 Tour de France General Classification:

1. Maurice De Waele (Alcyon): 186 hours 39 minutes 15 seconds
2. Giuseppe Pancera (La Rafale) @ 44 minutes 23 seconds
3. Joseph Demuysére (Lucifer) @ 57 minutes 10 seconds
4. Salvador Cardona (Fontan-Wolber) @ 57 minutes 46 seconds
5. Nicolas Frantz (Alcyon) @ 58 minutes

Chapter 4

1930–1934. A bold change to the Tour yields the golden years of French cycling

1930. Tour boss Henri Desgrange was steaming over the 1929 Tour. Maurice De Waele, even though he had taken ill in the Alps, had emerged the victor. At one point during the '29 Tour De Waele was unable to eat solid food and could only swallow water with a little sugar dissolved in it. His all-powerful Alcyon team had protected him, pushing him up mountains and blocking attacks. Collusion with other teams was assumed. Feeling that the trade teams were ruining his race and its integrity, Desgrange set about recasting the Tour de France.

Desgrange was never one to stick stubbornly to a formula that didn't work, even if it were his own brainchild. Desgrange searched for a new way to inject sparkle and competition into his race. He found it. He dispensed with the trade teams he hated so much. Not until 1962 would bicycle companies and other manufacturers again sponsor teams in the Tour de France. In the place of trade teams, he created a system of national and regional teams. Riders would now ride for France, Italy, Spain and other countries. To fill out the race, when needed, regional teams such as Normandy and Alsace-Lorraine also rode. At the inception of this system the riders would ride identical, yellow (of course) anonymous bikes.

The public instantly greeted the national team proposal as a fine idea. The team sponsors grumbled that they lost publicity during the most important race of the season. Moreover, they were still obliged to continue to pay the racer's salaries.

This presented a huge problem and a huge risk. No longer would the team sponsors pay the substantial expenses of running the teams during the Tour. The Tour organization would be responsible for transport, food and lodging, a huge undertaking. Where would the money come from? And suppose the bicycle manufacturers became sufficiently angry at Desgrange's move and withdrew their advertising from his newspaper and Tour sponsor, *L'Auto*? *L'Auto* was born out of just such an advertiser's rebellion 30 years before.

Desgrange had an audacious idea. He invented the publicity caravan. Companies could pay the Tour a fee to follow the Tour with their logo'd trucks and cars, advertising their products.

The publicity caravan took a while to get going. The Menier Chocolate company was the first to sign up, and was 1 of only 3 companies that participated in the caravan the first year. Today, even with trade teams back in the race, the caravan continues to be an important part of the color and magic of watching the Tour.

Desgrange also disposed of his team time trial format and went back to mass-starts. He dispensed with the riders-must-do-their-own-repairs and finish-with-the-starting-bike rules. Now a rider could get a bike from a following vehicle and receive assistance from his teammates. As we will see in the 1930 Tour, this had a huge effect on the outcome. With these changes Desgrange had officially recognized that professional bicycle racing is a sport contested by teams and won by individuals.

With the best French riders now all on one team, French teams were able to begin a run of 5 straight wins. At the time France possessed cycling talent with real depth. The 1930 team was filled with great riders: Charles Pélissier, André Leducq, Antonin and Pierre Magne, Victor Fontan and Marcel Bidot.

The Italian team included immortal riders Alfredo Binda and Learco Guerra. Belgium sent Joseph Demuysére, Aimé Dossche and Louis Delannoy. This was a race with truly worthy competitors.

The *touriste-routier* classification of independent riders was retained, with some of them put into regional teams.

Desgrange cut the distance from the 5,276 kilometers of 1929 to 4,818 kilometers. He also reduced the number of stages from a high of 24 in 1927 and 22 in 1929 to 21 in 1930. This gave him an average stage length of 229 kilometers. Compare this to 1916's (about the same in 1923) 360 kilometers and it becomes clear that the Tour was becoming a race with greater emphasis on speed and less on brute endurance.

The youngest of the 3 Pélissier brothers, Charles, was now an accomplished professional and a superb field sprinter. He beat Alfredo Binda to the line in Caen to notch the first win in the newly redesigned Tour. 3 years after his brother Frances held and lost the Yellow Jersey and 7 years after brother Henri won the Tour, another of the remarkable Pélissiers was in yellow.

28-year old Learco Guerra was in the second year of his professional career. He was already Champion of Italy and had placed ninth in the Giro that year, winning 2 stages. This was a man to be watched, but watching was not enough. Guerra escaped from the pack on stage 2 and beat Alfredo Binda, who led in the field, by 1 minute, 28 seconds. The young Italian with the thick, black shock of hair was the leader of the Tour de France.

Charles Pélissier was on a tear. He won the 57-man sprint in stage 3, beating Binda to the line in Brest. Guerra was still in yellow with Pélissier and Binda tied at the same time in second and third places. Pélissier was a determined sprinter who was not afraid to get rough in the final dash to the line. The judges relegated him to third place after he won the sprint in stage 6 in Bordeaux, for having given Binda's jersey a tug.

Binda's hopes for a win in the Tour were ruined when he crashed in stage 7, losing an hour. But Binda was a champion. Undeterred by his misfortune, the great man finally beat Pélissier in a sprint the next day.

So, after stage 8 and before the Pyrenees, here was the General Classification:

1. Learco Guerra
2. Charles Pélissier @ 12 seconds
3. Antonin Magne @ 1 minute 24 seconds

Antonin Magne descends the Tourmalet

___

Stage 9 from Pau to Luchon crossed the Aubisque and the Tourmalet. Benoît Faure, riding as a *touriste-routier* on the regional France South-East team set a hot pace. Nearly all were dropped including Guerra. Faure led over the crests of both the Aubisque and the Tourmalet but was eventually dropped by Binda, André Leducq, and Pierre and Antonin Magne. Binda won the stage and Guerra came in more than 13 minutes later. Charles Pélissier lost over 23 minutes that day.

The new General Classification:

1. André Leducq
2. Antonin Magne @ 5 minutes 26 seconds
3. Learco Guerra @ 11 minutes 42 seconds

The second day in the Pyrenees didn't change anything. All the leaders finished together behind Pélissier. The notable occurrence was Binda's abandonment.

Binda's entry in the 1930 Tour is interesting. He won the 1925, 1927, 1928 and 1929 Giros. The Giro organizers didn't want Binda to ride the 1930 edition, fearing he would make it uninteresting with his domination. They paid him the equivalent of the winner's purse to stay away.

Desgrange, meanwhile, wanted the magnificent Italian to ride the Tour. Binda demurred. Now, with no Giro in his 1930 schedule, Binda entertained offers from Desgrange to ride the Tour if Desgrange would pay him. A secret contract was agreed upon, which Binda revealed only in 1980, 6 years before his death. Binda's real objective for the year was to regain the World Road Championship, which he had been the first ever to win, in 1927. He succeeded that fall and went on to win it a third time in 1932.

Alfredo Binda is another in a long list of great Italian riders who did not find the structure and rhythm of the Tour to their liking. We'll meet Binda again later as the manager of the Italian team. It was he who had the difficult job of running the team that contained the hard to manage duo of Fausto Coppi and Gino Bartali.

Both Guerra and Antonin Magne lost some time on stage 14 to Nice with its Braus and Castillon climbs. Guerra won the next day and made up some of the loss.

So, before the Alps, this was how things stood:

1. André Leducq
2. Learco Guerra @ 16 minutes 13 seconds
3. Antonin Magne @ 18 minutes 3 seconds

Stage 16 from Grenoble to Évian with the Lautaret, Galibier, Télégraphe and Aravis passes is one of those days in racing in which a champion is forged on the anvil of misfortune. Let's take a look at this remarkable and famous day.

Fernand Robache, a Frenchman riding as a completely independent *touriste-routier*, was first over the Lautaret. Pierre Magne led over the Galibier with Benoît Faure, the *touriste-routier*, right with him. Guerra was only 6 seconds behind, followed by André Leducq, another 9 seconds back.

Leducq, throwing caution to the winds, flew down the Galibier and crashed. Sensing opportunity, Guerra kept going as fast as he dared.

Leducq had lost consciousness in the crash. Upon Leducq's awakening, Pierre Magne managed to get him back on his bike and rolling down the hill, his teammates riding with him. At the base of the next climb, the Télégraphe, Leducq broke a pedal and crashed again. Leducq wept, calling for his mother. Teammate Bidot managed to get a pedal from a spectator's bike. Leducq's leg was a bloody mess from the crash. He was probably suffering from shock after the 2 falls.

Surrounded by his teammates, he talked of abandoning. Pélissier would hear none of it. Jean-Paul Ollivier in *Maillot Jaune* relates:

"You don't give up when you've got the Yellow Jersey to take care of. Are you listening to me Dédé [Leducq's nickname]? We're all going to go flat out; you'll stick with us and we'll take you up to Guerra."

"There is also Demuysére," objected Leducq, thinking of the high-placed capable Belgian who was with Guerra.

Marcel Bidot answered, "Demuysére is an old nag! Come on, get on the saddle! I've had enough of seeing you blubbering like that. You're not a woman after all! Let's have a look at your knee! Stretch out your leg…now bend it…there's nothing broken. Let's go then, you'll warm up on the way!"

What man could resist such esprit-de-corps, such dedicated teammates desperate to help? Leducq remounted and the chase was on.

Guerra meanwhile was lashing himself and his breakaway companions, doing all he could to get as much time as possible on the chasing Frenchmen behind him. When Leducq restarted for the second time Guerra had a 15-minute lead, enough to give him the Yellow Jersey.

But, there were still 60 kilometers to the finish line in Évian. Guerra begged for more help from the others with him, but after four Alpine climbs and 270 kilometers, no one had any more to give.

Behind him, the French team was mobilized. As they had promised, Pierre and Antonin Magne, Charles Pélissier and Marcel Bidot, dragging the bloody Leducq, were riding like fiends possessed. After 2 hours of desperate, hard chasing, they caught Guerra near the finish. To make Guerra's misery complete, Pélissier led out Leducq who won the stage.

So here was the new General Classification

1. André Leducq
2. Learco Guerra @ 16 minutes 13 seconds
3. Antonin Magne @ 18 minutes 3 seconds

The fight for the General Classification was basically over at that point. Charles Pélissier continued his incredible sprinting streak by winning all of the final 4 stages.

The French team won the Tour, won 12 of the 21 stages and put 6 of their riders in the top 10 in the General Classification. Needless to say, the French were well pleased with the new format. Charles Pélissier, giving almost daily lessons in sprinting to the other racers, had won 8 stages.

Final 1930 Tour de France General Classification:

1. André Leducq (France): 172 hours 12 minutes 16 seconds

2. Learco Guerra (Italy) @ 14 minutes 13 seconds

3. Antonin Magne (France) @ 16 minutes 3 seconds

4. Joseph Demuysére (Belgium) @ 21 minutes 34 seconds

5. Marcel Bidot (France) @ 41 minutes 18 seconds

6. Pierre Magne (France) @ 45 minutes 42 seconds

1931. Desgrange increased the number of stages from 21 in 1930 to 24. This reduced the number of rest days to 3.

The French team, so completely dominant in 1930, retained its core of André Leducq, Antonin Magne and Charles Pélissier. Benoît Faure, who had ridden so well in the 1930 edition as a *touriste-routier*, was induced to become part of the French team. Faure had preferred to be, as he put it, a loner, rather than ride on the large teams. This was the only time out of his 7 Tour starts that Faure rode the Tour for a team. He turned down lucrative sponsorship offers from Alcyon, preferring to ride for less money for a smaller sponsor, Le Cheminot, during the rest of the year.

The Belgians, as usual, provided the major challenge to the French. Gaston Rebry, Julien Vervaecke, 1929 winner Maurice De Waele and Alfons Schepers assisted 1930's fourth place Joseph Demuysére. The Italian team with climber Antonio Pesenti could be expected to be tough as well.

Hubert Opperman, who was part of the confused entry of Australian and New Zealand riders in the 1928 Tour, was put on a team made up of 4 Swiss and 4 Australian riders.

The first notable occurrence was in the second stage. Desgrange had the *touriste-routiers* starting 10 minutes after the national teams. That didn't deter them. They would chase and often quickly catch the top men. Max Bulla was a *touriste-routier* who not only caught the big men, he won the stage and took the overall lead. Bulla has the distinction of being the first and, I think, the only *touriste-routier* to wear yellow. His glory was short-lived. The next day in the Dinan–Brest stage he lost a half-hour. Léon Le Calvez was the new leader.

Leading up to the Pyrenees, Italy's ace sprinter Raffaele Di Paco dueled with France's Charles Pélissier for stage wins and the lead. After stage 5 they shared the lead for a single day. Then Di Paco had it to himself before relinquishing it to Pélissier on stage 8.

All of these sprinter games jockeying for the lead ended on stage 9, the Pyreneen stage with the Aubisque and the Tourmalet. Last year's winner, André Leducq, didn't have the Tour-winning form he showed in 1930. One man was particularly well prepared. Antonin Magne, who had ridden as Leducq's *domestique* in 1930, was in superb shape in 1931 and was the acknowledged leader of the French team.

The Belgian Demuysére, in a leading group, went ahead of Magne over the 2 climbs. Magne took off after him and the other leaders on the descent of the Tourmalet. Magne caught the group and not knowing that Demuysére had flatted and was now behind, kept going, wanting to chase him down. The now-solo flying Frenchman kept pouring on the gas and arrived in Luchon a full 4 minutes, 42 seconds ahead of Pesenti and almost 8 minutes ahead of Demuysére and De Waele.

That ride brought Magne the Yellow Jersey with a large cushion given the new 3-minute time bonus for winning the stage. Here was the General Classification after stage 9:

1. Antonin Magne
2. Antonio Pesenti @ 9 minutes 32 seconds
3. Joseph Demuysére @ 10 minutes 44 seconds

The riders did not attack stage 10, with its 4 major climbs, with the same energy. 57 riders, including sprinters Pélissier and Di Paco, who won the stage, finished at the same time. Even Hubert Opperman, who usually suffered time losses on the descents, finished within a minute of the leaders.

Magne's grip on the race seemed secure. The Italians launched an attack in stage 14 from Cannes to Nice that put Magne and the French on notice that his lead was not safe and the race was far from over. With the Braus and Castillon climbs, 3 Italians—Pesenti, Eugenio Gestri and Felice Gremo—got away from the French. The chase was on and eventually Magne, having exhausted his help, had to go after them by himself. He never caught them. The Italians got the first 3 places in the stage and Magne's lead shrank to 5 minutes.

The next stage (2 days later), Di Paco and Pesenti tried again. Pélissier helped Magne reel them in. And then it was Demuysére's turn to take off. He gained 2 minutes, 30 seconds on Magne at the end of the day as the attacks continued.

Over the Alps the highly motivated and unified French team kept Magne out of trouble. There was no change to the podium of the General Classification. The last threat to Magne's lead came on the penultimate stage, from Charleville to Malo-les-Bains. This was to be a day over cobbles, the type that good Belgian riders master as part of their trade.

Magne, a man who worried incessantly that something might happen to take away his lead, couldn't sleep the night before the day on the cobbles. Knowing that they had not conceded the race, he had a real fear of the Belgians. He kept saying that the race was not won until the last turn of the pedal. His roommate, André Leducq, tiring of Magne's fretting, suggested that Magne read some of his fan mail.

Magne found this suggestion agreeable. One letter in particular caught Magne's attention:

"Monsieur Antonin Magne,

"I am writing to warn you that Rebry [one of the Belgian team riders] has written to his mother saying that he'll attack with Demuysére on the stage from Charleville to Malo-les-Bains."

The letter's postmark was from Rebry's village. Leducq, being an easier-going sort and not having a Yellow Jersey in the balance, laughed the letter off as a joke. Magne thought Leducq was probably right, but he was taking no chances. The next day was wet and cold. Combined with the pavé, this was the ideal place for Rebry to put the hammer down. Rebry had won Paris–Roubaix that spring and would be at home on this stage. Demuysére was also a Belgian tough guy as only the Belgians make them in bicycle racing.

Magne told his compatriots to stick to Rebry and Demuysére

and be ready for anything. 60 kilometers into the 271 kilometer stage the Belgian pair took off on a cobbled bend in the road. They instantly gained a gap. Leducq saw the move. He and Magne made a superhuman effort and got on their wheels. Rebry and Demuysére increased the pace. Magne hung on for dear life, refusing to do any of the work.

Magne fell. He remounted and regained contact with the pair. Upset that the Yellow Jersey was sitting on, refusing to pull, the Belgians maneuvered so that Magne got no shelter in the crosswind. With that, Magne consented to do some work.

Constantly the pair took turns attacking Magne, who fought to maintain contact. Rebry and Demuysére, with Magne refusing to be dropped, kept up the infernal place the entire balance of the stage, arriving at the finish 17 minutes, 34 seconds ahead of Leducq who led in the first chasing group. Even though Magne could not be dropped, the move wasn't entirely without gain for Demuysére. He moved up to second in the General Classification ahead of Pesenti.

To the best of my knowledge, the writer of the warning letter was never identified.

With the Belgians' gutsy attempt to gain time on Magne ending in partial failure, the Tour was really over. Pélissier won his fifth stage when he prevailed in the final stage into Paris. With this victory he and Di Paco were tied for 5 stage wins in the 1931 Tour.

Magne won to overwhelming French acclaim. The early 1930's were the glory years of French cycling. More was to come. Yet, the depth of the Belgian squad cannot be minimized. 4 of the top 6 riders in the final General Classification were Belgian. But it is the man in Yellow in Paris that we always remember. Five stages were won by *touriste-routiers*, including two by Max Bulla. This was the high point of the independent rider until Italy's Mario Vicini came in third as an independent in 1937.

The final 1931 Tour de France General Classification:

1. Antonin Magne (France): 177 hours 10 minutes 3 seconds
2. Joseph Demuysére (Belgium) @ 12 minutes 56 seconds
3. Antonio Pesenti (Italy) @ 22 minutes 51 seconds
4. Gaston Rebry (Belgium) @ 46 minutes 40 seconds
5. Maurice De Waele (Belgium) @ 49 minutes 46 seconds
6. Julien Vervaecke (Belgium) @ 1 hour 10 minutes 11 seconds

1932. The Tour added more and larger time bonuses for stage wins. A stage winner would get a huge 4 minutes, second place would get 2 and third would get a 1 minute bonus.

Desgrange shortened the Tour dramatically, going from 5,095 kilometers with 24 stages in 1931 to 4,520 with 21 stages in 1932. The average stage length remained about the same, 212 kilometers in 1931 and 215 in 1932. That compares to about 160–170 kilometers for an average modern Tour stage.

Since both Charles Pélissier, the demon sprinter and powerful locomotive of the 1930 and 1931 French teams and Antonin Magne, the 1931 winner were absent from the French team, one would think that France might have been fielding a weaker team. In those days France had such an abundance of talent that the 1932 team might be considered finer still than the previous ones. André Leducq, the 1930 winner and in fine condition, was joined by Roger Lapébie, Georges Speicher, Marcel Bidot, Maurice Archambaud, Albert Barthélemy, Louis Péglion, and Julien Moineau. Between Leducq, Speicher and Lapébie, I count 4 Tour wins. All of the French team riders finished the 1932 Tour, the only team to finish intact.

Italy raised the bar by bringing 3 Giro winners. 1932 Giro winner Antonio Pesenti returned. It was his aggression in the second half of the 1931 Tour that put Antonin Magne on the ropes. Francesco Camusso, the winner of the 1931 Giro, also came to try his hand. Luigi Marchisio, winner of the 1930 Giro, filled out the trio of accomplished Italian Grand Tour riders. Raffaele Di Paco, the only rider to consistently and effectively challenge Charles Pélissier in the 1930 and 1931 Tour's sprints helped round out an Italian team filled with gifted climbers.

And the Belgians who had fought almost "until the last pedal was turned" in 1931? Joseph Demuysére, second in 1931, returned along with 2-time world champion Georges Ronsse, Frans Bonduel, Jan Aerts and Gaston Rebry. This was a strong team, but as we shall see, not capable of riding as a unified squad.

The Belgians started off well enough on the first stage. Jean Aerts won the stage with Joseph Demuysére right on his wheel. Third place, German team member Hubert Sieronski, was 14 seconds back. The Belgians started the 1932 Tour the same way they did the 1931 edition, winning the first stage and claiming the Yellow Jersey at the first opportunity.

The Belgians may have had a good start, but on the second stage they foundered. Belgium is made up of 2 peoples, the French-speaking Walloons of the south and the Dutch or Flemish speakers who inhabit northern Belgium. There has always been tension between these 2 groups that usually just simmers. I can't find the details, but it seems that in the second stage the Flemish rider Aerts could not get support from his Walloon teammates when he needed it. Aerts lost almost 10 minutes in that stage, and with that time loss went the Yellow Jersey. The Italians Camusso, Pesenti and Marchisio also missed the winning move, finishing in the Aerts group. Kurt Stoepel won the stage and became the first German rider ever to lead the Tour de France.

Stage 3 was the longest stage of the 1932 Tour, a monster 387 kilometers that took the winner, André Leducq, almost 13 hours to complete. Stoepel was just 45 seconds shy of finishing with the lead group. With the generous time bonuses Desgrange was giving for stage wins, Leducq was now the leader, and Stoepel was 1 minute, 45 seconds back in second place.

The Tour hit the Pyrenees on stage 5 with the Aubisque and Tourmalet climbs being covered on the road from Pau to Luchon. The Italians tried to gain back the time they lost on stage 2. Pesenti won the stage, finishing with that rugged individualist, Benoît Faure, who was again riding as a *touriste-routier*. Francesco Camusso finished third, only 5 seconds back. The Italians had lost too much time in the first 4 stages to gain the lead with this victory. Leducq finished about 4 minutes behind Pesenti and thereby preserved his overall lead.

The next 2 stages allowed Leducq to pad his slim lead by getting consecutive second places and then a third place in stage 8. Stoepel stayed close to him, but the inexorable logic of the time bonuses allowed Leducq to continue to gain time. After stage 8, the General Classification stood thus:

1. André Leducq
2. Kurt Stoepel @ 6 minutes 5 seconds
3. Antonio Pesenti @ 14 minutes 34 seconds

Leducq lost some time in the Cannes–Nice stage with the Braus and Castillon climbs in the Maritime Alps. With the help of his team he survived a bad day in the mountains, usually the death-knell for anyone with Tour-winning ambitions. When Leducq flatted, teammate Georges Speicher (winner of the Tour the next year) gave him a wheel from his own bike. We'll see a sadder version of this heroic story in 1934 when René Vietto had to give a wheel to Magne.

Leducq again stamped his authority on the Tour when he won stage 11. At first it looked as if the jersey might change hands. Over the major climb of the day, the Col d'Allos, *touriste-routier* Benoît Faure went over first, chased by Francesco Camusso. They joined up and rode together, but it was more than 60 kilometers to the finish. Even though at one point their lead was enough to make Camusso the virtual Yellow Jersey, Leducq, Stoepel and eventually another 15 riders were able to catch them. By winning the stage Leducq not only saved his lead, he enhanced it with the 4-minute stage-winner's time bonus.

This was just a taste of what Leducq could do that year. Stage 13 was the Alpine Queen Stage with the Lautaret, Galibier and Télégraphe climbs. It was freezing cold and snowing on the Galibier. The picture I have of Leducq on the Galibier that year shows him obscured by the blowing snow, riding without gloves, in shorts and what must be a single wool long-sleeved jersey. Francesco Camusso was first over the Galibier. Pressing on over the snow-covered, fog-shrouded mountain, dragging the chasing riders, Leducq closed the gap to the flying Italian on the freezing descent. He then won the stage and stretched his lead to 13 minutes over Stoepel.

And from there Leducq continued to add to his lead. He won the stage exiting the Alps, stage 15 from Évian to Belfort. He was first across the line in stage 18 but was relegated for getting a helping push from his teammate Albert Barthélemy. Undeterred, he won the last 2 stages, exhibiting complete mastery of the Tour.

Now, let's look at the final 1932 General Classification:

1. André Leducq (France): 154 hours 11 minutes 49 seconds

2. Kurt Stoepel (Germany) @ 24 minutes 3 seconds

3. Francesco Camusso (Italy) @ 26 minutes 21 seconds

4. Antonio Pesenti (Italy) @ 37 minutes 8 seconds

5. Georges Ronsse (Belgium) @ 41 minutes 4 seconds

6. Frans Bonduel (Belgium) @ 45 minutes 13 seconds

Leducq won 6 stages, came in second twice and was third 3 times. This superb performance garnered Leducq 31 minutes in bonuses, while Stoepel had earned 7 bonus minutes, a 24 minute difference. As you can see, discounting the time bonuses the actual elapsed time between Leducq and Stoepel was nearly identical, with Leducq being ahead by only 3 seconds. Now one cannot say that they would have tied without the bonuses because a stage racer usually rides economically. Normally he does only what he must to gain and maintain the lead, using the rules to help his cause. If the time bonuses didn't exist, would Leducq have been able to press the advantage and gain more time? Likely, but that enters the realm of the hypothetical.

The Italians won 7 of the 21 stages. Di Paco couldn't equal his 5 stage wins of 1931, but his 1932 score of 3 is still impressive. In their ethnic disarray, even though they were bursting with talent, the Belgians couldn't do better than fifth.

It's worth looking at the time gaps in the 1932 Tour. Twentieth place Gaston Rebry, finished 1 hour, 39 minutes, 1 second behind Leducq. 10 years earlier, in 1922, twentieth place Jules Nempon finished over 12 hours behind winner Firmin Lambot. As Stephen Jay Gould wrote, this is the expected result. As a sport matures, the gaps in performance narrow. The same thing occurred in baseball. The range of batting averages in the professional ranks has narrowed over the decades, with the last .400 hitter being Ted Williams in 1941.

Writing in *L'Auto*, Tour boss Henri Desgrange went completely gaga over Leducq, writing page after page of worshipful prose. He found that Leducq's 1932 win when compared to his 1930 Tour victory showed a more complete rider. Leducq could do all that was asked of a rider of his era: climb, sprint and roll the gear. Desgrange wrote that Leducq became a more intellectual, thinking rider in this Tour. With all the bonuses in the offing, this cerebral riding was probably a requirement to win the 1932 edition. Leducq gained the Yellow Jersey on the third stage and kept it for the rest of the Tour. With the exception of stage 10, he maintained or increased his lead every stage. That made 2 victories for Leducq and 3 in a row for France.

This was André (Dédé) Leducq's last win in the Tour even though he kept racing until 1938. Let's take a last look at this fine rider before he became a *domestique* for others. He was world amateur champion at age 20. His 25 Tour stage wins remained the record until Eddy

Merckx smashed it with his 34. He loved women and they loved him. Many of the pictures of the handsome Leducq have a member of the fair sex looking at him admiringly. In addition to 2 Tour wins, he came in second in the 1928 Tour and won Paris–Roubaix and Paris–Tours.

1933. The 1933 Tour brought another innovation. Points would be accumulated in a competition for the first man over each mountain. The tougher the climb, the more points it would be worth. This was the birth of the "King of the Mountains" competition. The competition's first sponsor was Martini & Rossi of vermouth fame. While the competition started in 1933, the famous Polka-Dot jersey (*maillot a pois*) for the best climber was not introduced until 1975. Belgian racer Lucien Van Impe was the first to wear the *maillot a pois*.

Although he wanted racers to dig deeply for the stage win, Desgrange realized that his 4-minute bonus for a stage victory distorted the race. He reduced the winner's bonification to 2 minutes.

The Tour reversed direction in 1933. For the first time since 1912 the Tour went clockwise, Alps first. With a 4,396 kilometer, 23 stage Tour, the average stage length fell to 191 kilometers, down from 212 the year before.

Tour historian Jean-Paul Ollivier believes that the 1933 French team was the finest collection of pre-war riders in an era of back-to-back superb French teams. They had 2-time winner André Leducq, 1931 winner Antonin Magne and future winners Georges Speicher and Roger Lapébie. Filling out the team were Maurice Archambaud, Léon Le Calvez, René Le Grevès and super-sprinter Charles Pélissier. This was not just a magnificent collection of athletes. They had shown, since the beginning of the national team format in 1930, an esprit de corps that allowed them to dominate their rivals even in times of extreme difficulty.

The Belgians, always bursting with talent, had Georges Lemaire, Gaston Rebry, Jean Aerts, and Georges Ronsse on their team. They had power but had not addressed the split between the Flemings and Walloons (see 1932's stage 2).

Learco Guerra spearheaded the Italian effort, being now in the full maturity of his powers. In the 1930 Tour he came in second and if André Leducq had ridden for a lesser team, Guerra would probably have won the Tour that year. Since then Guerra had been world road champion and twice champion of Italy (earning a total of 4 Italian road championships over his career). In the 1933 Giro d'Italia, he abandoned on the sixth stage after winning 3 stages. Now he started the Tour with a good team that included Raffaele Di Paco and Francesco Camusso. Unfortunately for Guerra, most of his team abandoned by stage 11. Only 3 of the 8 starters on the Italian team finished the Tour. Guerra was mostly on his own. The talented climber Giuseppe Martano rode as an independent *touriste-routier*.

The Germans and Austrians were combined into one team. Kurt Stoepel, who had done so well the year before, was the most notable member of that team, which ended up losing most of its riders by stage 10.

Josephine Baker, the American expatriate entertainer, started the 80 racers on Tuesday, June 27.

Maurice Archambaud, a heavy, powerful rider nicknamed "Chubby Cheeks" by Desgrange won the first stage solo, beating the rest of the field by over $2\,^1/_2$ minutes. In the second Tour de France of his career he was in Yellow.

The 1933 Tour wouldn't be dazzled by a repeat month-long sprinter's shoot-out between Charles Pélissier and Raffaele Di Paco. In stage 3 Pélissier was behind a car that braked as he was accelerating to pass it. Pélissier crashed. He tried to continue, but being too badly injured, he finished outside the time limit and was eliminated.

After stage 3 and before 6 straight days of climbing, here was the General Classification:

1. Maurice Archambaud
2. Jean Aerts @ 6 minutes 32 seconds
3. Georges Lemaire @ 7 minutes 32 seconds

Both Aerts and Lemaire were on the Belgian team.

Learco Guerra had won stage 2 but it was in stage 6 that the powerful Italian locomotive, picked by Desgrange to win the Tour this year, began to make his mark on the Tour. He was first over the final climb of the day, the Tamié, and won the stage. All the other contenders finished with the same time. The winner's 2-minute bonus pulled Guerra up to third place in the General Classification, within 6 minutes, 24 seconds of Archambaud. Guerra won stage 7 the next day, also an important Alpine stage, and now was less than 5 minutes from the big Frenchman.

Vicente Trueba, called "The Flea of Torrelavega", went after this first King of the Mountains competition. Stage 7 had the Lautaret, Galibier and Télégraphe mountains. Trueba was first over the final 2. Little Trueba weighed just over 100 pounds. That meant he could fly up the mountains, often twiddling a miniscule gear at a terrific cadence. But he couldn't get down the other side of the mountain in good time to save his life. Because of this, he was always caught before the finish and never won a Tour stage.

Stage 8 from Grenoble to Gap had the Laffrey and Bayard climbs. Big Archambaud was able to separate himself from Guerra and beat him to Gap by over 4 minutes. This increased Archambaud's lead to almost 9 minutes. The day's stage winner was another French team member, Georges Speicher. Speicher later wrote that as the 1933 Tour was progressing, he felt his form getting better and better. By stage 8 he felt particularly good and was ambitious to do something to help Archambaud. Speicher made sure that the team's goal of putting more time between Guerra and Archambaud had been accomplished. Then, with Archambaud's approval, he took off for the stage win, doing the final descent far faster than Archambaud felt was worth the risk. It was good for the French team that Speicher won the stage, because Belgian Georges Lemaire was right on his wheel and came in second. Speicher's win deprived Lemaire of the victor's time bonus.

Everything changed the next day during stage 9 from Gap to Digne, with the Vars and Allos climbs. This stage gave the Belgians their fair shot at the Yellow. Trueba, the little Spanish climber, was first over the Vars. The pace on the Vars was too much at last for Archambaud who was dropped and had to ride the rest of the stage alone. Speicher won again, finishing in a group of 5 that included Trueba and Italian climber Giuseppe Martano. Belgian Georges Lemaire came in about $2\,^1\!/_2$ minutes later. Guerra flatted and couldn't capitalize on Archambaud's distress. He finished the stage 3 minutes, 40 seconds behind Speicher. Archambaud, whose chances for winning the Tour were damaged but not quite wrecked, finished about 16 minutes after Speicher.

So the General Classification now:

1. Georges Lemaire
2. Learco Guerra @ 23 seconds
3. Georges Speicher @ 2 minutes 56 seconds

Archambaud hadn't given up just yet. He won stage 11 that went from Nice to Cannes. With the time bonus he was in Yellow and had a very slim 44 second lead on Lemaire. One day later it went all wrong for him. He flatted and ended up losing 8 minutes. Speicher was enjoying his fine form and cruised in to Marseilles for both the stage win and, with the time bonus, the Yellow Jersey. Lemaire was still in second place, just 15 seconds back.

Leducq won the next 2 stages, denying the stage winner's time bonus to Speicher's competitors. With his chances for the Tour win gone, Archambaud joined the rest of the team in riding for Speicher. This was a team dedicated to winning the Tour. They liked each other and generally sacrificed themselves for the eventual team victory.

Stages 15 through 18 were 4 hard days in the Pyrenees. *L'Equipe* writes that with Lemaire being only 15 seconds behind Speicher, the talented Belgian team could have put Speicher in trouble. When Lemaire needed help, the capable Jean Aerts just rode right on by. The memory of his Belgian teammates' refusal to help him when he needed it—in stage 2 the year before when he was in Yellow—still burned. Aerts was in no mood to help those who would not help him.

Aerts ended up winning 2 of the Pyreneen stages and then 3 in a row on the road to Paris. It was a spectacular performance, but it came too late. He had lost too much time in the Alps to win the Tour.

As Lemaire foundered in the Pyrenees, Giuseppe Martano made sure he was in the front group in every stage and quickly rose in the General Classification.

After the Pyrenees, here were the standings:

1. Georges Speicher
2. Giuseppe Martano @ 5 minutes 8 seconds
3. Learco Guerra @ 7 minutes 1 second

Stage 22 was scheduled to finish in the Caen velodrome (like the finish in Paris–Roubaix). When too many riders arrived at the velodrome at the same time the officials decided to hold a 1-lap time trial for first place. René Le Grevès, 2 hours behind in the General Classification, won the stage.

Learco Guerra won the sprint for the final stage, stage 23. The 2-minute bonus moved him up to second place in the final overall standings.

The final 1933 Tour de France General Classification:

1. Georges Speicher (France): 147 hours 51 minutes 37 seconds
2. Learco Guerra (Italy) @ 4 minutes 1 second
3. Giuseppe Martano (*touriste-routier*) @ 5 minutes 8 seconds
4. Georges Lemaire (Belgium) @ 15 minutes 45 seconds
5. Maurice Archambaud (France) @ 21 minutes 22 seconds
6. Vicente Trueba (*touriste-routier*) @ 27 minutes 27 seconds

Vicente Trueba won the first-ever King of the Mountains competition with 134 points. 1931 Tour winner Antonin Magne was second with 81 points, and Giuseppe Martano third with 78.

Desgrange's national team formula for the Tour de France had produced 4 French winners in a row. Along with the French team, the fortunes of the Tour's sponsoring newspaper *L'Auto* soared as the French public eagerly sought news of their compatriots' exploits. *L'Auto*'s circulation spiked to 854,000, a record.

Speicher, who was as happy in a nightclub as anywhere, was not chosen to be a member of the French team for the World Championships that year. The selectors thought he would be too tired after winning the Tour. At the last minute one of the members for the French team dropped out. Needing someone to fill the spot and knowing generally where to look, the nightclubs of Paris were searched. They found Speicher and got him to Montléry the next morning in time to start the race. There, Georges did the rare double. He won the World Road Championship the same year he won the Tour. In 1935, 1937 and 1939 he was Champion of France. In 1936 he won Paris–Roubaix. And a final note, in 1938 he was kicked out of the Tour for holding onto a car on a climb in the Pyrenees.

1934. The 1934 Tour's story is one of the greatest and most famous in the history of racing. Its tale of noble sacrifice electrified French sports fans and created one of its most endearing and enduring heroes.

The Tour de France as we now know it was almost completely in place by 1933. The only major missing component was the individual time trial. Team time trials had been an integral part of the Tour in the late 1920s, but never had a rider been sent out as a lone man against the clock in the Tour. The origins of the inclusion of the time trial make for an interesting story and give another insight into the complex mind of

Henri Desgrange.

The newspaper *L'Auto* carried most of the costs of the Tour because of the introduction of the national team format in 1930. The burden grew with this change because the trade teams no longer covered the housing, travel and feeding of the riders while they raced the Tour. The basic purpose of the Tour de France was to stir up excitement for news of the Tour that *L'Auto* could then be in the best position to satisfy. Other journalistic competitors were eating into *L'Auto's* information franchise. One newspaper in particular gave *L'Auto* and its editor Henri Desgrange, who was also the Tour boss, cause for concern.

L'Auto was a morning paper, reporting the details of the previous day's stage in full. *Paris-Soir* was an evening paper and was getting the story of the day's stage, with results, into that same evening's edition. In order to make its deadline *Paris-Soir* had its writers report the race on the fly. As a stage progressed, the writers following the race would write a few pages and hand them off to be phoned in. Desgrange's paper, which had the results the following morning, was selling old news.

Desgrange, ever the competitor, countered by having his Tour stages start later in the day so the stages ended too late for the results to make the evening papers. *Paris-Soir* may have had some race details in their evening paper, but the final results had to wait for the next morning. Advantage Desgrange.

Paris-Soir's sports editor Gaston Bénac and his paper followed a hallowed tradition by starting a bicycle race. Not just any race. He started the Grand Prix des Nations, a time trial that eventually became the unofficial world championship of time trialing. Bénac's first edition was in 1932 and was not at all well received by the professional riders. Bénac had trouble getting enough of them to enroll in his first race. The sport of time trialing hadn't become the essential fixture that it is in today's racing scene. He did succeed, however. One of the main protagonists in the 1933 Tour, Maurice Archambaud, won the first Grand Prix des Nations. Raymond Louviot, also a French rider, won the 1933 Grand Prix des Nations.

If the patient reader has been following this Tour history from the beginning, one thing should be clear by now. Desgrange was adaptable. He was always willing to change his Tour if he thought he could improve it. He didn't seem to care where the idea came from. If it were a good idea, after a bit of consideration, he would use it. If an innovation didn't work, it was dropped. Seeing the success French riders were having in his antagonist's competition, Desgrange quite happily adopted the individual race against the clock for the Tour. He placed the Tour's first crono as the second part of a 2-stage day, late in the schedule of the 1934 Tour. The last 2 Tours (1932 and 1933) had ended up being very close affairs. Only the huge 4-minute time bonuses in the 1932 edition made Leducq's win seem big. A 90-kilometer time trial coming with only 3 stages to go could be decisive.

Many riders were unhappy with this new element. Climber René Vietto thought it just a test of dull, brutish horsepower when a bike race should be a contest that tested both head and legs. Vietto even cited Desgrange's book with that same title (*La Tête et Les Jambes*) to make his point. Others thought it would negate the effect of good teamwork since the individual time trial was, well, an individual effort. The rider's objections were met and overcome by 2 forces. This first was the power of the fine, exciting drama of a lone man on his bike in what has become known as the 'race of truth'. The second was the immediate success of French riders in the discipline. That sealed the time-trial's destiny as a crucial part of the Tour. It also gave new balance to the race as the powerful *rouleurs* could take time back from the smaller climbers who couldn't ride as fast on the flats. Climbing is a test of a rider's relative power output. Time trialing measures a racer's absolute horsepower. Now, to win the Tour, a racer had to have both qualities.

The French team for the 1934 Tour was another magnificent collection of outstanding athletes. The team's core was made up of Georges Speicher, 1933's Tour winner and World Champion, future Tour winner Roger Lapébie, previous Tour winner Antonin Magne, and Maurice Archambaud, who had held the Yellow Jersey for much of 1933's Tour. Rounding out the French squad were Charles Pélissier, René Le Grevès and a 20-year-old rider named René Vietto. Vietto, a hotel bellboy before he turned pro, had shown from the beginning a startling ability to climb. There was some debate about his inclusion in the team because of his youth but his talent silenced the naysayers.

Instead of riding as an independent *touriste-routier* as he had in 1933, gifted climber Giuseppe Martano headed an Italian team that did not measure up to his talent. Belgium sent a lackluster squad of whom only 2 found their way to Paris. The rest started abandoning in stage 2.

Of the 60 riders who started Tuesday, July 3 in Paris, the French national team was in a league of their own. The race was theirs to lose.

From the first stage of this clockwise Tour (Alps first), the French were off to the races. 1933 Tour winner Georges Speicher started where he had left off the year before by winning the first stage and again donning his Yellow Jersey. Speicher's time in Yellow was very short. The next day during the Lille to Charleville stage there was a split in the pack. 11 men beat the field to the finish by more than 15 minutes. Antonin Magne, "Tonin the Silent", winner of the 1931 Tour, was in this lead group. His second place that day gave him the lead in the General Classification. The Yellow Jersey stayed a French possession, passing from Speicher to his teammate Magne.

The French, from Speicher's stage 1 win, put on an impressive display of power. René Le Grevès won the second stage, Roger Lapébie took the third and fourth stages. Le Grevès and Speicher finished in a near dead heat at the end of stage 5. After looking at the photo finish the judges gave the stage win to Le Grevès but split the time bonus between them. Speicher took stage 6 with its climbs over the Aravis and the Tamié. All this time Magne kept a firm grip on the Yellow Jersey.

So, before the heavy climbing in the Alps, here was the General Classification:

1. Antonin Magne
2. Giuseppe Martano @ 7 minutes 57 seconds
3. Raymond Louviot @ 12 minutes 55 seconds

Stage 7 from Aix-les-Bains to Grenoble went over the great Galibier. There the ex-bellhop from Cannes showed what a brilliant talent he was. René Vietto won the stage with a $3\frac{1}{2}$-minute gap on the field. Giuseppe Martano was second, with Antonin Magne and several others right on his wheel. The rest of the field started coming in almost 12 minutes later.

The next day, stage 8 with the Laffrey and Bayard climbs, Martano was first but Magne was only 7 seconds behind. Vietto came in 21 seconds behind his leader.

Stage 9 was another Vietto showcase. He was first over both of the major climbs of the day, the Vars and the Allos. He continued down the road and soloed in for the stage victory. 3 days later Vietto finished off the Maritime Alps in the Nice to Cannes stage by being first over the

Braus, the Castillon and La Turbie. He beat Martano in the sprint thereby denying the Italian racer the time bonus that the stage win would have given him. Magne finished the stage 3 $1/_2$ minutes later. Magne still held the lead, but Martano had made the gap dangerously close. After the Alps and the 3 wonderful mountain stage wins by young Vietto, the General Classification stood thus:

1. Antonin Magne

2. Giuseppe Martano @ 2 minutes 5 seconds

3. René Vietto @ 29 minutes 51 seconds

During the first 2 stages Vietto had lost a lot of time with several flat tires. Barring that misfortune he would have been in serious contention for the lead. As we will see, misfortune should be Vietto's middle name.

The stages between the Alps and the Pyrenees were another series of French romps with victories in stages 12, 13, and 14 by Lapébie, Speicher, and Lapébie respectively.

The next stage, number 15 from Perpignan to Ax-les-Thermes, is the real beginning of the story of Vietto's sacrifice and his rise to immortality. On one of the earlier climbs of the day Magne tried to test Martano with an attack, but Martano was not to be dropped. The big climb of the day was the 25-kilometer long road up the Puymorens. René Vietto led Magne and Martano over the top. On the descent Magne crashed and broke the wooden rim of his front wheel. Seeing the Yellow Jersey's misfortune, Martano jumped away in an effort to put distance between himself and Magne.

"René, give me your bike," Magne demanded of Vietto

"No, but take my front wheel."

Vietto dutifully gave his team leader the front wheel of his bike. Unfortunately, Magne's frame was bent in the crash. When Georges Speicher—who had been behind on the climb—showed up, Magne took Speicher's bike. Magne was able to hook up with Lapébie and chase down Martano and the rest of the leaders. Magne limited his time loss that day to a mere 45 seconds and kept his Yellow Jersey. Vietto had to wait several minutes for the support car to bring him a replacement. He and Speicher finished together, 4 $1/_2$ minutes behind the stage winner Lapébie.

There is a picture of Vietto, weeping by the side of a mountain road, the front wheel of his bike missing. He knows that the Tour is going down the road without him. In some pictures of the scene a man in street clothes holds a smashed wheel in his hands. Vietto's anguish, 70 years later, still moves me when I see this picture. I wasn't the only one affected by the scene. The entire cycling world was touched by the scene of a man who made a huge sacrifice and was abject in the realization of the cost of that gift. The next day the newspapers proclaimed him *Le Roi René* (King René).

Things did not get better for the brilliant young climber. The next day, the stage from Ax-les-Thermes to Luchon was another big day of climbing with the Port, Portet d'Aspet and the Ares passes to overcome. Vietto was first over the Port and rode ahead of his team leader Magne who was keeping an eye on second place Giuseppe Martano. Over the next mountain, the Portet d'Aspet, Vietto was slightly ahead of Magne. He eased a bit so that he could be with Magne on the descent. Magne was still following Martano when he hit a rock and crashed. This time Magne wrecked his rear wheel. Vietto, thinking that Magne would be joining him shortly, continued. This was over a half-century before earphones. Often, in the "fog of war", riders are confused about what is actually going on in a race. A Tour course marshal on a motorcycle zoomed up ahead and told Vietto that his team leader had crashed and was stranded without any teammates. Lapébie was off the front and the rest of the team was well behind.

Hearing the news, Vietto turned around and rode back up the mountain against the tide of descending riders in order to reach his leader. Magne couldn't believe his good fortune. He grabbed Vietto's bike and took off after Lapébie who was now waiting for him and could help him regain the leaders. Adriano Vignoli, the stage winner, was long gone, but Magne and Lapébie did catch Martano and the rest of the riders who were up the road. Again Vietto had to wait for the service car to give him a new bike. He came in over 8 minutes after Vignoli, but only about 4 minutes after Magne, Lapébie and Martano. Vietto's selfless move preserved Magne's lead of 2 minutes, 57 seconds over Martano.

But, was everybody happy? Not Vietto, who had a sharp tongue. He complained that Magne didn't really know how to ride a bike and that Lapébie had taken off looking for a stage win instead of sticking with Magne. Magne, on the other hand, was profoundly grateful to both Vietto and Lapébie for saving his race.

The General Classification after stage 16:

1. Antonin Magne
2. Giuseppe Martano @ 2 minutes 57 seconds
3. Félicien Vervaecke @ 35 minutes 17 seconds

Stage 17 was where Magne sealed his victory in the 1934 Tour de France. Since the second stage he had been the leader, but Martano had been able to keep it close. Only great good fortune and a team that would do anything to make sure one of its own won the Tour had allowed Magne to keep the Yellow Jersey. On the road from Luchon to Tarbes, over the great Peyresourde and Aspin climbs, Magne built a lead that was almost invulnerable to challenge. Vietto was first over the Peyresourde but Magne led over the Aspin and came in alone, over 6 minutes ahead of Vicente Trueba, nearly 8 minutes ahead of Vietto. More tellingly, Martano wasn't able to stay with Magne and finished 13 minutes behind him. The gap in the General Classification between Magne and Martano was now 19 minutes, 47 seconds after time bonuses.

The next day, stage 18, Magne lost 4 minutes to Martano. Again, having a brilliant team was invaluable. René Vietto was first over the 2 major climbs, the Tourmalet and the Aubisque and won the stage with Lapébie coming in second. Martano was third, but Vietto had scooped up most of the time bonuses that were in play that day, minimizing Martano's possible time gain.

The French continued to win stages. The race for the Yellow Jersey was almost finished with the major climbing completed and the Tour heading back to Paris. There was one obstacle left in the way of Magne's likely triumph and that was the Tour's first individual time trial, 90 kilometers from La Roche-sur-Yon to Nantes. On the afternoon of Friday, July 27, Antonin Magne made history by winning the Tour's first individual time trial. He beat his teammate Lapébie, who came in second, by over a minute. He crushed Giuseppe Martano, besting him by 8 minutes. Magne's decisive time-trial win made it clear that he was truly the deserving victor.

The Tour was settled. Magne had taken the Yellow Jersey on the second stage and held it for the balance of the Tour. The time gaps between Magne and the rest of the peloton were huge, more like the Tours of a decade before. The French made the 1934 Tour their private property. Not only did Magne win the General Classification, the French team won 19 stages, King of the Mountains and Team General Classification. Yet, without Vietto's and Speicher's willingness to sacrifice everything for him, Magne's chances would have been doubtful. Would Martano have been higher up in the standings if he had not suffered two broken frames? Undoubtedly. But, to win a 3 week race one must have both strength and good luck.

The final 1934 Tour de France General Classification:

1. Antonin Magne (France): 147 hours 13 minutes 58 seconds
2. Giuseppe Martano (Italy) @ 27 minutes 31 seconds
3. Roger Lapébie (France) @ 52 minutes 15 seconds
4. Félicien Vervaecke (Belgium) @ 57 minutes 40 seconds
5. René Vietto (France) @ 59 minutes 2 seconds

Climber's Competition:

1. René Vietto: 111 points
2. Vicente Trueba: 93 points
3. Giuseppe Martano: 78 points

Vietto remained convinced until his death that he could have won the 1934 Tour if he could have kept riding up the mountain and left Magne to wait for a spare. I don't think so. Before the Tour hit the mountains he had lost a huge amount of time. He lost an additional near 10 minutes in the time trial. Vietto's class was real. He still won the King of the Mountains and came in fifth in General Classification. But he wasn't a complete enough rider to win the Tour. We'll run into "King René" again in this history. He will wear the Yellow for many days in the future, but he would never wear it in Paris as the overall winner.

Still, the French love a gallant man and Vietto was that. He became a hero and to this day is remembered with fondness for his sacrifices. He earned a terrific amount of money racing after the Tour because the French were so taken by his generosity. Sadly, he was swindled out of his winnings later in life.

Chapter 5

1935–1939. Only tainted officiating allows the French to win 1 Tour out of 5 amid Belgian hegemony

1935. Sometimes one looks at the start-list of a Grand Tour and it is clear, just plain obvious, how the race will turn out. Fortune then fools us and the result is one no one could expect.

The French team was brimming with talent. All 3 winners of the last 5 Tours, Magne, Speicher and Leducq were there. In addition, super-climber René Vietto and former Yellow Jersey Maurice Archambaud were on the 1935 French team. Roger Lapébie, who had played such an important part in Magne's 1934 win, as well as sprinter Charles Pélissier were not on the team. They rode as *individuels*, a different class from *touriste-routier*. If a member of the French team or any of the other teams had to quit, a rider competing as an *individuel* from that country could take his place. With all of this ability and experience there was no reason to doubt that the French spree of 5 straight Tour victories would be extended to 6.

The Belgians brought a fairly good team. Veterans Jean Aerts and Félicien Vervaecke (fourth in 1934), along with Romain Maes who had turned pro 2 years before, anchored the squad.

On paper the Italians looked powerful. Giuseppe Martano, Vasco Bergamaschi, Francesco Camusso, Mario Cipriani and Adriano Vignoli along with speedster Raffaele Di Paco were all accomplished riders. The team should have been tough competition. None of the starting Italian team finished the race. Two riders starting as Italian *individuels* did finish and as we shall see, one of them, Ambrogio Morelli did very well indeed.

93 riders started from Paris on Thursday, July 4. This was another clockwise, Alps-first Tour.

The Belgians started the Tour with a remarkable stroke of good luck. Romain Maes put a train between himself and the peloton in the first stage. By beating the closing of the road at a level crossing while the pack had to wait for the train to pass, Maes was able to come in almost a minute ahead of the peloton. Antonin Magne was in the 4-man group chasing Maes—with Charles Pélissier and Jean Aerts—but they were unable to catch the short, muscular Maes.

As the rules of the time required, Romain Maes is fixing his own flat.

The next day Maes had trouble with flat tires. At one point he was over 9 minutes behind the peloton. The Belgian team had to chase for 70 kilometers to get their Yellow Jersey back up to the field. At the end of the stage Charles Pélissier showed he still had lots of speed, winning the 30-man sprint. The time bonus for winning the stage pulled Pélissier to within 1 minute, 46 seconds of Maes, but no one expected Pélissier to be a contender for the Yellow Jersey in Paris. But then again, no one really thought that of Maes either.

It was on stage 4, from Metz to Belfort with the Ballon d'Alsace climb that the edges of the French machine started to look a bit ragged. Belgian Jean Aerts won the stage with Belgians Danneels and Neuville taking second and third. Roger Lapébie was the best placed Frenchman at tenth, coming in 2 minutes, 23 seconds after Aerts. Maes was now sitting on a 5 1/2-minute lead over Magne in the General Classification.

Monday July 8 was a truly brutal day of racing. It was a split stage. The first half was a 262-kilometer ride from Belfort to Geneva with a climb over the 1,320-meter Faucille. Archambaud won it, but the gap between Maes and Magne remained at 5 minutes, 29 seconds. That same afternoon the racers faced a 58-kilometer individual time trial. Italian sprinter Raffaele Di Paco won the time trial with Magne only 2 seconds slower. But the big story was that Maes did not crack. He lost only 38 seconds to Magne, one of the finest time trialists alive. The gap between Maes and Magne was about 4 minutes before the first day in the Alps.

Stage 6 crossed the Aravis and the Tamié, super-climber René Vietto's turf. He was first over both of the major climbs and took the solo win. René Le Grevès led in the field with Maes getting fourth in the field sprint. There was no change in the overall time between Maes and Magne. The Italian Bergamaschi was third, over 12 minutes down.

The Queen Stage of the Alps was stage 7. Going from Aix-les-Bains to Grenoble, it required that the riders pass over the Télégraphe, the Galibier and the Lautaret.

On the Télégraphe Magne was hit by a car. Badly injured, he was taken to the hospital in a farmer's cart. It was on the Galibier that the first true tragedy in the history of the Tour struck. Francisco Cepeda, riding as a Spanish *individuel,* crashed on the descent, fracturing his skull. Dying 3 days later, Cepeda became the Tour's first fatality.

With the abandonment of Magne, the net effect of the stage was to enlarge Maes' lead to over 12 minutes with Bergamaschi now in second place. Maes was showing that he had the power to compete in a Grand Tour, having survived many challenges: mechanical problems in the second stage, to the time trial and now the Alps.

Stage 9 reordered the podium. The Gap to Digne stage had the Vars and the Allos climbs. Scooping up the climber's points, Vervaecke was first over both of them. But it was René Vietto who won the stage with Francesco Camusso only a few seconds behind him. Maes came in 9 minutes later. Bergamaschi lost over a half-hour. Camusso was now in second place, 3 ½ minutes behind Maes. Through the Maritime Alps, Maes extended his lead over Camusso so that when the Tour emerged after stage 12 in Marseille, the General Classification stood thus:

1. Romain Maes

2. Francesco Camusso @ 6 minutes 11 seconds

3. Georges Speicher @ 10 minutes 24 seconds

The French showed that although they might be having trouble with the Belgian upstart in Yellow, as a team they still had the raw power to ride fast. Stage 13b was a team time trial and the French beat the Belgians by 27 seconds. The stage win gave Speicher the time bonus to bring him within 8 ½ minutes of Maes.

The next afternoon was the second of 3 individual time trials in the 1935 Tour. Maes was second to Maurice Archambaud. This extended his lead still further. Going into the Pyrenees, Romain Maes still topped the General Classification:

1. Romain Maes

2. Georges Speicher @ 10 minutes 22 seconds

3. Francesco Camusso @ 12 minutes 30 seconds

The first Pyreneen stage, from Perpignan to Luchon had the Puymorens, the Port and the Portet d'Aspet climbs. Félicien Vervaecke was first over all 3. Vervaecke and his compatriot Sylvère Maes (unrelated to Romain Maes) beat third place Oskar Thierback by over 13 minutes and the rest of the field by over 20 minutes. This made for a Belgian podium in the General Classification with Romain Maes leading, followed by Vervaecke and Sylvère Maes.

It was on the monster stage 16, Luchon to Pau, that Maes was finally put into difficulty. With the Peyresourde, the Aspin, the Tour-malet and the Aubisque compressed into 194 kilometers, the stage would be a hard test for any rider. The Belgians led over the first 3 climbs, then the Italians Ambrogio Morelli and Orlando Teani took over on the Aubisque. Morelli won the stage and, of course, the time bonus. Romain Maes depended upon his teammates Vervaecke and Jules Lowie to see him through this tough patch. They sheltered him and saved Maes' now diminished lead. Maes finished the stage in fourth place, 6 minutes, 19 seconds behind Morelli. With the major climbing now finished here were the standings:

1. Romain Maes
2. Ambrogio Morelli @ 2 minutes 30 seconds
3. Félicien Vervaecke @ 9 minutes 7 seconds

From here on, preserving his lead would be a matter of good luck. In the first half of the eighteenth stage Morelli lost a disastrous 10 minutes. That afternoon was the final individual time trial at La Rochelle. André Leducq won it, but Maes was second, only 7 seconds slower. There were still 2 more team time trials, but these had no effect on the podium of the General Classification. As the Tour came ever closer to Paris, Maes maintained his substantial lead over Morelli, which was now more than 15 minutes.

To cap a fairy-tale tour, Maes won the final stage in to Paris, alone, 39 seconds ahead of second place Vervaecke. He collapsed in tears into the arms of his mother. With that, Maes joined Maurice Garin, Philippe Thys, Ottavio Bottecchia and Nicolas Frantz in being the only Tour riders to that date to hold the lead of the Tour from start to finish. *L'Equipe* says that without Charles Pélissier and Antonin Magne, the terrific esprit de corps that had characterized the French national team since 1930 simply evaporated. Without this indomitable team spirit, they were taken apart by a Belgian who never again finished the Tour de France and was on a team that had only 3 finishers.

Final 1935 Tour de France General Classification:

1. Romain Maes (Belgium): 141 hours 32 minutes
2. Ambrogio Morelli (Italian *individuel*) @ 17 minutes 52 seconds
3. Félicien Vervaecke (Belgium) @ 24 minutes 6 seconds

4. Sylvère Maes (Belgian *individuel*) @ 35 minutes 24 seconds

5. Jules Lowie (Belgian *individuel*) @ 51 minutes 26 seconds

Climber's Competition:

1. Félicien Vervaecke: 118 points

2. Sylvère Maes: 92 points

3. Gabriel Ruozzi: 70 points

1936. In 1936 the old lion Henri Desgrange, now 71 years old, needed kidney surgery a few weeks before the Tour started. Indomitable, he tried to follow his beloved Tour. He had a car fitted up with cushions to mitigate his discomfort. Recognizing the seriousness of his condition, his family and doctors begged him not to direct the race. "My duty is to be with the Tour," he said. Being Desgrange, it was useless to try to dissuade him. But it was too much for the stubborn old man. After the second stage he handed the management of the race to Jacques Goddet, the son of Victor Goddet, the financial controller of *L'Auto* who had given his blessing to the start of the Tour back in 1903.

That was the last year Desgrange directed the Tour even though he visited the Tour and is listed as its Patron through 1939. He suffered declining health and died August 16, 1940 in his house on the French Riviera. Desgrange was always a competitor. In his final days as he was dying, he would force himself to walk across his bedroom with a stopwatch in his hand, trying to beat his previous time across the room.

This would be a good time to look back at Desgrange. The Tour was not his idea. It was Géo Lefèvre's. The idea of the newspaper *L'Auto* was not his, he was merely installed as its editor. Yet, he made both completely his with the strong force of his powerful personality. He created a brand new sport, stage racing. There were no rules for stage racing when he started. He had to make them up as he went. He was a dictator, but he was a scrupulous and fair one. Perhaps a benevolent dictator was needed in order to make sure this creation achieved a robust maturity.

He had no interest in advancing technology. His passion was the primitive struggle of a lone athlete against the terrain, elements, personal weakness and other equally dedicated competitors. The bicycle was almost an impediment to him. Mavic was producing aluminum rims by 1926, but Desgrange forbade them in his race until 1931, fearing that metal rims would not dissipate heat properly on long descents.

Gear changers were forbidden. Félicien Vervaecke would receive a 10-minute time penalty for using a derailleur on the Aubisque in the sixteenth stage of the 1936 Tour even though the *touriste-routiers* were using them and routinely beating the national team members to the tops of climbs. Desgrange may have been recovering at his home on the Riviera, but his rules were still in force.

I believe the Tour became the most important race in the world because of Desgrange's basic integrity and adaptability. He was always willing to change his race as opportunities to improve it presented themselves. He set the tone and the culture in the Tour de France that made everyone believe that the race was terribly hard but very fair. It was worth winning and no one could second-guess the victor. It is on this count that the Giro falls flat and why to this day the Giro is a very important Italian regional race rather than a contender with the Tour for the race that matters most in the world. I believe Henri Desgrange is, by far, the most important man in the history of cycling.

Before he retired, Desgrange made a number of changes in the 1936 Tour. He reduced the number of time trials to 5, but he made them all team time trials—there were no individual time trials this year. He increased the number of rest days from 4 to 6. But he also squeezed 3 stages into 1 day.

The rider and team enrollment system was changed yet again. He made the major cycling nations, France, Germany, Belgium and a strange combination of Spain and Luxembourg have 10-man teams. Switzerland, Holland, Romania, Yugoslavia and Austria competed with 5-man teams. The *touriste-routier* classification was discarded, but the classification of *individuels* was retained, though no longer as national *individuels*.

At this time France was undergoing profound changes. In 1936 the Popular Front coalition was elected to run France under Prime Minister Léon Blum. The Popular Front was made up of socialists, communists and other radicals, who instituted a 40-hour workweek and a 2-week vacation. It's amazing how a previous generation's seemingly extreme reforms can become today's basic human necessities. This paid 2-week vacation made it possible for more people than ever to watch the Tour.

The tensions between the European nations were growing. For decades Italy had been competing with Great Britain for influence and empire in East Africa. Italy under Mussolini, desirous of establishing an African empire, invaded Ethiopia in 1935. The world reacted with almost unanimous condemnation. I've never understood, however, how countries like France with her African and far-eastern colonies, Belgium with her stomach-turning record in the Congo, or Britain, suppressing Gandhi and the Indians working to throw off the colonial yoke, could be so outraged at Italy's only wanting to join the same club of colonial oppressors. For the purposes of this history, the result was that the Italians did not send a team to the 1936 Tour. The great Tour de France writer Pierre Chany put it thus, "The Italians had decided to stay away for political reasons. The country had engaged in a difficult war in Ethiopia and the fascist government, condemned by the League of Nations, had broken off relations with the outside world."

A group of Italians who said they were French residents, including Raffaele Di Paco and Jules Rossi, were allowed to enroll. Numbers 41 through 50 were reserved for them, but then Tour officials changed their minds and did not allow them to start.

The French team retained many of its core riders from its glory days in the first half of the 1930s. Antonin Magne, Georges Speicher, Maurice Archambaud and René Le Grevès, all with extensive Tour experience, planned to regain the winning ways they had known just 2 short years before.

Belgium fielded a superb team starting with last year's winner, Romain Maes. Sylvère Maes (no relation to Romain), who had ridden in 1935 as a Belgian *individuel* and finished fourth was now part of the Belgian team. Félicien Vervaecke, so valuable to Romain Maes on the climbs, returned. This was also the first Tour for Marcel Kint, "the Black Eagle", one of those super-tough Belgian roadmen who seem to be able to take anything a race or the elements will dish out.

Germany put 10 men on the road at the start. None made it to Paris. None of the 4-man teams of Austria, Romania and Yugoslavia was able to finish the Tour either. The first African in Tour history entered. Abd-el-Kader Abbes, an Algerian, rode as an *individuel*. He finished 42nd out of 43 finishers. Not bad when one considers that 90 riders started.

The beginning of the 1936 Tour is mostly remembered for its

terrible, torrential rains. The racers were forced to ride on streets flooded almost axle-deep at times. For 7 days the riders were lashed with terrible weather.

Paul Egli won the first stage making him the first Swiss rider in Tour history to wear the Yellow Jersey. The next day Maurice Archambaud was able to take advantage of his second place in the first stage. Egli missed the big move in stage 2, finishing almost 10 minutes behind the leaders. Archambaud regained the Yellow Jersey that he had last worn during the eleventh stage of the 1933 Tour. It must have felt good to put it on and finally again be a Frenchman back in the lead of the Tour de France. Notably, Antonin Magne, Sylvère and Romain Maes were all in the front group and retained their General Classification competitiveness.

The rains continued. Gaps continually opened up with the race being conducted under appalling conditions. Luxembourger Arsène Mersch took the lead from Archambaud after the third stage. The next day Archambaud won the stage and regained the lead when the Tour went over the Ballon d'Alsace. Again, Magne and Sylvère Maes stayed close to the action.

Before the real racing began in the Alps in stage 6 with the Aravis and Tamié climbs, the General Classification stood thus:

1. Maurice Archambaud

2. Sylvère Maes @ 3 minutes 37 seconds

3. Robert Wierinckx @ 3 minutes 44 seconds

The first Alpine stage didn't change the dynamics of the race as 17 riders, including almost all of the real contenders, finished together at Aix-les-Bains. The notable exception was René Vietto who quit after 2 broken chains.

Stage 7, with the Télégraphe prelude to the mighty Galibier, followed by the Lautaret climb, did alter the race, but did not change the top 2 places of the General Classification podium. Wierinckx lost his third place to Pierre Clemens of Luxembourg.

Romain Maes was first over the Télégraphe but then abandoned. Maes had been frequently ill the entire spring of 1936. He was dogged by a strange fever that came and went. He trained when he could and rested when he had to. He never consulted a doctor and lived on aspirin. He entered Paris–Roubaix and crossed the finish line first, but a judging error placed him second. The judges gave the win to Georges Speicher and they would not correct their mistake. There is a famous photograph of the 2 riders crossing the line, making the injustice to Maes very clear.

Owen Mulholland writes: "[Maes] never truly recaptured his old form. In Maes' own words: 'In the Tour de France, I attempted the impossible. But I was forced to abandon, incapable of breathing on the Galibier stage.' When he returned to Belgium and finally consulted a doctor he was informed that he was a victim of chronic bronchitis. The condition was so serious that he was ordered to quit racing for a year, if not more. At his peak he was described by [Tour historian] Théo Mathy, 'Romain Maes is an electric pile. He sleeps poorly. He doesn't recover easily. He has the class, but he lives on his nerves. With him, it's all or nothing.' "

Georges Speicher crashed descending the Galibier. His Tour was also over.

Stage 8 was one of the 1936 Tour's pivotal stages. The 194-kilometer stage from Grenoble to Briançon ascended the 900-meter Laffrey and then the 1,248-meter Bayard. It was too much for Archambaud, the man Desgrange had nicknamed "Chubby Cheeks". *Individuel* Jean-Marie Goasmat won the stage but in the first group of chasers a little over 6 minutes behind him were Magne, Sylvère Maes and Luxembourg rider Pierre Clemens.

This left the General Classification thus:

1. Sylvère Maes
2. Pierre Clemens @ 1 minute 10 seconds
3. Antonin Magne @ 1 minute 35 seconds

Magne, riding conservatively throughout the first part of the Tour, must have thought the situation perfectly manageable. There was a lot of Tour left and he was sitting less than 2 minutes behind Maes. The following day was a brutal stage going from Briançon to Digne. For the first time since 1927 the Tour included the Izoard. This massive mountain was followed by the Vars and the Allos. Magne attacked on the Izoard but was unable to shake Maes. Maes not only avoided being dropped, he was the first over the Izoard's crest. Later in the stage Maes flatted. But unlike their teams in the early 1930s, the Belgians now had that same team spirit that had earlier motivated the French. The Belgians, called the "Black Guard" for their team jerseys, resolutely worked to bring him back up to the front of the field. At the end of the stage the finishing group of 7 included Maes, Clemens and Belgian climber Vervaecke. It did not contain Magne. Magne lost about a minute on the day he had planned to take the Yellow.

Maes took another bite out of Magne in the final Alpine stage, number 11 from Nice to Cannes. This stage, over the Maritime Alps, cost Magne another precious minute.

So, here were the standings after the Alps and before the Pyrenees:

1. Sylvère Maes
2. Félicien Vervaecke @ 2 minutes 48 seconds
3. Antonin Magne @ 3 minutes 49 seconds

Between the Alps and the Pyrenees there were 2 team time trials. They presented a reversal of fortune from the previous year. In 1935, even though the French did not have a man who could win the overall lead, collectively they were still powerful and could win the team time trials. This year the Belgians won both of the intermountain team tests. The result was to push Antonin Magne ever further behind. Before stage 15, the first Pyreneen stage, Magne was still in third place, but now about 8 minutes behind Maes.

Even though the Perpignan to Luchon stage, so often pivotal in the Tour's history, included the Puymorens, the Port, the Portet d'Aspet and the Ares climbs, the podium didn't change. Maes, Magne, Vervaecke and Swiss rider Léo Amberg all finished together, a half-minute behind the winner, Sauveur Ducazeaux, another superb *individuel*.

But stage 16. That was the stage that finally decided the Tour. The 4 colossal mountains scheduled in the ride from Luchon to Pau were the Peyresourde, the Aspin, the Tourmalet and the Aubisque. Magne thought that this intimidating stage would be his last real chance to take back the lead, since this stage signaled the end of any substantial climbing. After that there were still 3 more team time trials, which had so far played to the advantage of the Belgians.

Magne just could not do it. He attacked Maes on the Tourmalet and blew up. He ended up losing 18 minutes when time bonuses and penalties were figured in. And Sylvère Maes? He won the stage after being first over the last 2 climbs, the Tourmalet and the Aubisque. Félicien Vervaecke had been policing Magne for his team leader when he flatted on the Aubisque. Vervaecke borrowed a derailleur-equipped bike to finish the stage, but a derailleur was still a forbidden piece of equipment for a national team rider. Only the *individuels* could use them. That's one reason why the *individuels* often did as well or better on the big passes in the mid to late 1930s. Vervaecke was penalized 10 minutes for using the gear-equipped bike. Magne also received a penalty, having gotten an illegal feed from retired French racer Victor Fontan.

After all the climbing, here's where things stood at the beginning of stage 17:

1. Sylvère Maes
2. Antonin Magne @ 26 minutes 13 seconds
3. Félicien Vervaecke @ 28 minutes 38 seconds

Stage 18b was another team time trial and the Belgians continued to pour it on. Magne lost another 2 minutes. The next day, another team time trial. The Belgians won again and this time let Vervaecke be first across the line. With the time bonus for winning the stage he was now sitting in second and Magne pushed to third place. This day, Friday July 31, was the first time the Tour had squeezed 3 stages into one day. It would be about 50 years before the riders would strike and end this particular abuse.

The penultimate stage was the final team time trial. The French dug deeply and finally won one. With that effort Magne pulled himself back up to second place. The Belgians, through excellent teamwork and the presence of a superb rider in Sylvère Maes kept the Yellow Jersey from stage 8 until the end.

The French did have a worthy successor to sprinter Charles Pélissier. French team member René Le Grevès won 6 stages. Not since the pre-war glory days of François Faber had the riders of Luxembourg done so well. 3 men from the tiny country made the top 10.

The final 1936 Tour de France General Classification:

1. Sylvère Maes (Belgium): 142 hours 47 minutes 32 seconds
2. Antonin Magne (France) @ 26 minutes 55 seconds
3. Félicien Vervaecke (Belgium) @ 27 minutes 53 seconds
4. Pierre Clemens (Luxembourg) @ 42 minutes 42 seconds

5. Arsène Mersch (Luxembourg) @ 52 minutes 52 seconds

Spanish climbers made their mark on the Climber's Competition:

1. Julian Berrendero: 132 points

2. Sylvère Maes: 112 points

3. Federico Ezquerra: 70 points

1937. 1937 was Jacques Goddet's first full year of control of the Tour. One of his first moves was to bow to the inevitable march of techno- logical change. Gear changers had been slowly improving in reliability since their introduction by Joanny Panel in the 1912 Tour. Henri Des- grange's reaction at the time to this technical improvement to the bicy- cle was his usual one. He banned them from the Tour. The truth be told, however, for years the racers shunned gear changers. They felt that a fixed-gear, single-speed bike was far more efficient.

Touriste-routiers and individuels, however, had been allowed to use gear changers for years. The situation grew ever sillier when the individuels began beating the stars to the tops of some mountains. So for 1937, national team members were allowed to ride the Tour with gear changers.

This is a bigger change than just a bit of an improvement to the bike. Until 1937 Tour riders rode bikes with double-sided rear hubs. There were two sprockets on each side of the hub. For the mountains one side might have and 18 and 20 tooth sprockets. The other would have a 22 and 24. A single 44 chainring was the usual front gear. A 50 x 16–20 was mounted for the flatter stages. To change gears a rider had to dismount his bike, loosen the wing nuts (Tullio Campagnolo was just inventing the quick release that year) and either move the chain to the other rear sprocket or flip the wheel around to get access to the other two cogs.

When to change gears? This was a crucial tactical question in those days. Pick the wrong moment to change gears and a racer could watch the other riders disappear down the road. In the 1920 Tour Firmin Lambot lied to Philippe Thys about the contours of the road up ahead to get Thys to change gears. Once Thys dismounted, Lambot took off. Angered, Thys chased Lambot down and made sure he beat Lambot in the sprint.

With the ability to change gears on the fly, clearly the tactics of mountain racing changed.

The 1937 Tour de France was a demanding monster. Goddet may have relented in the case of the gears, but there was no tendency to soften the cruel, hard character of the race. 31 stages were crammed into the 26 days of the Tour. On 3 separate occasions the riders had to ride 3 stages in a single day. I count 6 other days that had 2 stages each.

The Belgians brought back their 1936 Tour winner, Sylvère Maes. He was amply supported by a strong team that included climbing ace Félicien Vervaecke and Marcel "Black Eagle" Kint. A strong team indeed. Before their dramatic exit from the Tour in stage 17, the Belgians had lost only 1 of their 10 riders.

While political problems kept the Italians out of the 1936 Tour, they came back in 1937 with their hot new rider, Gino Bartali. Bartali had turned pro in 1934 and began winning races in 1935. 1936 was his breakout year with a victory in the Giro d'Italia. He did it with real authority, winning 3 stages as well as the climber's competition. Before coming to the 1937 Tour he again won the Giro as well as the Italian Road Championship. The rest of the Italian team was also strong, having such excellent riders as Francesco Camusso and Giuseppe Martano. Bartali was the odds-on favorite to win this edition of the Tour.

The French team sported several riders from the team's glory years of the early 1930s. Maurice Archambaud, René Le Grevès and Georges Speicher were lined up along with troublesome Roger Lapébie.

Lapébie and Tour Boss Henri Desgrange fought from Lapébie's very first Tour until Desgrange's retirement. These arguments sometimes kept Lapébie off the French team. In 1935 he rode as an *individuel* but quit the Tour during the twelfth stage. This abandonment caused yet more arguments with Desgrange. Lapébie, who had been third in the 1934 Tour, sat out 1936. With new Tour management for 1937 Lapébie was back in the saddle and part of the French attempt to keep the Belgians from gaining another Tour win. Yet, there were doubts about Lapébie's form. He had undergone back surgery for a lumbar hernia after riding the motorpaced 500-kilometer Bordeaux–Paris race. His entry in the Tour is amazing since Bordeaux–Paris was run on May 30 and the Tour started June 30.

This Tour continued the use of the *individuels*, a class of riders who rode the Tour on their own, completely responsible for their own food and accommodations. There were several fine riders in this class in the 1937 Tour. The best of them was the Italian Mario Vicini. Indeed, 12 of the top twenty finishers of the 1937 Tour were *individuels*.

While Gino Bartali may have been the favorite for this clockwise (Alps first) Tour, he let himself lose good chunks of time over the first 3 stages: 6 minutes here, 7 minutes there. Yet, when the race went up for the first time in stage 4 Bartali shone. He wasn't the first over the Ballon d'Alsace nor was he the first into Belfort. But he was second that day and that placing lifted him onto the General Classification podium. He was now sitting in third place, 10 minutes behind German team rider Erich Bautz who had won the stage and the Yellow Jersey. But, it was early yet. The best placed Belgian in that stage was *individuel* Ward Vissers, who finished seventh, over 5 1/2 minutes behind Bautz.

The first team time trial, stage 5b, let the Belgians shine and show that they still had lots of raw horsepower. Yet, though they won the stage, they couldn't gain any real traction. Over the 34 kilometer stage the French finished only 30 seconds behind the Belgians and the Italians were only another 7 seconds distant.

Before the Alps, the General Classification podium stood thus:

1. Erich Bautz
2. Maurice Archambaud @ 8 minutes 12 seconds
3. Léo Amberg @ 10 minutes 57 seconds

Stage 6 from Geneva to Aix-les-Bains was the first Alpine stage with the Aravis and the Tamié climbs. Bartali was first over the 1498-meter high Aravis but 26 riders came in together for the finish. The only real change was that Maurice Archambaud, the French team veteran who had been such an important part of the French teams of the early 1930s lost his place on the podium. He had won the second stage and had been sitting in second place in the General Classification. Yet, as had happened for the better part of the decade, the high mountains defeated him. The first bite of attrition hit the French team with the abandonment of Louis Thietard.

Stage 7 was another big Alpine stage with the Télégraphe and the Galibier. Bartali took the crest of the Galibier first, over a minute ahead of his immediate chasers and well ahead of the top General Classification men. Bartali won the stage and the Yellow Jersey. The French team was hit with more casualties. They lost former Tour winner Georges Speicher, and Maurice Archambaud abandoned after being struck by a car.

The General Classification stood thus after stage 7:

1. Gino Bartali
2. Ward Vissers @ 9 minutes 18 seconds
3. Erich Bautz @ 9 minutes 55 seconds

This changed drastically in stage 8, a 194-kilometer run from Grenoble to Briançon that included both the Laffrey and the Bayard climbs. While Bartali was crossing a bridge on the wheel of teammate Jules Rossi, Rossi crashed and sent Bartali into the river below. Teammate Francesco Camusso jumped into the river to pull him out. Upon emerging, Bartali was bleeding and covered with mud from the river. A blow to his chest made it hard for him to breathe. Yet Gino "the Pious" Bartali climbed back on his bike and struggled, with lots of pushing from sympathetic spectators, all the way to Briançon. Covered in mud and blood, he thrilled the fans with his determination. While his adventure put him almost 10 minutes behind the stage winner, he retained the Yellow Jersey.

The overall standings were now:

1. Gino Bartali
2. Erich Bautz @ 2 minutes 5 seconds
3. Léo Amberg @ 5 minutes 17 seconds

Yet Bartali had been hurt. Stage 9 from Briançon to Digne was a ferocious stage. The riders had to climb the Izoard, the Vars and the Allos, all over 2000 meters high. This is the stage where the events of the previous day manifested themselves. The injured Bartali was in no condition to defend his lead. Shepherded by teammate Camusso, Bartali finished 22 1/2 minutes behind the stage winner Roger Lapébie.

The stage results:

1. Roger Lapébie: 7 hours 27 minutes 43 seconds
2. Félicien Vervaecke @ 2 minutes 47 seconds
3. Pierre Gallien @ same time
4. Jules Lowie @ 3 minutes 16 seconds
5. Mario Vicini @ 3 minutes 28 seconds
16. Gino Bartali @ 22 minutes 33 seconds

The new General Classification:

1. Sylvère Maes
2. Mario Vicini @ 35 seconds
3. Roger Lapébie @ 1 minute 22 seconds

The Belgians must have been surprised at their good fortune. Their 1936 winner was in Yellow and the man sitting in second place was an *individuel* with no team. And the French team had lost yet another rider, René Le Grevès. The French were down to 6 riders. At that point the riders of the French team got together and appointed Lapébie as their team leader. He was the only one on the team with the strength to win and earn the rest of them some prize money.

The final Alpine stage, from Digne to Nice did not affect the standings: Maes remained in Yellow. Bartali abandoned as the riders approached the Pyrenees.

The first Pyreneen stage, a little 59-kilometer appetizer with the 1920-meter high Puymorens, didn't affect the race. The General Classification podium remained unchanged. But this was just the second of 3 stages in one day. The third stage of the day, from Ax-les-Thermes to Luchon climbed the Port, the Portet d'Aspet and the Ares. Still the General Classification podium remained:

1. Sylvère Maes
2. Roger Lapébie @ 2 minutes 18 seconds
3. Mario Vicini @ 5 minutes 13 seconds

Maes was unable to finish Lapébie off. Day after day Lapébie had been able to stay with the Belgian and maintain his position.

It was on stage 15 from Luchon to Pau that the entire 1937 Tour de France became complicated with politics and intrigue. The stage had 4 climbs, the Peyresourde, the Aspin, the Tourmalet and finally the Aubisque. All 3 of the General Classification leaders finished the stage together, 49 seconds behind Spanish climber Julian Berrendero.

But let's go back to the beginning of this stage because this stage sowed the seeds of what was to follow and really decided the outcome of the 1937 Tour.

A few minutes before the start of the stage, as Lapébie was warming up, half of his handlebars came off in his hand. The bars had been partially sawn through, sabotaged. With only a little time to get the bike repaired, there was a panic. The stage would start with or without the General Classification second-place rider. A new set was found and mounted on his bike. But, the new set didn't have a water bottle cage. In those days, bottles were not mounted on the frame. Lapébie believed that Belgians had tampered with his bike. There is no particular evidence pointing to anyone. To this day no one knows who did the deed.

Lapébie had to start the stage without water. That fact demoralized him. The strict rules regarding handing up water and food at only specific designated points meant that getting water early could cost him time penalties. He later recounted that he was mentally shattered from the morning's occurrences. Lapébie fought on, but at the top of the Peyresourde Sylvère Maes was 2 minutes ahead. Over the Aspin, Maes had 5 minutes. On the Tourmalet, ready to quit, Lapébie found a mountain spring and revived himself. While Lapébie was undergoing his resurrection, Maes flatted.

The Belgian team waited for their leader. Together again they worked to get him up to the Spaniard Berrendero, who had been first over each of the climbs so far.

Over the top of the Tourmalet Lapébie was almost 7 minutes behind Maes. The Belgians were exhausting themselves chasing the fleeing Spaniard. On the descent of the Tourmalet Lapébie did one of the heroic descents that sometimes make the difference between winning and losing the Tour. Maes was running out of gas and Lapébie was feeling better. Lapébie gained almost 4 minutes on the descent of the Tourmalet. In the next 15 kilometers Lapébie chased and caught Maes. Lapébie went on to win the field sprint. Lapébie at this point, at the end of the stage, should have been just 1 $1/_2$ minutes behind Maes in the General Classification.

So how did Lapébie, who was at one point exhausted and shattered, make it up to Maes and then beat him? On the climbs Lapébie had received lots of pushing from the spectators. The officials told Lapébie, over and over, that he would be penalized if he continued to get pushed up the hills. He replied to the judges that he was asking the crowds not to push him, but he was helpless in the face of their enthusiasm and therefore could not stop them. In fact, he later confessed, he was encouraging his partisans to help him up the mountains. He had been guilty of this in both the earlier Alpine stages and the Pyrenees.

That wasn't all of it. Lapébie had been holding on to cars on the climbs and drafting them on the flats. On the Aubisque, when he was closing in on Maes, he was lifted up the mountain by holding on to one automobile after another.

The officials penalized Lapébie with a firm slap on the wrist: a 1 1/2 minute penalty. The Belgians erupted in fury. Lapébie had cheated his way back into Tour contention and the penalty inflicted left him far better off than if he hadn't cheated and been penalized. The French riders threatened to leave the race if the penalty were increased.

So the General Classification after stage 15:

1. Sylvère Maes
2. Roger Lapébie @ 3 minutes 3 seconds
3. Mario Vicini @ 4 minutes 57 seconds

The next day, Stage 16 from Pau to Bordeaux, things grew ever more interesting. Maes flatted. Lapébie attacked and got a good gap. After getting his bike repaired, Maes chased, trading pace with Gustaaf Deloor. Deloor was a Belgian, but he was riding as an *individuel*. Not being a member of the Belgian Team, he was not allowed to assist Maes. This was strictly against the rules. As Maes closed in on the Lapébie group, they came to a level train crossing. The signalman lowered the gate just in front of Maes and Deloor right after Lapébie had gone through. Maes dismounted and got his bike under the barrier and continued the chase. He finished the stage 1 minute, 38 seconds behind Lapébie.

Because of the illegal help Maes got from Deloor, the officials penalized Maes 25 seconds. Feeling that the railway man had intentionally acted to delay Maes and angry at the penalty that now put Lapébie now only 25 seconds behind Maes, the Belgians quit the race. Maes, even though he was in Yellow, withdrew from a race he felt was being run in favor of the French.

Lapébie was now the leader of the Tour de France. The major climbing had been completed. The only impediment, besides the possibility of bad fortune, was the individual time trial in the penultimate stage, number 19b, where Lapébie was able to extend his lead still more. Léo Amberg, the Swiss rider who had been trading places with Francesco Camusso for the third spot on the podium ever since the withdrawal of Maes, won the time trial and earned third place in the

1937 Tour.

L'Equipe says that Lapébie's greater skill in using his derailleur significantly contributed to his winning margin. Vicini, who was not so adept, was forced to use gearing that at times wasn't optimal. The 1937 derailleur was a far from perfect device. As Lapébie came into the *Parc des Princes* velodrome for the finish of the final stage, his chain came off. A quick fix and he rode into history.

Does Lapébie's victory smell? It does indeed. He clearly cheated and the officials were obviously working to get a French victory, a rare lapse in Tour de France judging. I'm sure Maes felt that he was better off quitting while in Yellow rather than letting himself get slowly cheated out of it on the road to Paris.

Of the 96 starters, only 46 racers made it to Paris.

1937 Tour de France final General Classification:

1. Roger Lapébie (France) 138 hours 58 minutes 31 seconds
2. Mario Vicini (*individuel*) @ 7 minutes 17 seconds
3. Léo Amberg (Switzerland) @ 26 minutes 13 seconds
4. Francesco Camusso (Italy) @ 26 minutes 53 seconds
5. Sylvain Marcaillou (France) @ 35 minutes 36 seconds
6. Ward Vissers (*individuel*) @ 38 minutes 13 seconds

Climber's competition:

1. Félicien Vervaecke: 114 points
2. Mario Vicini: 96 points
3. Sylvère Maes: 90 points

1938. The Tour organization tinkered a bit with the Tour. The time bonuses were reduced to just 1 minute for winning a stage. From having as many as 5 team time trials in 1936, the Tour completely eliminated the event for 1938, being content with 2 individual time trials. A new climb was added to the roster of Alpine challenges, the Iseran, a 2,770-meter high giant.

The *individuel* classification was eliminated. Until 1938, a rider could enter the Tour as an individual and race at his own expense and try to seek his fortune. The 1937 second-place, Mario Vicini, was one of a long line of gifted men who gloried in their individuality. Yet, the

Tour couldn't quite leave about 20 rather good French riders out of the Tour just because they didn't make the national team. So, 2 new categories were set up, Cadets and Bleuets. 1930 and 1932 Tour winner André Leducq and near-Tour winner René Vietto, among others, were put in the Cadet class. Eventual tenth place Dante Giannello came from the Bleuets.

There were 3 powerful teams. The Belgian team was a squad of tough, experienced veterans. Sylvère Maes, who won the 1936 Tour and stormed out of the 1937 edition in fury over questionable judging, came back for another bite of the apple. As his teammate he had Félicien Vervaecke who had come so close to victory several times with a fourth and 2 third places. Vervaecke had been essential to the Belgian successes of the second half of the 1930s. Ward Vissers, Marcel Kint, Eloi Meulenberg and Jules Lowie filled out the strong Belgian squad.

The French didn't have a dominating Grand Tour rider. Antonin Magne and Georges Speicher were on the team, but Magne had been the winner of the 1931 Tour and Speicher was also well past his prime.

The Italians were easily in command. Gino Bartali was in Yellow when he crashed in the 1937 Tour, that crash eventually forcing him to abandon. Unlike 1937, Bartali didn't come to the 1938 Tour with a string of spring victories; his year, so far, had been low key. But no one doubted that he was the man to beat. He had a superb team with Mario Vicini (second, 1937 Tour), Giuseppe Martano, Jules Rossi, Aldo Bini and Vasco Bergamaschi (1935 Giro winner). The first great Italian Campionissimo, Costante Girardengo, was team director.

The first few stages of this counter-clockwise (Pyrenees first) Tour saw the major contenders lie low. André Leducq managed to get onto the General Classification podium after the second stage by staying up at the front and riding as brilliantly as ever, being only 52 seconds behind the Yellow Jersey, Jean Majerus.

Then, on stage 6b, Leducq got into a 6-man break that finished 1 minute, 40 seconds ahead of the field. That put this former Tour winner in Yellow again. The interlude was short-lived.

Stage 8 was a classic Pyreneen stage, from Pau to Luchon. The usual 4 mighty mountains stood in the way: the Aubisque, the Tourmalet, the Aspin and the Peyresourde. The 2 best climbers in the Tour, Bartali and Vervaecke bared their fangs, and their duel shattered most of the rest of the field. Vervaecke won the stage with Ward Vissers finishing with him at the same time. Bartali had been first over the first 3 climbs but ended up third, 55 seconds behind Vervaecke.

The change to the peloton was substantial. 7 riders were eliminated for not making the time-cutoff. Mario Vicini finished over 17 minutes behind Vervaecke. Spanish climber Berrendero was almost 18 minutes down. 2-time Tour winner Antonin Magne was about 20 minutes behind. André Leducq's days in Yellow were over when he came in over 25 minutes down. Sylvère Maes and Vasco Bergamaschi came in about a half hour after the winners.

Georges Speicher, the 1933 winner, was tossed from the Tour for holding on to a car on the climbs. The judges weren't going to have a repeat of 1937 when the Belgians had stormed out of the Tour because Lapébie had not been given more than a slap on the wrist for the same infraction.

The new General Classification:

1. Félicien Vervaecke
2. Gino Bartali @ 2 minutes 18 seconds
3. Jean-Marie Goasmat @ 5 minutes 9 seconds

Bartali had leaped from nineteenth in the General Classification to second. For all of his high placings in previous Tours, this was Vervaecke's first day in Yellow.

The next stage, after a rest day, was another day in the Pyrenees. Most of the good riders finished together. Bartali was able to gain some time on Vervaecke with a time bonus for being the first over the Portet d'Aspet.

Stage 10b, a 27-kilometer individual time trial, revealed some weakness in Bartali's armor. Vervaecke won the stage. Bartali finished nineteenth, almost 2 minutes slower. That put Bartali back at 3 minutes, 45 seconds behind Vervaecke.

By winning stage 11 and picking up a time bonus for being first over the Braus climb in stage 13, Bartali narrowed the lead to 1 minute, 15 seconds.

Stage 14 of the 1938 Tour de France is one of those historic, well-remembered days of racing. It was 219 kilometers going from Digne to Briançon in the high Alps. Along the way the riders had to climb the Allos, the Vars and the Izoard. By the time he was near the top of the first climb only the Belgian Ward Vissers was with Bartali. Bartali sprinted for the top to get the time bonus and dropped Vissers. He was now alone. At the top of the Vars he had 19 seconds on the new French revelation Victor Cosson. Bartali took off down the mountain, determined to win the Tour that day. He later wrote that his descent on the Vars gave him the Yellow Jersey. He flatted and while he was waiting for a new wheel he had to watch Mario Vicini pass him. He was alone again on the Izoard and stayed away for the rest of the stage, finishing 5 minutes, 18 seconds ahead of his teammate Vicini. Vervaecke lost 17 minutes, 22 seconds. Bartali earned 5 minutes, 43 seconds in time bonuses for his stage victory and for being first to the top of all 3 of the major climbs. Bartali was now in Yellow and solidly so.

The General Classification after stage 14:

1. Gino Bartali
2. Mathias Clemens @ 17 minutes 45 seconds
3. Félicien Vervaecke @ 21 minutes 30 seconds

The next day Bartali awoke feeling poorly. He had slept badly and was very nervous about the two climbs, the Galibier and the new-to-the-Tour climb, the Iseran. The Italian team director, Costante Girardengo, told him not to force himself if he felt weak. Bartali followed the advice and Vicini took the time bonus for being the first to the top of the Galibier, and Vervaecke led over the Iseran. On the descent of the Iseran Bartali let it go, descending for all he was worth. Before he reached the valley floor he was with the leaders. Marcel Kint won the stage but Bartali was third, only 12 seconds behind. The major casualties of the day were Mathias Clemens and Mario Vicini, both of whom finished in the major chase group that came in over 25 minutes after Kint. The effect of eliminating Clemens from the effective competition was to increase Bartali's lead still further. Vervaecke was now in second, a distant 20 minutes behind.

Bartali now had only 8 days left to defend his lead. There was only one more major climb, the Faucille in the next day's stage. Bartali was first over it and extended his lead to over 21 minutes.

The only other major obstruction was the 42-kilometer individual time trial in stage 20b. Vervaecke showed his class by winning it and beating Bartali by 1 minute, 50 seconds. With such a large lead, Bartali could afford to bleed a little time. The final stage of the Tour, from Lille to Paris, was the next day.

Mario Vicini and Gino Bartali together on the Galibier, stage 15.

As the riders approached the area of Paris in the final stage, André Leducq, winner of the 1930 and 1932 Tours, and Antonin Magne, winner of the 1931 and 1934 Tours, broke away. They came in to the *Parc des Princes* velodrome arm in arm, 5 minutes ahead of the field. The judges called it a tie for first place. This was the last Tour for the 2 racers who had symbolized the complete dominance of the Tour by the French in the first half of the decade. In 1938, the highest placed French rider was Victor Cosson who finished over 29 minutes behind Bartali.

Final 1938 Tour de France General Classification:

1. Gino Bartali (Italy): 148 hours 29 minutes 12 seconds
2. Félicien Vervaecke (Belgium) @ 18 minutes 27 seconds

3. Victor Cosson (France) @ 29 minutes 26 seconds

4. Ward Vissers (Belgium) @ 35 minutes 8 seconds

5. Mathias Clemens (Luxembourg) @ 42 minutes 8 seconds

6. Mario Vicini (Italy) @ 44 minutes 59 seconds

Climber's Competition:

1. Gino Bartali: 107 points

2. Félicien Vervaecke: 79 points

3. Ward Vissers: 76 points

1939. With conflict gathering in Europe, Italy, Spain and Germany did not send teams to the 1939 Tour. This meant, of course, that the defending champion, Gino Bartali, as well as the other superb Italians, would not start. Roger Lapébie, the 1937 Tour winner was injured and couldn't ride. Tour greats André Leducq and Antonin Magne had ridden their last Tour the previous year. Georges Speicher, the 1933 winner, even though he was the reigning French road champion, did not ride. Between them, Leducq, Magne, Speicher and Lapébie represented 6 Tour wins for France during the 1930s. With none of them riding in 1939, the way looked very good for the Belgians.

With the Spanish, Germans and Italians missing, the Tour had to fill out the peloton. Belgium sent two teams. Their "A" team was headed by 1936 Tour victor Sylvère Maes, and retained climber Félicien Vervaecke and strong-man Marcel Kint. 1935 Tour winner Romain Maes also rode for Belgium.

France was represented not only by the French team, but also by 4 regional teams. The National team was the home of the best French talent, but several of the regional teams had some real stars. Notably, the France North-East team had Maurice Archambaud who had worn the Yellow Jersey many times although he had never managed to bring it all the way to Paris. France South-East had René Vietto, the man who had famously sacrificed his chances for Antonin Magne in the 1934 Tour.

The 1939 Tour had a total of 5 individual time trials. One of them was the Tour's first mountain time trial, going up the 2,770-meter high Iseran.

The Tour tried a new rule, a sort of devil-take-the-hindmost. The last rider in the General Classification would be eliminated after each stage, starting with the second stage. Because it ended up threatening the first man to hold this Tour's Yellow Jersey after he was caught in a crash, the judges rather intelligently decided to ignore the rule. I wonder if they would have been so generous if the man threatened with elimination had been Belgian instead of Frenchman Amédée Fournier.

A 9-man breakaway won the first stage, led in by Amédée Fournier who rode for the France North-East team. Tucked in right with him was Romain Maes. By winning the first time trial the next day, 1935 Tour winner Romain Maes seized the lead. Maes didn't stay in Yellow very long at all. This was a 2-stage day, and that afternoon another rider from a regional team, Jean Fontenay of the France-West team made it into the front group that beat the field in by a half minute. So did René Vietto.

At this point, after stage 2b, all 3 riders on the General Classification podium were from the lesser-regarded regional teams:

1. Jean Fontenay
2. René Vietto @ 2 minutes 10 seconds
3. Eloi Tassin @ 2 minutes 11 seconds

Vietto was an intelligent man. He kept his head about him and in stage 4 he was in the winning break that came into Lorient almost 3 minutes ahead of the next riders. Vietto was at last in Yellow, despite his weak knee that he had permanently damaged in 1936.

As the race went counter-clockwise around the circumference of France, heading for the Pyrenees, Vietto hung on to his tiny, 6-second lead over Luxembourger Mathias Clemens.

Stage 8b, a 68.5-kilometer individual time trial, allowed Vietto, who was usually not good against the clock, to increase his lead. Mathias Clemens, who had been sitting in second place, only 6 seconds behind Vietto, had a terrible time trial. He came in 8 minutes behind the stage winner, Karl Litschi. This moved Albertin Disseaux of the Belgian "B" team up to second place in the General Classification, 58 seconds behind Vietto. Vietto, who had been suffering from bronchitis since stage 6, was not going to let the Yellow Jersey go without a fierce fight.

The 1939 Tour had only 1 Pyreneen stage, going from Pau to Toulouse, but it packed a real wallop since it included the Aubisque, the Tourmalet and the Aspin. Félicien Vervaecke, for years one of the mainstays of the Belgian efforts in the high mountains, could not finish the stage, abandoning with severe back pains. Ward Vissers, showing that he was not going to sacrifice his personal ambitions in favor of Sylvère Maes, took off with about 200 kilometers to go and rode away from the field, being first over all 3 of the major climbs. He beat a 4-man chase group that included Vietto and Maes by about 4 minutes. Maes was now in second place in the General Classification, 3 minutes behind the determined Vietto. The tension between Vissers and Maes was clearly apparent.

Vietto was able to add another 22 seconds to his lead in the third time trial, stage 10b.

The General Classification now stood thus:

1. René Vietto
2. Sylvère Maes @ 3 minutes 19 seconds
3. Lucien Vlaemynck @ 6 minutes 6 seconds

The standings stayed that way until stage 12b when Maes and Maurice Archambaud broke away and came in $1\,^1/_2$ minutes ahead of Vietto's 11-man chase group. The lead was narrowed to just under 2 minutes.

And so things stood with Vietto defending his lead with all the energy he could muster. Stage 15 from Digne to Briançon was a classic Tour Alpine stage with the Allos, the Vars and the hulking Izoard on the day's schedule. Vissers was first over the Allos and the Vars. 10 kilometers from the crest of the Izoard, Maes, who had been holding his fire for much of the Tour, took off. Only Pierre Gallien, riding for the France North-East regional team was able to stay with Maes for a while, but no one could stay with him that day. Maes finished alone, 12 minutes ahead of Vissers. René Vietto's efforts in attaining and defending his lead for 16 stages had exhausted him. He came in 17 minutes after Maes.

The new General Classification showing that Maes was now solidly the Yellow Jersey:

1. Sylvère Maes
2. René Vietto @ 17 minutes 12 seconds
3. Ward Vissers @ 21 minutes 31 seconds

In this one stage Maes had gone from second place to forging a 17 minute lead. It was a masterful performance whose outcome he had predicted before the stage began.

The next day had 3 stages crammed into 1 day. The first one was 126 kilometers over the Galibier. Vietto was able to stay with Maes but Vissers collapsed, losing over 10 minutes and his place on the podium.

That afternoon was the Tour's first mountain time trial, up the 2,770-meter Iseran. Again Sylvère Maes displayed his mastery, winning the 64.5-kilometer hill climb and taking another 4 minutes out of Vissers and 10 minutes out of Vietto. This stage more or less settled the Tour. The General Classification after the stage 16b time trial:

1. Sylvère Maes
2. René Vietto @ 27 minutes
3. Lucien Vlaemynck @ 31 minutes 16 seconds

As the Tour headed to Paris, Maes was able continually to add to his lead over the exhausted Vietto. Even on the final stage Maes padded his lead by another 2 minutes. This was Sylvère Maes' second Tour victory, with the first in 1936. He probably would have won it in 1937 if the officiating had been up to the normal high standards of the Tour. Contemporary observers wrote that Maes' victory was more of an individual effort than most Tour victories given that there were 5 individual time trials and that the leading riders were usually isolated from their teams in the mountains.

With an average speed of 31.986 km/hour, the 1939 Tour set a new record.

The final 1939 Tour de France General Classification:

1. Sylvère Maes (Belgium): 132 hours 3 minutes 17 seconds
2. René Vietto (France South-East) @ 30 minutes 38 seconds
3. Lucien Vlaemynck (Belgium B) @ 32 minutes 8 seconds
4. Matthias Clemens (Luxembourg) @ 36 minutes 9 seconds
5. Ward Vissers (Belgium) @ 38 minutes 5 seconds

Climber's Competition:

1. Sylvère Maes: 86 points

2. Ward Vissers: 84 points

3. Albert Ritserveldt: 71 points

The 1939 Tour ended July 30. Germany invaded Poland September 1. The Soviet Union joined the partitioning of Poland by invading from the East on September 17. The Tour de France would not return until June 25, 1947.

Chapter 6

1947–1952. Italian and Swiss domination in the early post-war Tours would have been complete except for a bold move by Jean Robic in the final stage of the 1947 Tour

The story of the Tour and its sponsoring organization during and just after the war is affected by the fierce politics and partisanship generated by the conflict and the occupation.

In August of 1939, shortly after that year's Tour ended, *L'Auto* announced the basic framework of the 1940 Tour. But with the September 1939 German invasion of Poland and the May 1940 invasion of Holland, Belgium and France, there could be no Tour. By the end of June, northern France was conquered, occupied and ruled by Germany. As part of the surrender agreement southern France remained unoccupied and was ruled by a collaborationist French government called "Vichy". The great French World War One hero, Henri Pétain, headed the Vichy government. The divided system for ruling France remained in place until 1942. When the Allies invaded North Africa, Hitler decided that he needed to occupy southern France to protect his flank. He voided the 1940 agreement and sent his soldiers into the south. They remained in place until France was freed when the Allies advanced in 1944 and 1945.

Racing continued in a hit and miss way all over Europe throughout much of the war. The Giro d'Italia was run in 1940, but was then discontinued until 1946. The Tour of Switzerland was suspended for 1943, 1944 and 1945. The Tour of Spain missed 1943 and 1944. Paris–Roubaix skipped 1941, 1942 and 1943. Italy's Tour of Lombardy was held without interruption except for 1943 and 1944.

The Germans wanted "normalcy" in their occupied territories. France without the Tour wasn't normal. They asked Jacques Goddet to restart the Tour de France, offering to open the border between German-occupied France and Vichy France. With Tour founder Henri Desgrange's health failing, Goddet had taken over both the post of editor of *L'Auto*—which owned and ran the Tour de France—and the job of running the Tour. Henri Desgrange, the father of the Tour de France, had held both of those jobs.

Throughout the German occupation Jacques Goddet refused to run the Tour de France. There were several truncated stage races and a race omnium series held during that period, the *Circuit de France* and the *Grand Prix du Tour de France* being the most notable. Goddet ran the latter race but he made it clear that it wasn't the Tour de France. Goddet walked a tightrope. He thought Pétain was doing the best possible thing for France by cooperating with the Germans, saving France needless destruction from a protracted battle with the Germans that she could not win. So he wrote editorials praising Pétain, and put on races, but denied the Germans the greatest of all cycling competitions.

When Paris was liberated in 1944, the authorities shuttered *L'Auto* because it had continued publishing during the occupation.

Jacques Goddet was not going to be stopped that easily. He went across the street and founded *L'Equipe* in 1946. With this new tool he was able to work on re-launching the Tour de France. Since *L'Auto* no longer existed, the ownership of the Tour de France was up in the air. The French cycling federation decided to have a race shoot-out between the organizations applying to take over the Tour. The other newspaper competing for the right to run the Tour, *Sports*, combined with another Parisian paper, *Miroir Sprint*, to put on the 5-day *Ronde de France* to try to win federation approval.

Goddet's test race was the Monaco–Paris or *La Course du Tour de France* and it had 5 stages. Goddet got help from another publication, *Le Parisien Libéré* as well as the *Parc des Princes* velodrome. The success of his test race, and the politics of Goddet's association with newspaper owner and resistance fighter Emilien Amaury tipped the balance in

Goddet's favor. He won the right to put on the Tour de France.

Things were very tight in those early post-war years. During a time of rationing, a calorie-gobbling, gasoline-burning bicycle race presented problems. Race fans sent food to their favorite racers, something far more valuable than mere money. The government had given its approval to the races in those hard times hoping to improve French morale.

Among the other terrible losses of World War Two, the entire cache of the official Tour de France records and photos was lost. They were shipped out of the *L'Auto* offices in 1939 for safekeeping in southern France. They disappeared in transit and no one knows what happened to them.

1947. Buoyed by their 1946 test-race success, *L'Equipe* announced the 1947 Tour. It was to be full-blown affair with 21 stages covering 4,640 kilometers with 5 rest days. There would be no days with split stages. National teams were still used but Germany was not invited and wouldn't be for another decade. The Italian team was made up of Franco-Italians living in France. The war wounds were still too raw to bring in a real Italian national team or consider inviting a German team.

5 of the 10 teams entered were French regional squads. Of foreign nationalities, only Belgium, France and the ersatz Italian team were composed of riders of just those countries. Holland's team had 2 Italians living in France, including Fermo Camellini. Switzerland had to combine with Luxembourg to make up its team.

René Vietto, the favorite for 1947, led the French team. The last year the Tour had been run, 1939, Vietto had come in second. He was no longer the hot yet inexperienced young rider who famously gave up his wheel to Antonin Magne in 1934. He was now an accomplished veteran of 33 who had been the subject of 3 knee operations. The war had taken his best years as it did to so many other men and women. For all the years and wear and tear he was still a superb athlete. He had worn the Yellow Jersey in previous Tours, but never as far as to Paris. He deeply yearned to achieve that elusive goal.

The France-West regional team had a strange, talented, difficult and some say foul-mouthed man, Jean Robic. Utterly sure of his abilities, he was furious at being left off the French national team. Robic usually raced with a thick leather helmet because he had fractured his skull in Paris–Roubaix. Being very short with big ears, and possessing a difficult temperament, the helmet added to an appearance that invited nicknames. "Old Leatherhead" was used often, as was "Biquet" which means, contrary to Robic's acerbic personality, "Sonny" or "Sweetie".

The first postwar Tour stage started at Paris' Palais Royale. Future Tour winner Ferdy Kübler won almost 7 hours later in Lille.

Vietto captured the Yellow Jersey after a long breakaway on the second stage, 182 kilometers from Lille to Brussels. He had a 3 minute, 28 second lead in the overall standings on second place Raymond Impanis.

Robic made his way to the higher rankings in the General Classification with a solo win in stage 4. Vietto's lead was now about a minute and a half over Italian Aldo Ronconi. Robic was sitting in sixth place at 15 minutes.

Going into stage 7, the first Alpine stage, the rankings were unchanged. This stage had 4 big climbs culminating in the 1,326 meter high Col de Porte. Robic was first over the final 2 climbs and won the stage with a 4 1/2 minute lead over Italian rider Pierre Brambilla. Vietto came in 8 minutes, 24 seconds after Robic and almost 3 minutes after Aldo Ronconi who had been sitting in second place in the General Classification. Vietto lost his lead and Robic had cut his deficit in half.

The General Classification after stage 7:

1. Aldo Ronconi
2. René Vietto @ 1 minute 29 seconds
3. Pierre Brambilla @ 4 minutes 12 seconds
4. Jean Robic @ 7 minutes 14 seconds

Stage 8 was another day in the high Alps with the Glandon, Croix de Fer, Télégraphe and Galibier. The Glandon and Croix de Fer climbs, both now mainstays in the Tour's catalog of mountains, were new this year to the Tour. Fermo Camellini blazed away for a solo win, being first over the last 3 major mountains. Brambilla came in 8 minutes later for second place. Vietto and Ronconi followed after another 2 1/2 minutes. Robic had a bad day, finishing over 16 minutes after Camellini.

Stage 9 had the Izoard, Allos and Vars mountains. Robic was first over the Izoard. Vietto matched him by cresting the Allos first and then Robic led over the Col de Vars. On the descent Robic flatted and was badly delayed. Vietto won the stage and regained the Yellow Jersey. Robic came in over 6 minutes later, and was now in fifth place in the General Classification, over 18 minutes behind Vietto.

The next day Vietto faltered in the final Alpine stage. Fermo Camellini won it with Vietto over 6 minutes behind. Robic was seventeenth, over 13 minutes off the pace.

So, the General Classification after the Alps:

1. René Vietto
2. Fermo Camellini @ 2 minutes 11 seconds
3. Pierre Brambilla @ 3 minutes 4 seconds
4. Aldo Ronconi @ 3 minutes 25 seconds
5. Jean Robic @ 25 minutes 5 seconds

Old Leatherhead, Jean Robic, leads on a climb in the 1947 Tour.

The situation stayed unchanged as the Tour went across southern France. Even after the first Pyreneen stage, nothing was altered in the top ranks of the General Classification, except Edouard Fachleitner's solo win in stage 11 which moved him into fifth place.

Stage 15 from Luchon to Pau was a classic day in the Pyrenees.

The riders had to face the Peyresourde, the Aspin, the Tourmalet and the Aubisque. Almost from the gun Robic attacked. On the Peyresourde Robic was away, at first with Vietto, Brambilla, Apo Lazaridès and Primo Volpi. Robic kept the pressure on his companions and before long Robic was riding away alone. He continued his escape and ended up riding almost 190 of the day's 195 kilometers on his own. He beat Vietto, Brambilla and Ronconi by 10 minutes, 43 seconds. Because of the time bonuses given for being the first over the 4 big passes, Robic gained a total of 15 minutes, 13 seconds.

The new General Classification:

1. René Vietto
2. Pierre Brambilla @ 1 minute 34 seconds
3. Aldo Ronconi @ 3 minutes 55 seconds
4. Edouard Fachleitner @ 6 minutes 46 seconds
5. Jean Robic @ 8 minutes 8 seconds

After the Pyrenees the situation remained stable for a while. Vietto held his lead until stage 18, nursing his 94-second lead in the General Classification. In stage 19 he ran into the longest individual time trial in Tour history. The 139-kilometer brute cost Vietto 15 minutes. He was never to wear Yellow in Paris. Italian Pierre Brambilla, after doing well in the time trial, was now in Yellow. The little Breton Robic, coming in second in the time trial, had moved up to third. Brambilla probably felt that with 2 stages to go, the Tour was his.

Here was the General Classification after the time trial:

1. Pierre Brambilla
2. Aldo Ronconi @ 53 seconds
3. Jean Robic @ 2 minutes 58 seconds
4. René Vietto @ 5 minutes 6 seconds
5. Edouard Fachleitner @ 6 minutes 56 seconds

In the final stage, a mostly (and that word mostly is important) flat run from Caen to Paris, the peloton was subjected to a series of tough, hard attacks. On the Bonsecours hill, as the race was leaving the city of Rouen, Jean Robic managed to get away from Brambilla. Brambilla didn't or couldn't react at first, being boxed in by other riders. He did manage to get just near Robic when Fachleitner counter-attacked. Robic dug deeply into his reserves and made contact with Fachleitner. Brambilla chased, but could not close the gap to the pair. He knew he was watching his Tour de France ride away.

Fachleitner wanted to drop Robic and get up to riders further up the road, thereby gaining enough time to surpass Robic and possibly win the Tour. Robic is famously to have said to him, "You can't win the Tour, Fach, because I'm not going to let you go. Work with me and I'll pay you 100,000 francs." The deal was made. Robic and Fachleitner powered away from Brambilla. Robic rode into the Yellow Jersey. Belgian Brik Schotte won the stage but Robic beat Brambilla, Ronconi, Vietto and Camellini by over 13 minutes. Robic became the first man to gain the final General Classification victory on the final day. The only time he had possession of the Yellow Jersey in the 1947 Tour was when he donned it on the final podium. It wasn't done again until Jan Janssen won the Tour in the final time trial in 1968.

Robic was a difficult man. He was not well liked by his fellow racers or the Tour organizers. He felt that being left off the French national team for the 1947 Tour and having to race on a regional French team was a slur on his abilities. He was married shortly before the Tour started and had promised his new bride a victory in the Tour as a dowry. Even under those idyllic circumstances, he started the race with a chip on his shoulder. It might have been his promise to his wife or just his disagreeable nature that caused him to attack the Yellow Jersey in that final run-in to Paris. But Jean Robic never lacked for courage or audacity. He was only 5 feet tall but he had a complete arsenal of abilities. In addition to being a superb road racer he was both French and World cyclo-cross champion. To commemorate his Tour victory there is a monument with his likeness on the Bonsecours hill.

We'll meet Old Leatherhead again.

Final 1947 Tour de France General Classification:

1. Jean Robic (France-West) 148 hours 11 minutes 25 seconds
2. Edouard Fachleitner (France) @ 3 minutes 58 seconds
3. Pierre Brambilla (Italy) @ 10 minutes 7 seconds
4. Aldo Ronconi (Italy) @ 11 minutes
5. René Vietto (France) @ 15 minutes 23 seconds

Climber's Competition:

1. Pierre Brambilla: 98 points

2. Apo Lazaridès: 89 points

3. Jean Robic: 70 points

1948. The 1948 Tour would be a straightforward 4,922 kilometers in 21 stages, again with no split stages. There was one new rule. Between the third and the eighteenth stages, the last man in the General Classification was to be eliminated.

The Italians came back to the Tour. But whom to bring? With two mighty powerhouses, Fausto Coppi (1947 Giro d'Italia winner) and Gino Bartali (1938 Tour winner) available, the selection of the team was fraught with difficult politics.

Coppi was enjoying very good form. That spring he won Milano–San Remo and came in second in the Belgian Het Volk. He abandoned the Giro at stage 18 after winning the sixteenth and seventeenth stages. Those were mountain stages, and Coppi had won them alone, both by several minutes. Coppi was always very sensitive to any sort of preference or favoritism given to others at his expense. He felt that the Giro judges were complicit in allowing Fiorenzo Magni's cheating. They gave Magni nominal penalties that did not negate the advantage he gained breaking the rules. Much like the Belgians furious at Roger Lapébie's flagrant cheating in the 1937 Tour, Coppi quit rather than be defrauded.

Bartali's condition wasn't nearly as scintillating that May as Coppi's, but he acquitted himself well enough in the Giro, coming in eighth and winning the King of the Mountains prize.

There were hard feelings between Coppi and Bartali that grew out of this Giro and the press's exploitation of the rivalry between the two. Coppi had been a *domestique* of Bartali. When Coppi started to assert his independence from Bartali in 1941, the friction began and grew with the passing years. These combined sources of bitterness caused Coppi to refuse to participate in the Tour. That made Gino Bartali the Italian team captain by default. It had been 10 years since his last Tour win. His legs, at 34, were even older by a year than Vietto's and Vietto had wilted in 1947.

Moreover, the French team had the rapidly rising Louison Bobet. Bobet had not yet matured into the great racer who would win 3 Tours in a row. Still, although he was young, he was an extremely formidable rider. The French team also included last year's winner Jean Robic and René Vietto.

There were 4 regional French teams as well as a second Italian and a second Belgian team. An international team made up of Italians, a Pole, Swiss and Belgians was included to fill out the 120-man peloton.

Bartali won the first stage, which was run in a terrible downpour. He lost the Yellow Jersey the next day when the peloton broke up under the pressure of the day's attacks. Bobet was in the winning break of 3 and now only 13 seconds behind the leader, Jean Engels. Delayed by a crash, Bartali came in with the better part of the field over 4 minutes later.

Bobet was riding with both his head and his legs. In stage 3 he again made it into the winning break. Only 23 years old, he was now the Yellow Jersey. He lost the lead the next day, but when the Tour rolled into Biarritz in stage 6, Bobet won both the stage and the overall lead with a narrow 11-second lead over Belgium's Roger Lambrecht.

The next day, stage 7 from Biarritz to Lourdes, took the riders over the Aubisque. Bartali finally showed his form, winning the stage with 1947's winner Jean Robic. Bobet was third, only 3 seconds slower. Bartali had lost so much time in the first 6 stages that this only lifted him to twelfth place, almost 20 minutes behind Bobet. Bartali, deeply religious, took the opportunity at the shrine of Lourdes to ask the Pope for a special blessing for both himself and his team. When he prayed to the Virgin that evening, he asked not that she help him win but that he be protected from falling. In the 1937 Tour he had crashed badly while in the lead and had to abandon.

The next day was the final day in the Pyrenees. Even though it contained some of the most fearsome climbs possible, the Tourmalet, the Aspin, the Peyresourde and the Ares, 24 riders led in by Bartali finished together. All the big names were there: Vietto, Brambilla, Guy Lapébie (Roger Lapébie's brother), Lambrecht, Bobet, Stan Ockers and Robic. So, after the Pyrenees, here was the General Classification:

1. Louison Bobet
2. Roger Lambrecht @ 9 minutes 18 seconds
3. Lucien Teisseire @ 9 minutes 23 seconds
4. Gino Sciardis @ 9 minutes 59 seconds

5. Guy Lapébie @ 16 minutes 4 seconds

8. Gino Bartali @ 18 minutes 18 seconds

On stage 10, one of the days on the way to the Alps, Lambrecht was able to cut Bobet's lead to just 29 seconds when Bobet missed a big winning break.

By stage 12, Bobet had increased his lead over Bartali to more than 20 minutes. Even though Bartali had won 2 stages in the Pyrenees and appeared to have ever improving form, Bobet's lead over Bartali was substantial.

Then fate intervened.

In Italy, the leader of the Communist party, Palmiro Togliatti, had been wounded in an assassination attempt. He was hit with 4 bullets as he was leaving the Chamber of Deputies in Rome. In reaction, all of Italy was seething, gripped in a general strike. Furious Communists seized radio stations and factories. Given the unstable situation back home the Italian riders figured that they would ride the first Alpine stage and then quit and return to Italy.

The evening of that day, a rest day for the Tour, the Italian Premier phoned Bartali in France. He told Bartali of the near revolutionary air in Italy. Italy needed a distraction. A stage and Tour win would save Italy. "This is important, Gino, no longer just for you but for Italy, for everyone. If you win the Tour it will take everyone's mind from our troubles here. It could save the country!"

Bartali had earlier told a reporter that he would win the Tour, despite his age. He wasn't so sure when he talked to his Prime Minister. "I am not a magician. The Tour isn't over until Paris and there's still a week to go," he replied.

The next day had the Allos, the Vars and the 2,360-meter high Izoard. Last year's Tour winner, Jean Robic, was first over the first 2 climbs. But on the Allos, in cold, rainy weather Bartali attacked and dropped everyone else. Robic went over the Allos with only a 30-second lead. Bartali was a wonderful descender and sped by the Frenchman. On the Izoard Bartali was in his element, soaring away. He came into Briançon alone, over 6 minutes ahead of Belgian Brik Schotte, over 10 minutes ahead of Vietto and over 18 minutes ahead of Bobet.

Bobet was still in Yellow, but he had a lead of only 1 minute, 6 seconds over Bartali.

The next day, stage 14 was even harder with the Lautaret, Galibier, Télégraphe, Croix de Fer, Porte, Cucheron and the Granier. Again Bartali rode a tour de force, first over the last 4 climbs and the day's winner with a solo victory. He came in almost 6 minutes ahead of the next rider, Stan Ockers. 10 years after his last Tour victory, Bartali was again in Yellow with an 8-minute lead over Bobet.

Stage 15 was the final Alpine day with a climb new to the Tour, the Forclaz. Again Bartali soloed to victory. Now the young Bobet was almost 14 minutes in arrears. Third place Brik Schotte was over a half-hour behind. In 3 days Gino Bartali had crushed the entire Tour de France peloton.

In Italy, everyone was rapt as the word of Bartali's wonderful accomplishments came over the radio. Togliatti regained consciousness and asked that the general strike be ended. The crisis had passed.

Stage 17 was another of those huge individual time trials that the Tour used during that era. This one was 120 kilometers long. Lambrecht won it. Bartali came in twenty-eighth, losing almost 12 minutes. Bartali could bleed that much time without worrying, so large was his lead.

At that point, the Tour was settled. When the race came into Paris, Bartali had done what no racer had done before or since, win the Tour 10 years after winning a previous Tour.

1948 Tour de France final General Classification:

1. Gino Bartali (Italy): 147 hours 10 minutes 36 seconds
2. Brik Schotte (Belgium) @ 26 minutes 16 seconds
3. Guy Lapébie (France South-West-Central) @ 28 minutes 48 seconds
4. Louison Bobet (France) @ 32 minutes 59 seconds
5. Jean Kirchen (Holland-Luxembourg) @ 37 minutes 53 seconds

Climber's competition:

1. Gino Bartali: 62 points
2. Apo Lazaridès: 43 points
3. Jean Robic: 38 points

1949. In 1949, the Italians demonstrated that they weren't done showing the French how to ride a stage race. They had punished the peloton with Bartali in 1948. In 1949 they brought another superb team with both Gino Bartali and Fausto Coppi. Team manager Alfredo Binda would have his hands full keeping their fierce rivalry from blowing up the team. If he could get them to momentarily forget their antagonism and keep them racing for Italy, the Italians would be unstoppable.

Coppi had been having a superb post-war run. In 1940 he won the Giro d'Italia. During the war he was interned as a prisoner of war. Back to racing after the war's end, in 1946 he won Milan–San Remo and the Tour of Lombardy as well as taking second to Gino Bartali in the Giro, missing the win by only 47 seconds. He did get 3 stage wins in the '46 Giro.

In 1947 Coppi won the both the Giro and the Tour of Lombardy. In 1948 he again won Milan–San Remo, the Tour of Lombardy and the King of the Mountains in the Giro. As we saw in 1948, he quit the Giro, furious at what he saw as tainted officiating, and then refused to ride the Tour.

Comparing riders from different eras is a risky business subject to the prejudices of the judge. But if Coppi isn't the greatest rider of all time, then he is second only to Eddy Merckx. One can't judge his accomplishments by his list of wins because World War Two interrupted his career just as World War One interrupted that of Philippe Thys. Coppi won it all: the World Hour Record, the World Championships, Grand Tours, Classics as well as time trials. The great French cycling journalist Pierre Chany says that between 1946 and 1954, once Coppi had broken away from a peloton, the peloton never caught him. Can this be said of any other racer? Informed observers who saw both ride agree that Coppi was the more elegant rider who won by dint of his physical gifts as opposed to Merckx who drove himself and hammered his competition relentlessly by being the very embodiment of pure will.

Raphaël Géminiani—whom we will meet several times as this history unfolds in the 1950s—compared Merckx and Coppi. He raced against Coppi and watched Merckx. In the first chapter of his book *Les Routiers-Flingueurs*, Géminiani makes his feelings clear by titling it "Fausto Coppi, Champion of Champions". Géminiani starts by listing the ways in which Coppi was ahead of his time and established standards that have been followed ever since. Coppi was scientific in his approach to diet, training and teamwork. Géminiani also notes the completeness of Coppi's talent with his success in all disciplines of the sport. After all this, "Gem" says, to quote Francis Pélissier, "'Tell me who was second'…and this question remains valuable in a career that was even more magnificent than that of Merckx. Merckx beat many excellent racers, but not the super-champions as Coppi did." (translation by Owen Mulholland).

1949 was to be Coppi's year. He had been putting off riding the Tour de France. Finally, he agreed that fate was not to be denied. By the time he was to go to France he had already won the 1949 Giro in fine style, beating Bartali by 23 minutes, 47 seconds.

The national team system showed its potential for problems with the 1949 Italian Tour team. It was very powerful, with 1948 Tour winner Gino Bartali and 1949 (and now 3-time) Giro winner Coppi on the same team. Who is to be the leader? Who would sacrifice himself for the other? The story of the 1948 World Championships at Valkenburg, Holland, didn't bode well for the team. Coppi and Bartali just marked each other, letting others go down the road. Finally, too far behind to be in contention, they both quit. The Italian Cycling Federation, furious that the 2 had let their rivalry override their responsibilities as members of the Italian team, gave them both symbolic (it was the end of the season) 3-month suspensions.

The great Italian *campionissimo* Alfredo Binda was the manager of the Italian team. He was saddled with the onerous task of keeping these 2 wary competitors together and winning the Tour for Italy, a big job for any man. Getting them together for a meeting he had to talk to the 2 of them for hours. Binda explained to the 2 champions why Italy needed a Tour victory and that both of them had to follow his orders unquestioningly. He managed to get them to agree to ride on the same team and even had them put in writing that they would obey him. Each rider would get 5 devoted *domestiques*. Given that Coppi and Bartali used bikes with different and incompatible gear systems, this was a practical measure as well as a confidence giving measure to the 2 riders. Binda promised to lead the team without favoritism. Still, Coppi was very unhappy with the situation. He publicly complained that a team with a divided leadership is inherently weak. He also accused Bartali of having poor team spirit. Things were not starting well. Binda said it was like putting a cat and a dog in the same sack. The tension between the 2 wasn't a pose for the newspapers. It was deep, real and unending.

There were other teams, of course. The French team still had

René Vietto as well as the rapidly improving Louison Bobet and Raphaël Géminiani. The Belgians had Stan Ockers and Rik Van Steenbergen. But the horsepower was on the Italian side. This was their race to lose.

As the race went to Belgium and then counter-clockwise across northern France both Coppi and Bartali let themselves give up time in big chunks: 2 minutes here, 12 minutes there. By the time the fifth stage started Mario Ricci was the best placed Italian, in third place, 6 minutes, 42 seconds behind race leader Jacques Marinelli of the French regional Ile de France team. Neither Coppi nor Bartali were in the top 15 places in the General Classification.

Then Binda was subjected to a real-life Italian opera by his difficult pair of riders.

On stage 5 Coppi broke away with the Yellow Jersey Jacques Marinelli, and 5 others. With a 6-minute lead on the field, a spectator caused Marinelli and Coppi to crash. Marinelli was unhurt, his bike was undamaged, and so off he sped. Coppi's bike was wrecked. He was offered a bike from the Italian team car, but it wasn't his personal spare bike and he refused to take it. He threatened to quit unless he had his own bike.

Then Bartali caught up to Coppi, saw the problem, and decided to wait until Coppi could get a suitable bike. Eventually, team manager Alfredo Binda showed up with Coppi's bike. Bartali and Coppi rode off in pursuit.

But Coppi slowed, complaining of hunger and exhaustion. He was finally barely riding at a walking pace. Bartali, feeling he couldn't wait anymore, took off. Coppi lost over 18 minutes that day. It turned out that Coppi felt that Binda was playing favorites by not following Coppi who had been in the lead break. He didn't want to race on a team in which Bartali was the favorite receiving the higher level of support.

It was a long, long night for Binda. Binda was able to convince Coppi that he had been delayed and that he wasn't playing favorites by not following him. The story is that Coppi's disbelief of Binda's explanation was broken by the appearance of a blind man as the 2 were arguing. The sightless (but by no means unseeing) man walked into the hotel room with his dog. He told Coppi that he had named his dog "Fausto" and that he would never betray his dog and his dog would never betray him. With that cryptic explanation given, the blind man left. Coppi reflected for a moment and then accepted Binda's story.

Coppi was in such magnificent form that the loss of the 18 minutes on the one stage and the total deficit of 36 minutes to Marinelli didn't deter him. 3 days later he won the seventh stage 92-kilometer time trial beating the Yellow Jersey by 7 $1/_2$ minutes. Coppi was now sitting fourteenth in the General Classification, down 28 minutes on Marinelli. Bartali was seventh at 20 minutes.

The day before the single Pyreneen stage, 2 of Coppi's teammates, Fiorenzo Magni and Serafino Biagioni got into a break with Raymond Impanis and Edouard Fachleitner. They beat the field by 20 minutes, earning Magni the Yellow Jersey.

Stage 11: Fausto Coppi on the Tourmalet.

Stage 11, the first Pyreneen stage with 4 monster climbs, allowed Coppi to cut his deficit in half. He broke away with 1947 Tour winner Jean Robic and Lucien Lazaridès. The 2 French riders beat Coppi to the finish by a minute, after he was slowed by a flat tire. After a day that had included the Aubisque, the Tourmalet, the Aspin and finally the Peyresourde Coppi now was sitting in ninth, 14 minutes, 46 seconds behind Magni who was still in Yellow.

As the Tour rode across southern France towards it appointment with the Alps, the General Classification remained stable with Magni retaining the Yellow Jersey.

Stage 16, from Cannes to Briançon with the Allos, Vars and

Izoard was the first day in the Alps. On the Izoard Coppi and Bartali broke away. The 2 of them were in a class by themselves. They were minutes ahead of the chasing Jean Robic and still further ahead of the rest of the field. Bartali flatted on the Izoard and Coppi waited. Resuming, the pair continued their destruction of the field coming in 5 minutes ahead of Robic. The rest of the peloton didn't start arriving for another minute and a half. This being Bartali's birthday and Coppi feeling completely confident now of his powers, Coppi allowed Bartali to take the stage win. Because of the time losses related to stage 5, Bartali was still ahead of Coppi in the General Classification and now donned the Yellow Jersey. Coppi was now sitting in second place, 1 minute, 22 seconds behind his Tuscan teammate.

On the seventeenth stage, from Briançon to Aosta, the 2 men did it again. On the final climb of the day, the Petit St. Bernard, Coppi and Bartali broke away. After the descent Bartali flatted. Again Coppi waited. Then Bartali fell. This time, with 40 kilometers to the finish, Binda told Coppi to go on alone. He left Bartali and rode an epic solo ride for the stage victory and the Yellow Jersey. Bartali came in 5 minutes later. Robic led the first chasers in over 10 minutes after Coppi finished. The General Classification after Stage 17:

1. Fausto Coppi
2. Gino Bartali @ 3 minutes 53 seconds
3. Jacques Marinelli @ 12 minutes 8 seconds
4. Stan Ockers @ 18 minutes 13 seconds
5. Jean Robic @ 20 minutes 10 seconds

There were 2 more Alpine stages, but neither had the heavy climbing of the first 2. The top 5 in the General Classification remained unchanged.

The final challenge was the huge 137-kilometer individual time trial from Colmar to Nancy. This immense test on the Tour's penultimate stage sealed the Tour in a commanding fashion for Coppi. He won it in a way that left no doubt that he was the deserving victor. His nearest competitor was Bartali who was 7 minutes slower. Marinelli lost over 11 minutes. Robic, a competent time trialist, lost over 13 minutes.

Coppi had done what no man had done before. In attempting the Tour for the first time in his career, he had won the Giro d'Italia and the Tour de France in the same year. He was clearly the finest living rider. And, perhaps the best ever.

Final 1949 Tour de France General Classification:

1. Fausto Coppi (Italy): 149 hours 40 minutes 49 seconds
2. Gino Bartali (Italy) @ 10 minutes 55 seconds
3. Jacques Marinelli (France-Ile de France) @ 25 minutes 13 seconds
4. Jean Robic (France) @ 34 minutes 28 seconds
5. Marcel Dupont (Belgium) @ 38 minutes 59 seconds

Climber's competition:

1. Fausto Coppi: 81 points
2. Gino Bartali: 68 points
3. Jean Robic: 63 points

1950. After the 1948–1949 display of Italian power, the French were to be denied victory in their own Tour for years to come. 1950 and 1951 were the great years of Swiss racing. The team the Swiss sent to the Tour in 1950 was only 6 men strong, but it had Ferdy Kübler, whose growth as an effective stage racer took time. He won the first stage of the 1947 Tour and then went on to win the fifth stage before being eliminated when the Tour hit the Alps.

The next year Kübler won the Tours of Romandie and Switzerland and the Swiss Road Championship. His time-trialing ability was made clear with a second place in the Grand Prix des Nations, at that time the unofficial world championship of time trialing. In 1949 he won the Tour of Switzerland in grand style, winning 4 stages and coming in second in 3. He abandoned the 1949 Tour de France on the eighteenth stage after winning the fifth stage and coming in second on stage 7.

In 1950, both Kübler and the other Swiss great of the era, Hugo Koblet, hit their stride. Koblet had a fantastic spring in which he won the Tour of Switzerland and became the first non-Italian to win the Giro d'Italia, with Kübler fourth. Kübler was chosen to be the leader of the 6-man team that Switzerland sent to the Tour.

In July, 1950 Coppi could not ride the Tour because he was still recovering from a bad Giro crash that resulted in a broken pelvis. Coppi's fragile bones caused him recurring problems. It has been speculated that the regular enforced rest that his fractures caused might have been one reason why he was such a dominating rider. The other racers were forced to fulfill a demanding, season-long schedule that left them exhausted. Coppi got regular respites from the enervating requirements of his profession. Think of Lance Armstrong, guided by modern sports physiology, how he carefully dosed his efforts and chose his challenges. Armstrong would retire from a racing season as soon as his goals were met. Perhaps, accidentally, Coppi was following the same path.

The aging eagle of Italian cycling, Gino Bartali, now 36, was chosen to lead the Italian team. Fiorenzo Magni, who had worn the Yellow Jersey for several days in 1949, was also on the Italian team.

Raphaël Géminiani had been reluctant to ride the Tour for the French team after the poor performance and hence meager financial returns for the team's 1949 effort. In 1949 half of the French team abandoned on the tenth stage and their best placed rider, Apo Lazaridès, came in tenth. Géminiani was now in his fifth year as a pro and while a major win had eluded him, he was considered among the most accomplished French stage racers. He preferred to lead a regional team where he could choose his fellow riders and keep whatever prizes he might win. Team manager Jean Bidot (brother of later national team manager Marcel Bidot) was able to cajole Géminiani into riding with the understanding that Géminiani would be the sole leader and that the prize money that the team earned would be distributed according to who earned it. Louison Bobet, Apo Lazaridès and Jacques Marinelli would be on the team to back him up. Jean Robic, the 1947 winner who had been so incensed at being put on a regional team that year found himself back on a regional team.

Belgium, with Stan Ockers, Raymond Impanis and Roger Lambrecht would not be a pushover.

Right after the 1950 Tour was over Ferdy Kübler gave his thoughts to *L'Equipe* as to who and what constituted the major obstacles in the 1950 Tour. Although he deeply desired to win the Tour in order to complete the Swiss hat-trick started by his compatriot Koblet, his previous failures to do well in the Tour made him apprehensive about his chances. He considered Gino Bartali a man who was always a threat. Magni was also worrisome. The Luxembourg racer Jean Goldschmidt who had been second in the Swiss Tour, beating Kübler by almost 17 minutes, gave Kübler ample reason for concern. And of course, Louison Bobet was getting better every year.

The first stage confirmed Kübler's suspicions of Goldschmidt's form. The Luxembourg rider won the stage and the Yellow Jersey. He kept it until stage 3, when he missed the winning break of 7. The lead passed to Bernard Gauthier, a rider on the regional France South-East team.

Things stayed that way until stage 6, the first of the 1950 Tour's 2 individual time trials. This one was 78 kilometers long and it allowed Kübler to open his account with a serious deposit. Kübler won the stage with Magni only 17 seconds slower. Bobet lost almost 3 minutes and Bartali over 4.

The General Classification after the stage 6 time trial:

1. Jean Goldschmidt
2. Bernard Gauthier @ 47 seconds
3. Ferdy Kübler @ 49 seconds
4. Fiorenzo Magni @ 2 minutes 37 seconds
7. Louison Bobet @ 5 minutes 23 seconds
11. Gino Bartali @ 6 minutes 9 seconds

The very next day Gauthier joined a 12-man escape group and left Goldschmidt over 10 minutes behind. That was the end of Goldschmidt's days in Yellow.

When Fiorenzo Magni won stage 8, he confirmed the strength of the Italian squad. They had won half the stages contested so far. Magni was enjoying wonderful form and he clearly had an excellent team to support him. The chosen leader of the Italian squad was Bartali, and the Italian riders had pledged to support him. But Magni was clearly the man with the horsepower to win the Tour in 1950.

It was stage 11 that completely changed the course of the Tour. Going from Pau to St. Gaudens, it was a typical big Pyreneen stage, being 230 kilometers long and crossing the Aubisque, Tourmalet and Aspin.

The French fans lining the roads of the day's climbs were not in a good mood. For 2 straight years the Italians had been dominating their Tour. They saw no reason why this day's climbs would change that unpleasant tendency and they didn't like it at all.

Robic set about doing what he could to alter the situation. He escaped on the Aubisque while the rest of the riders marked Bartali. Over the top of the mountain he had a lead of about 3 minutes. He crashed but remounted and continued on. He began to feel the results of his early efforts as well as his crash, and he weakened on the Tourmalet. The French rider Kléber Piot was the first of the leading riders who crested the Tourmalet. The crowds on the side of the road began to insult the riders and jeer them. On the final mountain they began to throw small stones, bottle caps and other objects.

As the front group containing Bartali, Robic, Bobet and Ockers neared the summit of the Aspin they found their way blocked by a photographer. Bartali and Robic, in the front, were unable to avoid their human obstacle and crashed. Robic ruined his front wheel.

The spectators ran to help the 2 riders back on their bikes. But, as might be expected, not all of them wanted to see Bartali win. As he was trying to remount his bike he was kicked and punched. Bartali later said another spectator wielded a knife, but that may have been a picnicker who happened to have a sandwich knife in his hand at the time. Adding to the confusion, some in the melee were drunk. Tour boss Jacques Goddet arrived and started to beat the unruly spectators away with a stick. Bartali had to have been aware of the hostile atmosphere of the crowd as he rode the final 2 climbs. Convinced that the crowd had bad intentions toward him, he leaped upon his bike and sped off with Magni.

Consumed with fury at the treatment he received at the hands of the French fans, Bartali rode like a man possessed. He was able to catch the lead break and win the stage. Teammate Fiorenzo Magni who was in this break donned the Yellow Jersey.

The General Classification at the end of the stage:

1. Fiorenzo Magni
2. Ferdy Kübler @ 2 minutes 31 seconds
3. Louison Bobet @ 3 minutes 20 seconds
4. Raphaël Géminiani @ 3 minutes 25 seconds
5. Stan Ockers @ 3 minutes 37 seconds
6. Gino Bartali @ 4 minutes 17 seconds

Furious at the rough handling he had received, Bartali could not forgive the French mob. At St. Gaudens he told the team manager, Alfredo Binda, that he was withdrawing from the race and that the rest of the Italian squad should also quit. There were 2 Italian teams in the Tour. The best riders were in the Italian National Team and a second team called the Italian Cadets contained lesser riders. Bartali said all of the Italians should abandon the Tour and go home. Quitting was a hard thing for Magni who was enjoying spectacular form and was the man in the Yellow Jersey.

Binda and Bartali were up most of the night. Bartali was adamant that by continuing he would be encouraging the bad behavior of the crowds. The Tour organization proposed various compromises, even offering the Italians neutral gray jerseys to hide them from the crowds. Bartali wouldn't budge. A few of the other members of the team wavered, especially the Cadets and Adolfo Leoni, winner of the second stage. Not all the Italian riders were happy to be under Bartali's thumb. It has been said that the man in the Yellow Jersey, Magni, didn't decide until the next morning to quit and stand beside the man he had pledged to help win the 1950 Tour. His decision was made harder because several of the Italians said they would be willing to continue and ride to help Magni keep the Yellow Jersey all the way to Paris.

All the Italians did quit. A later stage of the Tour had been scheduled to end in the Italian town of San Remo. That had to be changed. The rage of the Italians screaming for revenge made the necessity of changing the route obvious to all concerned. The stage in question was re-routed to end in Menton in France.

The lucky recipient of this withdrawal was the Swiss rider Ferdy Kübler who had been quietly sitting in second place. He was now the Tour leader. For his first day in the lead he refused to wear the Yellow Jersey out of respect for Magni. He wore it the next day and from then on.

2 days later Kübler was able put his stamp of authority on the Tour. Stage 13 was run in terrible heat from Perpignan to Nîmes. Marcel Molines won it, beating the next rider, Georges Meunier, by over 4 minutes. But more importantly for the Tour, Kübler broke away with Stan Ockers and Marcel Hendrickx. French team leader Bobet failed to join the move and came in 4 minutes, 9 seconds after Kübler.

Before we leave stage 13, we can't forget Abdel Khader Zaaf, a member of the North African team made up of Algerian and Moroccan racers and how Molines came to win the stage. About 15 kilometers into the stage, Zaaf and Molines, both members of the North African team, broke away. Since the pack didn't want to race hard in the blistering heat, the pair got a good gap on the field.

With less than 20 kilometers to go Zaaf started to wobble on his bike, zigzagging across the road. Concerned for his safety a race official pulled him from the race. Molines—close to the end of the stage and riding with a large lead over the pack—continued on alone. Zaaf was not to be deterred by the race official who tried to stop him. He restarted, fell off his bike, gave up and fell asleep. When he awoke he realized that he was in a race, an important race, the Tour de France. He remounted his bike and took off in pursuit of the peloton. But he was going the wrong way. Clearly Zaaf had something wrong with him. An ambulance was called. Zaaf later claimed that upon awakening a spectator had revived him with wine. Being a devout Muslim he said he was unused to alcohol. Most observers think given his pulse of 160 and the necessity to pump his stomach, it was probably a combination of drugs, exhaustion and dehydration. Molines as noted above went on to win the stage. Zaaf, as the rider who rode the wrong way, became famous for a while, then faded away and returned to Algeria.

The General Classification after stage 13 now had this order:

1. Ferdy Kübler
2. Stan Ockers @ 1 minute 6 seconds
3. Pierre Brambilla @ 9 minutes 1 second
4. Louison Bobet @ 10 minutes 58 seconds

Stage 15 from Toulon to Menton along the southern coast of France had another of those famous moments in Tour history. The pack was feeling unmotivated as it rode by the Mediterranean Sea. Half the peloton left their bikes to take a momentary respite from the summer's heat by taking a dip in the sea in their cycling clothes. Tour Boss Goddet was upset and ordered the riders back on their bikes to continue racing.

The next day's stage to Nice, with 2 hard climbs, allowed the 4 best riders to still further distance themselves from the field. Kübler won the stage with Bobet, Robic and Ockers finishing with him at the same time. The rest of the peloton was over 4 minutes behind. With the time bonus for the day's stage Kübler was now 2 minutes ahead of Ockers and almost 12 minutes ahead of Bobet. At this point it is generally believed that Ockers and Kübler had formed an alliance with Kübler riding to win the overall victory and Ockers racing for the Climber's prize.

It was on stages 18 and 19 that the final drama of the 1950 Tour was played out with Bobet refusing to give up. These were the high Alpine stages. A 98-kilometer time trial was coming up near the end of the Tour. Time trialing was a discipline in which Kübler held a big advantage. These 2 days in the Alps were Bobet's only chance to take the Tour back from the Swiss rider. He knew he would have to take chances if he were to regain the advantage. As Danton said, "*De l'audace, encore de l'audace, et toujours de l'audace*" (audacity, more audacity, ever more audacity).

Stage 18 crossed the Vars and the Izoard. Near the top of the Vars Bobet got clear with a lead that was less than a minute. He was still alone at the start of the Izoard ascent. He finished that climb with a minute's lead over Kübler. The weather turned nasty as Bobet took terrible chances on the descent. With his big 12-minute cushion over Bobet, Kübler didn't have to take the same risks. Bobet finished almost 3 minutes ahead of Kübler and Ockers.

The General Classification had tightened a little, but Kübler was still in the driver's seat:

1. Ferdy Kübler
2. Stan Ockers @ 2 minutes 56 seconds
3. Louison Bobet @ 6 minutes 46 seconds
4. Jean Robic @ 16 minutes 53 seconds

Bobet still had another mountain stage to try to wrest those almost 7 minutes from Kübler, who was riding a controlled, intelligent, tactical race. Bobet's last chance was stage 19 from Briançon to St. Etienne with 3 major climbs: the Lautaret, St. Nizier and the Grand Bois. 2 of his Team France teammates, Pierre Molineris and Apo Lazaridès broke away with a racer from the France Central-South-East team, Marcel Dussault. They crested the Lautaret ahead of the field. Bobet attacked in the feed zone and took off with his teammate Raphaël

Géminiani. If all went well, Bobet would have half the French team with him to assist him in riding away from Kübler. Bobet soon dropped Géminiani. He caught Lazaridès and the others, but they could not take the determined Bobet's hot pace. Soon Bobet was alone with a 2-minute lead on Kübler.

Kübler knew he had to chase. He took off with several riders in tow including second place Stan Ockers and his Belgian compatriot Raymond Impanis. Kübler rode like a demon. He wasn't content to simply catch the now flagging Bobet. He yelled in triumph as he passed him and worked to increase his lead. Géminiani had managed to tag onto the Kübler group and won the stage but Kübler now had a solid, comfortable lead.

A day of rest followed those 2 brutal days in the mountains. Stage 20 was a 98-kilometer individual time trial from St. Etienne to Lyon. Kübler had won the stage 6 time trial and there was no reason to believe he was in any way weakening as the Tour progressed. At the first time check at 20 kilometers Kübler was already leading. Wearing a smooth leather cap and riding in his ungainly style, Kübler performed magnificently. He beat Stan Ockers by over 5 minutes and Bobet by almost 9 minutes. With 2 stages to go, Kübler had won the 1950 Tour de France in grand style.

The final 1950 Tour de France General Classification:

1. Ferdy Kübler (Switzerland): 145 hours 36 minutes 56 seconds
2. Stan Ockers (Belgium) @ 9 minutes 30 seconds
3. Louison Bobet (France) @ 22 minutes 19 seconds
4. Raphaël Géminiani (France) @ 31 minutes 14 seconds
5. Jean Kirchen (Luxembourg) @ 34 minutes 21 seconds

Climbers Jersey:

Louison Bobet: 58 points

Stan Ockers: 44 points

Jean Robic: 41 points

Kübler was an erratic personality who goaded the other riders in his terrible French. Here is how Les Woodland told about one such incident:

"Kübler enjoyed taunting riders and managers, dropping back to team cars to warn in broken French, 'Ferdy attack soon, you ready?' And then, a few minutes later, 'Ferdy big horse. Ferdy attack now. Your boys ready?' When he once more dropped back to tell Raphaël Géminiani, 'Ferdy attack now, France ready?', the Frenchman said in deliberate, equally bad French, 'Ferdy shut up now or Ferdy get head knocked in.' "

In an interview with *L'Equipe*, Kübler recently answered his critics who said his victory was only the result of the Italian pullout.

"I took the Yellow Jersey in the eleventh stage after the Italians quit the Tour at St. Gaudens. People said I owed my victory to their departure. But, on the contrary, it was harder for me as I had been riding with Magni and Bartali. I was the third man behind them, and when they left, I found myself alone. The next day, I took the jersey and I never let it go."

1951. For the first time the Tour headed inland to the Massif Central, crossed Mont Ventoux and, unusually, started outside Paris. Until 1951 the Tour's route had followed the hexagonal outline of France, never venturing into the interior. Only one other time, in 1926, had the race not started in Paris. The 123 riders from 12 national and French regional teams set off on the 4,692 kilometer, 24-stage race going counter-clockwise (Pyrenees first) around France starting in Metz.

We saw that in 1950 Swiss cycling had hit a new peak with the powerful twin engines of Ferdy Kübler and Hugo Koblet.

Kübler and Koblet could hardly have been more opposite. Kübler with his large nose and smile that turned into a demonic grin when he was making a big effort was known as the "pedaling madman" or the "the Eagle of Adilswil" for the Swiss village where he grew up. Hugo Koblet was tall, beautiful like a Greek god, with undulating fair hair, clear eyes, and inimitable elegance. He was incredibly gifted. Koblet was nicknamed the "*Pédaleur de Charme.*" *L'Equipe* called him "Apollo on a Bike." His effortless grace on a bicycle combined with his natural talent was in marked contrast to Kübler, who would thrash his bike into submission, white foam around his mouth, pedaling with an ungainly riding style.

Koblet made his name as a pursuiter. He was Swiss champion at the discipline every year from 1947 to 1954 and was the bronze medalist at the World Championships in 1947. In 1951 he was offered a place on the Swiss Tour team that did not include Kübler. With Koblet clearly the finest rider on the team, there would be no competition for team leadership.

Ferdy Kübler had a standout year in 1951, winning the World Championship, Liège–Bastogne–Liège, the Fleche Wallonne, and the Tours of Romandie and Switzerland. He also came in third in the Giro. Even without riding the Tour, Kübler's 1951 would have been a fine career for almost any other racer. It has been suggested that had Kübler ridden the Tour in 1951, he was to ride in support of Koblet. For that reason it was said that Kübler declined to ride the Tour that year.

Koblet's main rival should have been Fausto Coppi, but the legendary Italian had just buried his beloved brother Serse. That loss left Coppi in no condition for the Tour. Coppi's terrible grief manifested itself at one point in the Tour in a wave of nausea and vomiting.

The French had a team that could win the Tour, with Jean Robic, Louison Bobet and Raphaël Géminiani. Bobet was in good form. He was Champion of France and had won Milan–San Remo and the Critérium National. The French papers said Bobet was the favorite to win the Tour. Team strategy decided that Géminiani and Bobet would be co-leaders of the French team.

The Belgians had Stan Ockers leading their team. This was a superb field. Whoever wanted to win this Tour would have to earn it. Nobody expected Koblet, the playboy from Zurich, to be the final victor.

Among the French regional teams was Afrique du Nord, a team made of Algerian and Moroccan riders, which included Algerian Abdel Khader Zaaf, who had become something of a celebrity with the fans in 1950.

Koblet showed either his bravado or naiveté on stage 1 when he attacked nearly from the gun. He was brought back by the peloton after 40 kilometers of chasing. A cautious truce fell between the main contenders.

Over the next 5 stages they crossed northern France. While the main contenders eyed each other cautiously, lesser riders took the glory and gained real time. In stage 4 Roger Levêque, a rider for the regional West-South-West team, broke away with 85 kilometers to go. His stage win earned him second place in the overall standings, a little over 2 minutes behind the Yellow Jersey, Bim Diederich of Luxembourg. By the end of stage 6 Levêque was in Yellow, having joined the day's winning break. The highest placed of the fancied contenders, Stan Ockers, was more than 13 minutes back.

Stage 7, an 85-kilometer Individual Time Trial between La Guerche and Angers, let Koblet lay down the gauntlet. He won the stage with an average speed of 40.583 kilometers an hour and moved up into third place on the General Classification.

The results of the time trial were not so clear at first. The time-keeper initially believed that Louison Bobet had bested Koblet. By his calculations Levêque was no longer the Yellow Jersey. Koblet and his manager protested that evening to Tour boss Jacques Goddet. Their concern was probably not that Levêque would unjustly lose his Yellow Jersey. They didn't want to give Bobet, a real threat to win the Tour, an unearned stage victory and a free full minute in bonus time. They showed Goddet that by virtue of the intermediate timings, Bobet's winning was a near impossibility. The timekeeper relented, Koblet was given the stage win, and Levêque had his Yellow Jersey returned. Koblet's pace was so fast that 12 riders were eliminated from the Tour for failing to make the time cutoff.

The stage results:

1. Hugo Koblet: 2 hours 5 minutes 40 seconds
2. Louison Bobet @ 59 seconds
3. Fausto Coppi @ 1 minute 4 seconds
4. Fiorenzo Magni @ 2 minutes 52 seconds

The General Classification was now:

1. Roger Levêque
2. Gilbert Bauvin @ 1 minute 19 seconds
3. Hugo Koblet @ 7 minutes 2 seconds
7. Louison Bobet @ 8 minutes 31 seconds
8. Fausto Coppi @ 9 minutes 6 seconds
11. Fiorenzo Magni @ 10 minutes 54 seconds

During the next 3 stages the race headed inland for the first time in Tour history and into the leg-sapping Massif Central. Raphaël Géminiani won stage 9. Ockers, Koblet and the rest of those who dreamed of Yellow in Paris finished just a little over a minute behind him. The next day, stage 10, Spanish rider Bernardo Ruiz was first over all 3 of the day's major rated climbs and then won the stage. He left most of the field over 7 minutes behind.

After stage 10, Levêque was still leading. Bauvin had closed to within 36 seconds of him. The eventual King of the Mountains winner, Raphaël Géminiani, was showing fine form and moved into fourth place overall at 6 minutes, 44 seconds. Koblet dropped back to sixth at 7 minutes, 7 seconds. Bobet, Coppi and Magni were clustered just a few minutes behind Koblet.

It was in stage 11 that Hugo Koblet became a Tour immortal. It was a transitional stage before the Pyrenees and the Alps. Conventional wisdom said that an attack here would be the equivalent of suicide. Koblet had no time for conventional wisdom. On the thirty-seventh kilometer with 135 kilometers to go, in baking hot weather, he escaped the peloton on a small climb with the French rider Louis Deprez.

The other contenders for the General Classification must have smiled to themselves at this act of folly. The Tour rookie was going to burn himself out with both the Pyrenees and the Alps yet to be climbed. After a few kilometers Deprez found Koblet's pace too fast and dropped back. The Swiss rider was now on his own. However, when the gap rose to 4 minutes the laughter ceased and the peloton began to chase back in earnest.

Bobet flatted. The 2 members of the French team who were working the hardest to pull the fleeing Swiss back were told to halt their efforts and go back to pace Bobet back up. Until Bobet and his team-mates rejoined the peloton, only the Italians were working to recapture Koblet. The chase lost its momentum for a while.

With 70 kilometers to go Koblet still had a 3 minute lead. Now the big guns were taking serious turns at the front of the peloton. Coppi, Bartali, Bobet, Robic, Ockers, Magni, and Géminiani added their weight to the chase. The finest riders in the world were cooperating with each other, taking pulls at the front of the chasing peloton. Yet this group of cycling immortals still could not make an impression on Koblet's lead.

135 kilometers after he had made his attack Hugo Koblet entered the finish city of Agen. In the final kilometers of his great escape as he held off the entire peloton Koblet's face had shown no stress from the mighty effort. Before crossing the finish line Koblet took a sponge,

wiped his face, and combed his hair. He had used the comb as a psychological weapon before. In the Tour of Switzerland he had combed his hair on the hardest climb to give the impression of ease. In reality he was suffering with hemorrhoids. But it fooled his rival, François Mahé, who gave up trying to stay with him.

Koblet then calmly got off his bike and started his stopwatch to see what advantage he gained over the rest of the field, a move that was not just for show. He had reason to distrust the timekeepers as his experience in stage 7 shows. He wanted no repeat of that mistake. 2 minutes and 35 seconds later the rest of the peloton finally crossed the line, exhausted and astonished by Koblet's great escape.

Without exception the peloton and press poured praise onto Koblet. "That was a performance without equal. If there were two Koblets in the sport I would retire from cycling tomorrow... If he climbs like he races on the flat, then we can say good-bye to the Yellow Jersey. None of us will wear it. If he doesn't have any problems, then we can all start looking for another job," said Raphaël Géminiani. It was after this stage that singer Jacques Grello coined the phrase "*Pédaleur de Charme.*"

L'Equipe described the elite pack of riders chasing Koblet as "...skeptical and disconcerted at first, then utterly mortified and fiercely vindictive." There was another error in timing. This time it deprived Bauvin of his rightful evening in Yellow after Koblet's great ride.

The General Classification after stage 11:

1. Roger Levêque
2. Gilbert Bauvin @ 36 seconds
3. Hugo Koblet @ 3 minutes 27 seconds

Stage 12 was the start of another great Tour legend. On the last day before the Pyrenees, the Tour took another unexpected twist. A 10-man breakaway gained 18 minutes, 16 seconds on the peloton and Wim Van Est, "Iron William" as he was known to his fans, was in the Yellow Jersey.

Stage 13, from Dax to Tarbes, included both the Tourmalet and the Aubisque. Van Est, the first Dutchman to wear Yellow, was not going to give up the lead without a fight.

He turned pro in 1949 at the age of 26. In 1950 Van Est won

Bordeaux–Paris. In 1951 he was selected for membership in the Dutch national Tour de France team. Van Est had grown up poor and had never traveled. This was the first time he had ever seen, much less ridden up a major climb. Knowing that he wasn't a climber, he went off early so that he could finish with the leaders and keep his Yellow Jersey. He had never done a mountain descent and did his best to follow the line of the experienced riders.

Close to catching Ockers and Coppi, he flatted near the top of the Aubisque. Remounting, he joined Magni and tried to hold his wheel on the descent. Van Est crashed, remounted, and continued down the mountain. The descent of the Aubisque is considered very difficult with its hairpin turns hidden behind sharp corners.

He went too fast into a decreasing radius turn and lost control of his bike. He went flying off the side of the cliff and ended up 20 meters (70 feet) below. Trees broke his fall. He was able to grab one and by not moving much, fell no further.

Looking way down below, people could barely see that he was waving his arms. He was alive! How to get him out? There were no ropes. But there were tubular tires.

The mechanics and riders got together, made a rope of linked tires, and sent someone down the sheer cliff to rescue Van Est. When he got back up to the road, his first question was about his bike. He wanted to resume racing. He was forced to get into the waiting ambulance and go to the hospital for an examination. This was a bitter pill for the man in Yellow. He was fine, just a few bruises and scratches. The entire Dutch team quit in solidarity.

Van Est went on to win more Tour stages and wore Yellow for a while in both the 1955 and the 1958 Tours.

Meanwhile the race forged on. Raphaël Géminiani was the first man to go over the Aubisque and then got into the winning move of the day along with teammate Nello Lauredi, Serafino Biagioni of Italy and Gilbert Bauvin. Indeed, Géminiani was first to cross the line but was judged to have broken the rules and was relegated back to fourth place. The result was that Biagioni took the stage and Gilbert Bauvin was finally in Yellow. Koblet, Coppi, Ockers and Magni finished 9 minutes, 14 seconds back. Koblet was now down to fifth on General Classification, nearly 13 minutes behind the leader and over 6 minutes behind Géminiani.

Coppi, Géminiani, and Koblet on the Tourmalet, stage 14.

Stage 14. Once again the dramatic backdrop of the Pyrenees served as a breathtaking stage for the Giants of the Road. The 142 kilometers between Tarbes and Luchon included the Tourmalet, Aspin and Peyresourde climbs. Coppi managed to forget his grief and display his awesome powers. He was the first man to cross the Aspin and Peyresourde while the field behind him was utterly shattered. Koblet punctured before the top of the Tourmalet, but calmly waited for service before chasing back his rivals. In a great chase back, Koblet eventually caught Coppi and out sprinted the Italian legend to take the stage and the Yellow Jersey.

The General Classification now stood thus:

1. Hugo Koblet
2. Gilbert Bauvin @ 21 seconds
3. Raphaël Géminiani @ 32 seconds
4. Fausto Coppi @ 5 minutes 9 seconds
12. Louison Bobet @ 17 minutes 40 seconds
13. Stan Ockers @ 18 minutes 45 seconds

Stage 16 saw more drama on what was supposed to be a transitional stage. With the Alps yet to come, Koblet, Marinelli, Géminiani, Barbotin and Lazaridès attacked. Koblet won his third stage and only Géminiani at 1 minute, 32 seconds was still in contention for the Yellow Jersey. Coppi, overcome with the feelings of grief over his brother's recent death suffered a day of misery in the heat. He was dropped by the leading riders, eventually stopping and vomiting. Other accounts have attributed his problems to food poisoning. Bartali and Magni stayed with him to the finish line. Coppi ended up losing over 33 minutes, and was now out of the top 15 in the General Classification.

Stage 17, 224 kilometers between Montpellier and Avignon sent the Tour over Mont Ventoux for the first time in Tour history. On the climb 12 riders, all favorites, formed a leading break. By the time the group was halfway up the mountain only Raphaël Géminiani, Gino Bartali and Lucien Lazaridès were left at the front. Coppi and Magni were already 5 minutes in arrears. Koblet had suffered a derailleur problem and was limiting his losses riding in a high gear. Manager Bidot told Géminiani to slow the break because Bobet was closing in on them. With that help Bobet was able to bridge the gap. Pierre Barbotin made a tremendous effort to join the leading men, but with 2 kilometers to go Lazaridès (whose brother Apo was also riding in the race) attacked and was the first rider to cross the summit. Gino Bartali followed him. On the descent, Koblet caught up with the leading 5. In the closing kilometers Bobet attacked and won the stage by nearly a minute. That win galled Géminiani and from then on he raced not to beat Koblet but to be ahead of Bobet.

Over the next 2 stages Koblet maintained his 1 minute, 32 second advantage over Géminiani.

On Stage 20 Fausto Coppi gave another virtuoso performance. The Italian, now well out of overall contention, attacked early in the stage with Roger Buchonnet. He climbed the mighty Izoard and Vars alone. Koblet, seeing the danger of Coppi on a solo tear, responded and finished third that day. Raphaël Géminiani's challenge for the Yellow Jersey was over when he ended up over 7 minutes behind Koblet. The Swiss rider seemed destined to win the Tour on his first attempt.

Hugo Koblet must have relished Stage 22. It was the final Individual Time Trial, over 97 kilometers starting from Aix-les-Bains and finishing in Geneva, Switzerland. The *"Pédaleur de Charme"* was at his very best. Setting off at 2:32 p.m., Koblet started to reel in the riders who had already set off. He caught the great Gino Bartali who had started 8 minutes before him. As he passed Bartali, Koblet slowed and took his water bottle and placed it in the carrier of the struggling Italian. "Take it, Gino, there is still some left!" he said. In a previous race, Koblet had been dehydrated had asked Bartali for water. Gino had calmly had a drink and, then, looking at Koblet, emptied the remains of the bottle on the road.

At 5:11 p.m. Koblet entered the Frontenex Stadium in Geneva to immense cheers from the huge crowds. He had won the time trial by almost 5 minutes. He beat Coppi by 7 $1/2$ minutes and Bobet by almost 13.

Koblet won the 1951 Tour by 22 minutes from Raphaël Géminiani. He never again reached such heady heights. It was a complete triumph for Koblet and his Swiss team. Second placed Raphaël Géminiani joked, "chasing after these white crosses [the Swiss National Jersey], you could end up finishing at the Red Cross!" Géminiani said that he was actually the winner. When he was asked about Koblet, he replied, "He doesn't count. I'm the first human." It has been speculated that had the French been more unified and worked harder to beat Koblet rather than each other, Géminiani might have won the Tour. I think that unlikely given the ease with which Koblet was able to handle his rivals no matter what the challenge.

1951 Tour de France final General Classification:

1. Hugo Koblet (Switzerland): 142 hours 20 minutes 14 seconds
2. Raphaël Géminiani (France) @ 22 minutes
3. Lucien Lazaridès (France) @ 24 minutes 16 seconds
4. Gino Bartali (Italy) @ 29 minutes 9 seconds
5. Stan Ockers (Belgium) @ 32 minutes 53 seconds

Climber's Competition:

1. Raphaël Géminiani: 66 points
2. Gino Bartali: 59 points
3. A three-way tie between Coppi, Koblet and Bernardo Ruiz at 41 points

Koblet reveled in his newfound fame and fortune. "Money used to slip through his fingers like water," said one teammate, "Hugo couldn't say no to anyone. Sponsors always wanted him for some occasion or party, journalists wanting this or that story, groups of pretty women permanently waiting for him at the finish line." His flamboyant lifestyle was hugely expensive and in complete contrast to his rival and compatriot Ferdy Kübler. With the glamour of a modern-day rock star, Koblet would arrive at races driving a Studebaker, while Ferdy would arrive by train, third class. "Ferdy looks after his money; if there were a fourth class, Ferdy would take it," commented Charly Gaul.

In a time of post-war economic growth, the big stars benefited from direct sponsorship—indeed, we'll see how Raphaël Géminiani did a great deal to open up sponsorship for riders. Pontiac Watches capitalized on Wim Van Est's tumble on the Aubisque and ran the ad, "His heart stopped but his Pontiac kept time." For all his Studebakers and elegance, Koblet was astonished when an Italian businessman greeted him after a race and presented him with a check for one million lire. The businessman had to explain that it was Koblet's commission from a company that had produced a "Koblet" comb.

But unlike the true greats, Koblet could not remain focused on his racing.

"This flamboyant behavior made him lazy in his training. I remember we planned a training ride on the Klausen Pass and said we would meet at his house at 7:30 a.m. He agreed. We showed up, buzzed the door…nothing. We buzzed for 7 minutes and finally he comes to the window, obviously still asleep! He lets us in and says he has to make some calls and we should go down to the coffee shop till he is ready. We go down there and now it's one hour later. He then comes up and says he forgot about some meeting he has to do but will be done by 10:00 o'clock. We said forget it and left without him. This happened so often we gave up riding with him. Yet in the mountains he could drop us all on the few kilometers he trained," commented teammate Gottfried Weilenmann.

Following the Tour, Koblet accepted an offer to ride the Tour of Mexico. He was fascinated by exotic Central America and it suited his sense of adventure. Koblet was greeted by the President of Mexico and enjoyed the hospitality and the parties. One episode demonstrates his prodigious talent. Koblet had hardly ridden for a month and had been partying non-stop. On a mountainous stage in the Sierra Madre he left half an hour before the Mexican amateurs for a 200 kilometer solo race. The heat was intense and the Mexicans were enthusiastic about trying to catch the Tour de France winner. Nevertheless Koblet crossed the line 30 minutes, 35 seconds ahead of the chasing peloton.

While in Mexico, he contracted an illness that caused him kidney and lung problems that would plague him for the rest of his life. Koblet was never quite the same cyclist again.

A crash on the descent of the Aubisque in the Tour de France in 1953 caused Koblet more health problems and from then on his career went into a slow decline. While track racing with old friend Fausto Coppi in Colombia in 1957 the idea of emigrating to Argentina with thoughts of car franchises and other schemes was discussed (Coppi was trying to establish his bike frame business there). In 1958 Koblet hung the bike on the nail and moved to Argentina in search of fortune. He became homesick and returned to Europe but found it difficult to settle. His wife and great love, the model Sonja Bühl, had divorced him and his good looks were starting to fade.

On November 6th, 1964, witnesses saw a white Alfa Romeo speeding along the road to Esslingen at about 140 kilometers an hour. The weather was perfect, the road was good but the car plowed straight into a tree. Koblet had been alone in the car. Doctors operated on him for 4 hours. Koblet was only 39 when he died. By a bizarre twist of fate, the doctor who was first at the scene and later confirmed his death was named Kübler. To this day it is debated whether or not Koblet had committed suicide.

Years later when the 80-year-old Ferdy Kübler was asked about Koblet, the old man was nearly moved to tears as he remembered his friend and rival. The old man's reply was simple: "How lucky I was to have ridden with a great champion like Koblet."

1952. The Tour organizers, in their usual, almost oxymoronic way, continued the Tour tradition of breaking with tradition. In 1951 the Tour had ventured into the central part of France for the first time. In 1952 the 4,827 kilometer route with its 23 stages made a clockwise (Alps first) helix that again brought the race right through the center of France. This allowed the Tour to include a new climb, Puy de Dôme. 2 other new summits were included, L'Alpe d'Huez and Sestriere. All 3 were to be hill-top finishes in this Tour, favoring good climbers. A stage finish at the top of a mountain is a standard part of every Tour today, but in 1951 it was new.

The individual time trials, which had been in the 78–120 kilometer range in the post-war years, were shortened. It was decided that they had been too influential deciding the outcome of the last 2 Tours. Kübler attributed his 1950 victory to his ability to win the time trials. Possibly it was also thought that both of the great Swiss riders, Kübler and Koblet, were too good at them, hurting French chances, but I am only guessing here. The first time trial, stage 7, was 60 kilometers and the stage 22 crono was 63 kilometers.

The race was in no small way shaped by the riders who didn't come. Louison Bobet, Ferdy Kübler and Hugo Koblet, 3 of the world's finest stage racers, were unable to ride the Tour in 1952, all for health reasons. Fausto Coppi had no such problems. Coppi, although 33 years old, was in superb form. That spring he again won the Giro, capturing 3 stage wins in the process. He also came in second in Paris–Roubaix and fourth in the Tour of Romandie. It was his intention to avenge his tenth place in the previous year's Tour and again do what no one else had ever done, win the Giro and the Tour in the same year.

He was prepared to win and had a superb team to help him. He had the 38-year old Bartali with him. Coppi was still wary of Bartali and it again cost the Italian team manager, Alfredo Binda, no small effort to convince Coppi to ride on the same team with Bartali. This was despite the obvious fact that Bartali had lost his edge and was no longer the dominating master of the mountains. That said, he was still a formidable rider, having won the Italian Road Championship and taken fifth in the Giro. Other superb riders on the Italian squad included Fiorenzo Magni, Alfredo Martini and Andréa Carrea.

The French team had wonderful riders in Raphaël Géminiani and Jean Robic. The Belgian squad had Stan Ockers, second in the 1950 Tour and fifth in 1951. Yet, the Italians were the team with the power. Without riders of the caliber of Koblet, Bobet and Kübler, there was no counterbalance to Coppi, who was unstoppable when his form and morale were good.

Belgian classics ace Rik Van Steenbergen won the first stage and kept the lead for 2 days. Each day for the first 6 stages the peloton broke up with big time gaps between the stage winner—sometimes solo, sometimes with a small breakaway group—and the pack. When the pack completely came apart in the fourth stage, none of the top French riders was close to the front. Géminiani almost single-handedly towed his group for 100 kilometers. Robic spent the time sheltered, letting his teammate do the work. At the end of the stage Robic tried to sprint away but gained nothing but a few minor placings. That evening in the hotel Robic told reporters about how smart he had been, letting Géminiani do all the work. By saving his energy Robic said he was the smarter rider and now in a good position to win the Tour. Enraged upon hearing the little man's bluster, "Gem" held Robic's head face down in the hotel room sink. Robic never again rode for the national team.

Stage 5 had the first 9 riders scattered across the landscape with almost 10 minutes separating the winner, Bim Diederich, and the peloton. Coppi was second in the stage and now fifth overall. On stage 6, Fiorenzo Magni, who was forced to retire from the 1950 Tour while wearing Yellow, escaped and beat second place Tino Sabbadini by over 5 minutes and the peloton by over 7. This put Magni in the lead by a narrow margin over Nello Lauredi.

The General Classification after stage 6 and before the first individual time trial:

1. Fiorenzo Magni
2. Nello Lauredi @ 12 seconds
3. Robert Vanderstockt @ 13 seconds
4. Alex Close @ 2 minutes 56 seconds
5. Fausto Coppi @ 6 minutes 18 seconds
6. Andréa Carrea @ 6 minutes 29 seconds
9. Gino Bartali @ 9 minutes 3 seconds

The Italians had 4 riders in the top 10.

Coppi won the stage 7 time trial that went from Metz to Nancy. Magni wasn't able to keep his narrow lead. Lauredi regained the Yellow Jersey, which he had won on stage 3 and held until Magni wrested it from him. This moved Coppi up to third place, 3 minutes, 43 seconds behind Lauredi. Magni was second, down only 10 seconds.

Stage 8 had the year's first real climbing with the Tour's entry into the Vosges Mountains in eastern France. The day's ascents included the Ballon d'Alsace, important in Tour history as the first mountain to be part of the Tour. Raphaël Géminiani, France's best climber excepting

Louison Bobet, won the stage. Magni was second, and with the bonus time earned from that placing retook the Yellow Jersey. His slim 20-second lead over Lauredi would be very hard to defend.

The next day's stage took the Tour into Switzerland with a finish in Lausanne. A break of 8 riders got away. Andréa Carrea of the Italian team, ever watchful, made sure he was in the break. Carrea was absolutely devoted to Fausto Coppi and was his most loyal domestique. By the end of the stage the break had gained over 9 minutes on the pack with Swiss rider Walter Diggelmann first of the escapees across the line. Carrea went to the hotel after the stage was finished, only to be summoned by the police. Shocked, he asked what he had done wrong. He was due for an even greater jolt. The police told him that he was the leader of the Tour and he was to be awarded the Yellow Jersey. This was not only an extraordinary surprise for a man who was there to labor for his *campionissimo*, it scared him. He was terribly afraid of how Coppi would react. Crying, he apologized to Coppi, trying to deflect what he thought would be Coppi's terrible anger. In fact, Coppi was indifferent to Carrea's moment of glory. Coppi knew that with the next day's finish at the top of L'Alpe d'Huez the standings would completely change. Coppi was confident that given his present form, there was no one alive who could offer him any real challenge.

Stage 10 was 266 kilometers that went from Lausanne to top of the new L'Alpe d'Huez climb. At the first switchback of the Alpe 1947 Tour winner Jean Robic attacked. Only Coppi could go with him. They rode together for several kilometers. With 6 kilometers to go Coppi rose up out of the saddle and rode away from a man who was one of the finest climbers of his age. At the top of the then-potholed road Coppi was 1 minute, 20 seconds ahead of Robic and 3 minutes, 22 seconds ahead of Stan Ockers. He had placed his stamp of authority on this Tour and made it his.

The General Classification after the stage 10 climb to L'Alpe d'Huez:

1. Fausto Coppi
2. Andréa Carrea @ 5 seconds
3. Fiorenzo Magni @ 1 minute 50 seconds
4. Nello Lauredi @ 5 minutes 1 second
5. Alex Close @ 7 minutes 6 seconds

6. Stan Ockers @ 13 minutes 25 seconds

7. Gino Bartali @ 13 minutes 57 seconds

The Italians had captured the top 3 places, keeping 4 riders in the top ten.

After a rest day, stage 11 was a classic Alpine stage with 4 big climbs: the Croix de Fer, the Galibier, the Montgenèvre and the finish at Sestriere. The French, especially Géminiani, started attacking Coppi hard on the Galibier. He answered the French attacks with one of his own and easily escaped. After being first over the first 3 mountains he was still alone on the final climb to Sestriere. He arrived 7 minutes ahead of the Spanish climber Bernardo Ruiz. The carnage he left was amazing: 9 minutes, 33 seconds ahead of Ockers, over 11 minutes ahead of Robic, almost 18 minutes ahead of Géminiani and over 23 minutes ahead of Lauredi. It was an extraordinary performance. Alex Close of Belgium was now in second place to Coppi in the General Classification, 19 minutes, 57 seconds behind. This was an athletic performance that has few equals in the history of any sport.

With his huge lead Coppi could now relax a bit and ride conservatively. The next day, stage 12, a group of riders who didn't threaten his leadership broke away. Even so, with the day's 4 climbs in the Maritime Alps Alex Close lost another 4 minutes to Coppi. Coppi now had a 24-minute lead. Bartali rode as a true member of the Italian team. When Coppi flatted—he suffered 3 flats in a 20 kilometer stretch of road that day—Bartali generously gave Coppi his wheel. Bartali said that he was at the service of the team leader. The long fight was truly over.

The Tour organization felt that with Coppi's runaway victory, the racing would turn flat and the public would lose interest. They doubled the prize money for second and third places to keep the participants actively, aggressively racing. There was a complication also mitigating the intensity of the competition. Géminiani rode for Bianchi in 1952, the same as Coppi. While the Tour teams were national teams, riders were often reluctant to forget their trade team relationships which were their bread and butter for most of the year. For this reason Géminiani would hold his fire if it threatened his teammate Coppi. Understandably, Géminiani was left off the French team for the World Championships that fall because the selectors feared he would ride for Coppi and not for France. Finding the Bianchi sponsorship restrictive, Géminiani changed teams the next year.

As the Tour rode in stifling heat across southern France for its appointment with the Pyrenees, little changed in the General Classification.

The first Pyreneen stage, number 17, had the Ares, Peyresourde and the Aspin climbs. The stage showed Coppi's confidence. When Géminiani—fourteenth in the General Classification at 52 minutes— broke away on the descent of the Peyresourde, Coppi let him go. Géminiani was able to win the stage and partly salvage some French pride. But Coppi still had his solid 25 minute lead. The next day had the Tourmalet and the Aubisque. Coppi was first over both climbs but he took his time on both descents, allowing other riders to catch him. He sprinted away for the stage win, beating Stan Ockers by 4 seconds and capturing the time bonus. Coppi was now 27 minutes ahead of second-place Ockers.

There were still 2 final bumps in Coppi's way. The first was the hilltop finish at Puy de Dôme, a steep climb up an extinct volcano in France's Massif Central. Again Coppi soloed to victory and extended his lead to over 31 minutes.

The next day was the 63-kilometer individual time trial from Clermont-Ferrand to Vichy. Normally Fausto Coppi excelled in this discipline. He seems to have ridden it rather leisurely, letting Magni win the stage and Ockers take back a little time. Coppi finished fourteenth, just about 3 minutes behind Magni. It didn't affect the final standings. Coppi had the race in the bag.

Coppi never rode the Tour again. He left his record at 3 starts and 2 victories.

Final 1952 Tour de France General Classification:

1. Fausto Coppi (Italy): 151 hours 57 minutes 20 seconds
2. Stan Ockers (Belgium) @ 28 minutes 17 seconds
3. Bernardo Ruiz (Spain) @ 34 minutes 38 seconds
4. Gino Bartali (Italy) @ 35 minutes 25 seconds
5. Jean Robic (France) @ 35 minutes 36 seconds
6. Fiorenzo Magni (Italy) @ 38 minutes 25 seconds

Climber's competition:

1. Fausto Coppi (Italy): 92 points

2. Antonio Gelabert (Spain): 69 points
3. Jean Robic (France): 60 points

Chapter 7

1953–1956. The French finally unite behind 1 man and win 3 in a row and then get a surprise win that they oddly find unwelcome

1953. In so many ways the 1953 Tour de France represented a break from the past. There was a changing of the guard that had been promised but had taken so long to happen. No longer were the pre-war greats like Coppi and Bartali and others the dominant riders. Every rider who finished in the top 10 at the end of the 1953 Tour had turned pro after the war.

The 1953 Tour, like the 1952 version, was a counter-clockwise helix that about finished in the center of France with the final stage a 328 kilometer almost dead-north shot from Montluçon in central France up to Paris. At 4,476 kilometers it was almost 400 kilometers shorter than the 1952 Tour. This resulted in a final elapsed time that was 21 hours shorter than the year before. The average speed set a new record going from 31.9 kilometers an hour in 1952 to 34.6. A new age was dawning.

This was the 50th anniversary of the Tour de France. To mark the occasion a new competition was introduced, the Green Jersey for the best sprinter. Called the Grand Prix Cinquentenaire, points were awarded to the best-placed finishers of each day's stage. Because there are many more opportunities in a Tour for a sprinter to win than a climber, the competition favored the speedsters. To this day the quickest men in the peloton fight hard for the honor of wearing the Green Jersey. The competition has been refined over the last half-century. Today's Tour gives more points to the flat stages than to the mountain stages to emphasize that it is an award designed for the quick.

Fausto Coppi, winner in 1952, didn't come to the 1953 Tour. Sources give conflicting reasons for his absence. One author writes that Coppi gave the Italian team managers an ultimatum. He would not ride the Tour with Bartali on his team. This seems ungracious and unlikely to me in light of Bartali's generous team riding the previous year. Cycling journalist Sven Novrup writes that Tour management had the final say in teams chosen, and that after Coppi's overwhelming dominance in the 1952 Tour, they simply did not invite him.

There are further complications in this Coppi story. With Coppi there always are. Coppi wanted to win the World Road Championships that were to be held at the end of August in Lugano, just over the Italian border in Switzerland. Some writers say that he did not want to ride the Tour because it would interfere with his preparation for the championships and Coppi was very careful about his training and riding. He ended up winning the Lugano Worlds in commanding style, coming in alone, 6 minutes and 22 seconds over Belgium's Germain Derycke. Of the 70 starters, only 27 finished that day.

And there was the "Woman in White". She was not yet so named in the press, but Coppi was engaged in an affair with Giulia Locatelli. He was spending more time with her than with his wife and family. A trip to the Tour would take time away from Giulia.

Clearly Coppi was in magnificent form. He had already won the 1953 Giro, taking the lead from Hugo Koblet in the penultimate stage. I wanted to sort this all out because Coppi's absence made a big difference in the race's outcome. Tour scholar Owen Mulholland thinks that none of these reasons are really wrong and none really conflict with each other. While it's all sort of fuzzy, each probably contributed to giving him justification to miss the Tour. Coppi never rode the Tour de France again.

The French had been suffering. With the exception of the Lapébie's tainted 1937 victory and Robic's 1947 win, Belgian, Italian and Swiss riders had dominated their Tour for decades. Who would bring back those wonderful years of the early 1930's when the French were the greatest stage racers in the world?

The French team was loaded with good riders. Louison Bobet would be making his sixth attempt to win the Tour. Bobet's best performance to date was his third to Ferdy Kübler in 1950. But this was a team filled with Indian chiefs, each with his own ambitions. This was the problem that had plagued post-war French teams: none of France's wonderful riders wanted to sacrifice his chances for another racer. Also on the French team was Raphaël Géminiani, a superb climber who had understandable claims to team leadership with his fourth place in 1950 and second in 1951. Nello Lauredi had worn Yellow. Lucien Teisseire had his own aspirations. Team manager Marcel Bidot had a challenge on his hands as great as Binda had when he had to keep the peace between Coppi and Bartali. Bidot spent much of the 1950's wrestling with his ambitious, difficult riders.

The French regional teams were also formidable. Jean Robic was back on a regional team even though the year before he was the only rider capable of going with Coppi, albeit only partway, on the ascent of L'Alpe d'Huez. Gilbert Bauvin, Jean Malléjac, Roger Hassenforder, François Mahé, Jean Forestier and a rider new to the Tour, André Darrigade, all excellent racers, were placed on regional squads. The regional teams raced aggressively, some angrily, with many of the riders feeling that they had a point to prove: that they belonged with the best on the French national team. Robic's grudge-driven 1947 win is an excellent example of what a regional rider could do when both talent and outrage meet.

The tested duo of Gino Bartali and Fiorenzo Magni anchored the Italian team. Bartali was well past his prime but Magni was Italian Road Champion and still had another Giro win in his future. He should have been a real threat.

The Luxembourg team sported a rider new to the Tour, Charly Gaul. He won't get any print from me for this year, but in time he would become recognized as the greatest climber of the 1950s and according to many, the greatest climber ever.

The Swiss team was led by 1951 Tour winner Hugo Koblet. He was coming off a second place (to Coppi) in the 1953 Giro. Koblet had led the General Classification during most of the Giro. It was on the penultimate stage on the Stelvio that Coppi had taken the leader's Pink Jersey from Koblet and cinched the win. Since the illness that Koblet contracted in Mexico following his 1951 Tour win, he was not the same natural, perfect, powerful rider who had astonished the world in 1951.

Stage 1 gives us an excellent case in point. After trying to launch one of his blistering early-in-the-stage attacks he was easily brought back. The field later broke apart and the day's winner, Swiss rider Fritz Schaer, finished in a 4-man break that included French rider Nello Lauredi. Only 3 minutes behind these 4 were several attentive racers: Jean Robic, Raphaël Géminiani and Italian rider Giancarlo Astrua. This move foreshadowed the unfolding of the 1953 Tour. Koblet finished 10 minutes down along with most of the main field which contained Bobet, Bartali, Malléjac and Belgian contender Alex Close.

Schaer went on to win the second stage, giving him a 1-minute lead on Dutch rider Wout Wagtmans in the General Classification. As the race rolled across northern France Schaer finally had to relinquish the Yellow Jersey after the fourth stage when he missed the winning break. The lead passed to regional team rider Roger Hassenforder. Hassenforder, falling ill, could not defend the lead. Schaer took it back in the ninth stage, the last one before the race hit the hard climbing in the Pyrenees.

Here was the General Classification after stage 9:

1. Fritz Schaer
2. Wout Wagtmans @ 1 minute 2 seconds
3. Jacques Renaud @ 3 minutes 30 seconds
4. Thijs Roks @ 3 minutes 55 seconds
5. Gilbert Bauvin @ 4 minutes 40 seconds

Stage 10 took the race from Pau over the Aubisque and then the second-category climb to the finish at Cauterets. Spanish rider Jesus Lorono was first over the Aubisque and soloed in for the stage victory. Robic, signaling his ambitions and fine form, led Schaer and Astrua in about 6 minutes later. Bobet followed only a few seconds later. Tragically, after losing time to Lorono on the first climb, Koblet crashed on the descent of the Aubisque, breaking several ribs.

Stage 11 with the Tourmalet, Aspin and Peyresourde would be a profound test for the riders. Robic was always an audacious rider. He escaped on the first climb, the Tourmalet, and stayed away the rest of the stage. He never got very far ahead of his chasers and at the end Bobet was able to close within 1 minute, 27 seconds of him. But "Old

Leatherhead" was in Yellow again. Schaer showed that he was a complete rider by finishing fourth.

Here was the new General Classification:

1. Jean Robic
2. Fritz Schaer @ 18 seconds
3. Gilbert Bauvin @ 1 minute 50 seconds
4. Giancarlo Astrua @ 7 minutes 12 seconds
5. Louison Bobet @ 9 minutes 12 seconds

Let's pause a moment. Robic has another couple of interesting stories. There are so many of them. Remember, he wasn't riding for the French National Team in the 1953 Tour. He was riding for a regional French team, France-West. The manager of the team, Léon Le Calvez (who had ridden on the great French Tour teams of the 1930's), knew he had a good rider in Robic, but Robic could not get down the hills quickly. He could make great time on the climbs and then lose it on the other side. It wasn't a matter of being a skilled descender. He was very small, only 5 feet tall. Like many of the great climbers, he just didn't have the mass to get down fast.

Le Calvez had a plan. The evening before the first climbs in stage 9 he had molten lead poured into a water bottle—water bottles were aluminum at that time. At the top of the climb it would be secretly passed to Robic who would then have an extra 9 kilograms of mass to aid in his descent. It had to be done secretly because handing up food and water could only be done at the designated feed zones. The ruse (effectively doubling the weight of his bike) probably helped Robic on the descent of the Tourmalet. He was able to get down the mountain fast enough to stay away and don the Yellow Jersey.

I haven't been able to track it down, but I remember years ago reading a story about Robic in which a spectator complained that Robic had thrown a bottle and hit him in the head. The answer he was given was that if that were true, the spectator would be dead because the bottle weighed 9 kilos (20 pounds).

The next day a break of 24 riders got clear. Tour newcomer André Darrigade won the first of his 22 Tour stage victories that day. Robic, not being in the break, lost his lead. A rider on his team, Francois Mahé, was keeping an eye on the action and did finish with Darrigade's group. Mahé now assumed the lead. That leadership was short-lived. The following day, stage 13, was the real turning point in the 1953 Tour. This stage crossed southern France from Albi to Béziers as the Tour headed for the Alps.

With the Alps looming, the French team knew they had to blunt Robic's challenge. French team manager Bidot had his men attack from the gun. As planned, a 9-man break loaded with French team riders won the stage. In it were Lauredi, Géminiani, Bobet and Rolland of the French team along with Alex Close, Wout Wagtmans, Joseph Mirando, Jean Malléjac and Giancarlo Astrua. Robic missed the move and then crashed while chasing. He finished seventy-third, 38 minutes behind the stage winner Nello Lauredi. Barring a miracle, Robic's chances for a win were eliminated. He retired from the Tour the next day.

Stage 13 results:

1. Nello Lauredi
2. Raphaël Géminiani
3. Louison Bobet
4. Antonin Rolland
5. Giancarlo Astrua

all finishing with the same time

This left the General Classification thus:

1. Jean Malléjac
2. Giancarlo Astrua @ 1 minute 13 seconds
3. Louison Bobet @ 3 minutes 13 seconds
4. Gilbert Bauvin @ 4 minutes 24 seconds
5. Alex Close @ 4 minutes 41 seconds
7. Nello Lauredi @ 5 minutes 55 seconds
11. Raphaël Géminiani @ 8 minutes 15 seconds

Bobet was extremely upset, to say the least, because he lost the 1-minute bonus that winning the stage would have brought him. But he was unfair. The finish was on a cinder track and Lauredi tried to lead Bobet out. Bobet wasn't comfortable on a track and couldn't hold Lauredi's wheel. Géminiani then tried to help but Bobet was now out of gas. Géminiani and Lauredi needed to keep pushing hard to keep other riders from gaining the time bonuses up for grabs. That evening Bobet confronted Géminiani. Géminiani did not retreat from his belief that he had sprinted correctly and Géminiani had no obligation to slow to allow Bobet to win the stage which seemed to be beyond his strength that day. When Bobet accused Lauredi and Géminiani of working together to steal the stage win from him, Géminiani threw the dinner table to the ground and grabbed his fork. Bobet, in tears, ran away. With relations within the team now poisonous, a meeting of the French team was held. Manager Bidot asked the riders who among them could win the Yellow Jersey in Paris, meaning who on the team could win the Tour. Only Bobet raised his hand. Bobet said that he could win the Tour if the others in the French team would rally around him and protect him. Offering up a plan that the Italians had been using since Coppi, Bobet promised the other riders on the team all of his Tour prize money if he won. A formal contract was drawn up. While initially dubious, all the riders signed the agreement. Now they were a team.

Over the next 4 stages the General Classification changed little except that Bauvin dropped to ninth place.

Stage 18 is etched in the history of the Tour. It was 165 kilometers from Gap to Briançon crossing the Vars and the 2,360-meter Izoard. Bobet knew this was the time to strike. Both climbs are terribly hard, especially the Izoard. One of Bobet's teammates, Adolphe Deledda, went clear on the Vars with two other riders. Bobet stayed with the other leading climbers as they ascended the Vars. Spanish rider Jesus Lorono attacked. The alert and very capable Bobet jumped on his wheel and the pair disappeared up the mountain. Bobet was a good descender and dropped Lorono on the way down the Vars. Meanwhile Deledda, upon being told that Bobet was on his way, eased up and waited for his captain. The two hooked up and took off across the 20-kilometer valley floor leading to the Izoard. In doing so they caught and then dispatched Deledda's two original breakaway companions. Bobet and Deledda, knowing the importance of the moment were men on a mission. Deledda, fulfilling the team contract in both letter and especially in spirit, buried himself towing Bobet to the foot of the Izoard. Upon being delivered by an exhausted Deledda to the great mountain Bobet flew up the Izoard as if he had wings. Bobet had finally arrived as the premier stage racer in the world. As he crested the Izoard there was a very well known cycling fan by the side of the road. Fausto Coppi with his mistress Giulia Locatelli ("The Woman in White"), was watching the race. As he rode past the great man, Bobet shouted thanks to Coppi for coming.

Bobet hurtled down the other side of the mountain and despite a flat tire, arrived in Briançon almost 5 1/2 minutes before the next rider, Dutchman Jan Nolten. Lorono came in another 30 seconds later. Géminiani finished almost 11 minutes after Bobet. Lauredi was at 12 minutes and Magni 13. Bobet had shown his mastery and the French had finally found their man.

The post-Izoard (stage 18) General Classification:

1. Louison Bobet
2. Jean Malléjac @ 8 minutes 35 seconds
3. Giancarlo Astrua @ 9 minutes 48 seconds
4. Alex Close @ 11 minutes 55 seconds
5. Fritz Schaer @ 14 minutes 57 seconds

The race had been completely blown apart.

The stage 20 individual time trial, 70 kilometers between Lyon and St. Etienne, proved that Bobet was far more than just a superb climber, he was a truly deserving victor. Bobet won the stage and almost doubled his lead on Malléjac. With only 2 stages left the race, after 5 attempts, was his.

To celebrate the Tour's 50th anniversary, a gathering of previous Tour winners was waiting to greet Bobet in the *Parc des Princes* velodrome for his victory lap in Paris. The first Tour winner, Maurice Garin, was there. Also in attendance were Gustave Garrigou, Lucien Buysse, Philippe Thys, Romain and Sylvère Maes, André Leducq, Antonin Magne, Georges Speicher, Roger Lapébie and Ferdy Kübler. Although he never won the Tour but was perhaps the most deeply loved of all by the fans, Eugéne Christophe also attended.

Bobet's victory was not only the triumph of perseverance. Bobet was willing to suffer incredible pain in order to ply his craft of bicycle racing. He was susceptible to boils his entire career. They would break out not only on his seat, but sometimes all over his body. This awful malady struck Bobet in the 1948 Tour. During the 1953 Giro boils forced him to retire on the last stage. He had them lanced and had recovered enough to ride the Tour. The boils reappeared in the Pyrenees and again a doctor had to lance them. This agony would haunt Bobet year after year.

With an eleventh place, Gino Bartali finished his last Tour. He rode the Tour 8 times, starting in 1937, finishing 6. He won twice, in 1938 and 1948. Both times he also took the climber's prize. Bartali retired from racing a year later. He lost and gave away most of his money but always retained his famous religious piety. Gino Bartali passed away in 2000.

Final 1953 Tour de France General Classification:

1. Louison Bobet (France): 129 hours 23 minutes 25 seconds

2. Jean Malléjac (France-West) @ 14 minutes 18 seconds

3. Giancarlo Astrua (Italy) @ 15 minutes 2 seconds

4. Alex Close (Belgium) @ 17 minutes 35 seconds

5. Wout Wagtmans (Holland) @ 18 minutes 5 seconds

Climber's Competition:

1. Jesus Lorono: 54 points

2. Louison Bobet: 36 points

3. Joseph Mirando: 30 points

The first-ever points competition for the Green Jersey, lowest total wins:

1. Fritz Schaer: 271 points

2. Fiorenzo Magni: 307 points

3. Raphaël Géminiani: 406 points

1954. The Tour went back to roughly 4,800 kilometers with 2 days of split stages. Indicative of the intensity of the racing in the 1954 Tour, the average speed was still higher than the record set the year before when the race was 400 kilometers shorter. This was a savage Tour. From the start, the level of aggression was almost as much as the racers could stand even without the presence of one of the most important teams in cycling.

The Italian federation did not send a team to the Tour after the 1954 Giro's "Bernina Strike". I know this is a book about the Tour de

France but this is an interesting cycling story. I am thankful to the great Giorgio Albani (highly accomplished racer as well as Director of Merckx) for relating the story.

It was very important to the Giro organizers that Fausto Coppi ride their race. He was the biggest star and his presence was deemed essential. To induce Coppi to ride they paid the *campionissimo* a large sum of money. This was not a secret. The other riders knew and were deeply resentful. After the first stage Coppi ate a bad plate of oysters and became quite ill. He lost 11 $^1/_2$ minutes the next day. So now there was an angry peloton and the Giro was stuck with an expensive Coppi who could not race. The Giro Boss, Giuseppe Ambrosini, asked the riders to save the race by actively and aggressively competing. Fiorenzo Magni and several others wanted to help. They fought hard that day and tried to make a brilliant race of it. As a professional and one of the greatest riders of the age, Magni expected to be recompensed in a generous way by Ambrosini. Ambrosini gravely disappointed Magni and the others with what they considered an insufficient repayment for their efforts. They then deadened their efforts.

With this lack of competition, Swiss team domestique Carlo Clerici insinuated himself into a break in stage 6 that beat the field by over 30 minutes and thus gave him the Giro's lead. Clerici was a good enough rider to defend his Pink Jersey, especially with a slow-moving and surly peloton to beat. On the third to the last stage Coppi, who earlier had fallen ill, pulled a lot of time out of Clerici. It was expected now that bellicose and hard-driving competition would be restored to the race. Surely Coppi would deliver the *coup de grace* the next day. He didn't. Instead, Coppi and the peloton, still striking, rode easily over the Bernina pass and allowed Clerici to cement his victory.

When the race entered the Vigorelli Velodrome in Milan the derisive whistles from the crowd were so loud that the riders could not hear the bell signaling the final lap. The Italian federation was incensed and handed Coppi a 2-month suspension. Additionally, they refused to send a team to the Tour. Perhaps the Italians would not have been allowed to come to the Tour anyway because they had begun to accept "*extra-sportif*" sponsors, that is sponsors outside the cycle industry. This was new and considered harmful to the sport at the time. Attitudes do make surprising changes over time.

As an afterthought to the Bernina matter, it is important to realize that the Tour de France has also resorted to pay-to-play in the past. Desgrange had a secret deal to pay Alfredo Binda to ride the Tour. And, during Coppi's domination in the 1952 Tour the prize money for second and third place was doubled to keep the other racers competing.

Of the 1954 Tour's 110 entrants, 60 were French: 10 on the National team, 50 on regional French squads.

The French national team was almost the same as the previous year's. But this year there could be no disagreement as to who the team leader would be. With Louison Bobet's commanding victory in the 1953 Tour he was the obvious designated captain. Raphaël Géminiani, owner of one of the sport's finest tactical minds as well as a superb rider, would now be riding for Bobet instead of against him.

Regional squads contained the ever aggressive Jean Robic as well as Gilbert Bauvin, Jean Dotto, and Jean Malléjac. The Belgian team had both Stan Ockers (second in 1950 and 1952) and Alex Close (fourth in 1953).

Tour legend Charly Gaul anchored the Luxembourg team but Gaul still needed another year to develop into the climber who could strike fear bordering on panic into the hearts of the other riders. This year he could get into the top 10 of a stage only once. This was also the first Tour for Federico Bahamontes. This legendary Spanish rider would become not only one of the monumental riders in cycling's history, but also one of the great eccentrics of the sport. As Jean Robic fades from the scene "Baha" will keep the story of the Tour interesting in the coming years, I promise.

The Swiss team would more than make up for the absence of the Italians. For starters they had their 2 Tour winners, Ferdy Kübler and Hugo Koblet, as well as that year's Giro winner Carlo Clerici. Fritz Schaer who had worn Yellow for a while last year and finished with the sprinter's Green Jersey was a very accomplished rider who filled out the powerful core of a formidable team that had no intentions of rolling over for the French.

The 1954 Tour was counter-clockwise (Pyrenees first), starting in Amsterdam. This was the first foreign start for the Tour and what a start it was. Koblet started throwing high heat (if I may be allowed to mix my sports analogies) and the pack broke up under the pressure. In the front group of 19 were the day's winner Wout Wagtmans and Ockers, Robic, Koblet and the almost always attentive Bobet. Missing the move and coming in 9 minutes later: Kübler, Gaul, Malléjac, Lauredi, Mahé and Bahamontes.

The pack broke up again the next day as the Tour went from Beveren in Belgium to Lille, France. This time the break was smaller, but the big guns were there: Bobet (the stage winner), as well as both Swiss contenders Kübler and Koblet. Bauvin, Wagtmans, Robic and Géminiani made the break as well. The effect of such a powerful, fast-moving group forming a break was dramatic. The chasing field was spread over the road coming in solo and in little groups between 10 seconds and 30 minutes after the winner. By winning the stage Bobet pulled himself to within 1 second of race leader Wagtmans. The third stage didn't affect the top standings in the General Classification.

After 3 tough Northern European stages the Tour was already sorting the wheat from the chaff:

1. Wout Wagtmans
2. Louison Bobet @ 1 second
3. Gilbert Bauvin @ 31 seconds
4. Hugo Koblet @ 1 minute 1 second
5. Jean Robic @ same time

The next day, Sunday, had 2 stages. Stage 4a was a short 10.4-kilometer team time trial. The Swiss with their powerful masters of the race against the clock, Koblet and Kübler, won. The French were 47 seconds slower. The regional France West team with Robic, Mahé and Malléjac was better than some of the national teams and came in third, 1 minute, 44 seconds off the pace. Bobet was now in Yellow.

The new General Classification:

1. Louison Bobet
2. Wout Wagtmans @ 35 seconds
3. Hugo Koblet @ 51 seconds
4. Gilbert Bauvin @ 59 seconds
5. Fritz Schaer @ 1 minute 1 second
6. Jean Robic @ 1 minute 26 seconds
7. Wim Van Est @ 6 minutes 54 seconds

The General Classification top 7 places contained 3 former Tour winners (Bobet, Koblet and Robic) and 3 former or future Yellow Jersey owners (Wagtmans, Schaer and Van Est). This kind of accurate sorting generally happens when the racing is really tough and only the strongest can rise to the top.

Stage 4b, like all the road stages so far, ended in a break. Van Est won it but the top 6 places didn't change; Van Est was now down only 1 minute, 47 seconds. The next day the Swiss again raced with guns blazing. Kübler led in a 15-man break. Still, the top echelons of the General Classification were unchanged except that Jean Robic was forced to abandon after a bad crash.

Ding-dong, the Swiss kept banging away at it. In stage 6, France Ile-de-France rider Dominique Forlini led in Koblet and Kübler with Schaer just 2 seconds behind them. Bobet still had the lead but Koblet was now second at only 17 seconds. Schaer followed at 59 seconds and Kübler was third, albeit a bit distant at 5 minutes, 58 seconds. Wagtmans had dropped to sixth at 7 minutes, 52 seconds. Through sheer relentless aggression the Swiss occupied 3 of the top 4 places in the General Classification.

Two days later the Swiss (and the French) let one get away. A break made up of some good riders who were not thought to be Tour General Classification contenders escaped, among them Fred De Bruyne and Jean Stablinski. Nestled among the fast-moving group that beat the field by over 8 minutes was Wagtmans. He regained the Yellow Jersey that Bobet had taken from him 5 stages before.

Now the race headed due south for the Pyrenees in 2 big leaping stages. Gilbert Bauvin (riding for the France North-East-Center regional team) won stage 10. This wasn't an easy day for Koblet. After crashing he needed the help of his Swiss teammates to engage in a long, hard chase to regain contact with the crucial Bobet-Wagtmans group. Koblet kept his dangermen in reach but this is not how the Swiss wanted to spend the day before the high mountains. Bauvin's stage win moved him to second in the General Classification.

So, before the heavy climbing the standings stood thus:

1. Wout Wagtmans
2. Gilbert Bauvin @ 39 seconds
3. Louison Bobet @ 1 minute 2 seconds
4. Hugo Koblet @ 1 minute 19 seconds

5. Fritz Schaer @ 2 minutes 1 second

8. Ferdy Kübler @ 7 minutes

Still, none of the road stages had ended with the pack sprinting together. Every stage so far in this Tour had ended in a break.

Stage 11, from Bayonne to Pau crossed the Soulor and the Aubisque. Bahamontes was first over the Aubisque, but this was years before Bahamontes had the legendary conversation with Coppi wherein Coppi convinced him that he could win the Tour. Bahamontes was interested in the climber's prize which, in his native Spain, was more highly esteemed than the Yellow Jersey at this time. In his early Tours Bahamontes would fly up the mountain and then descend slowly, waiting for the others. That day, Bahamontes was caught and dropped, finishing thirty-fifth. The elite group that finished in the lead included Ockers (the day's winner), Kübler, Bobet, Schaer, Wagtmans, Gaul and Géminiani. The main casualty of the day was Koblet, suffering from the previous day's crash and hard chase. He was nineteenth and lost 1 minute, 54 seconds. It was worse than that. He crashed twice getting off the Aubisque. The next day offered no respite to the suffering Swiss racer who only a few short years before had been called the "Pedaler of Charm."

Stage 12, 161 kilometers from Pau to Luchon made the riders go over the Tourmalet, the Aspin and the Peyresourde. This was another day of aggression that pushed the men to their limits. Bahamontes was first over the Tourmalet. Bobet led over the Aspin. Bahamontes went over the final mountain in front and finished together with Malléjac, only 1 second behind Bauvin. Bobet fought to limit their advantage, losing 1 minute, 59 seconds. The rest? They were scattered across France. Kübler lost 7 minutes, Schaer almost 11, Wagtmans over 18 minutes. Koblet, exhausted and sore from his crashes suffered terribly. Early in the stage he lost a huge chunk of time climbing the Tourmalet. As the stage progressed he crashed 3 times, losing even more time. Koblet finished the day sixty-fourth, almost 27 minutes behind the winning trio. He fell to thirteenth in the General Classification, 31 minutes behind the new Yellow Jersey, Gilbert Bauvin.

With racing in the Pyrenees over after stage 12 here was the General Classification:

1. Gilbert Bauvin

2. Louison Bobet @ 3 minutes 52 seconds

3. Fritz Schaer @ 13 minutes 40 seconds

4. Ferdy Kübler @ 14 minutes 52 seconds

5. Wout Wagtmans @ 19 minutes 20 seconds

6. Jean Malléjac @ 20 minutes 16 seconds

There were no pretenders in this group, all were worthy racers. The huge time gaps after only 2 days in the mountains speaks volumes about the intensity of the racing in this Tour. Instead of several days of racing flattish roads in southern France on the way to the Alps the Tour headed into the Massif Central. There was only 1 stage between the Pyrenees and the Massif stages to give some respite from the mountains. So far there had been no rest day. The 1954 Tour's only rest day wouldn't come until after stage 16.

Stage 14 in the Massif had a series of 4 second and third category climbs. 23 of the best riders broke clear with Bahamontes first over the final 3 mountains. This should not have affected the race except that Bauvin flatted on the second climb, the 1,030 meter-high Montjaux. He was unable to regain contact with the Bobet-Bahamontes group and lost 8 minutes and the Yellow Jersey. Bobet was again the leader.

Two days later Bauvin had another terrible day. On stage 16 he lost 20 minutes and dropped to 6th in the overall. After stage 17 and with the Tour having finished the hilly country of the Central Massif, the race stood at the foot of the first of the Alpine stages. Here were the standings:

1. Louison Bobet

2. Fritz Schaer @ 9 minutes 44 seconds

3. Ferdy Kübler @ 10 minutes 30 seconds

4. Jean Malléjac @ 16 minutes 54 seconds

5. Jean Dotto @ 20 minutes 4 seconds

6. Stan Ockers @ 22 minutes 25 seconds

7. Gilbert Bauvin @ 22 minutes 36 seconds

Without winning a single stage Bobet had built a huge lead.

The Romeyere was the first major climb of the first day in the Alps. Bahamontes took off in a white heat, panicking Bobet and the other leaders who felt they had to keep the Spaniard in check. When they got to the top of the mountain they found Bahamontes sitting on a wall eating an ice cream that a spectator gave him. Over the years his explanation for this behavior has changed: he wanted to play a joke on the others, he needed mechanical assistance. At the heart of the matter was Bahamontes's fear of descending. Once while riding alone as an amateur he had fallen down a ravine into cactus and no one knew of his plight. He never wanted to repeat that episode and so waiting for the others to arrive and give him company on the descent made sense to him. Bahamontes finished the day forty-ninth, 10 minutes behind the Bobet group.

Stage 18 proved that Bobet's 1953 Tour win was no fluke. There were 3 major climbs. Bahamontes led over the first, the Laffrey as well as the second, the Bayard. Now they were at the base of the mighty, 2,360-meter high Izoard, the same mountain that Bobet had used to win the Tour the year before. At the foot of the climb there were about 40 riders still with Bahamontes and Bobet. Bobet fearlessly took the point and slowly burned the entire peloton off his wheel. When he pulled into Briançon he was alone. The next rider, Ferdy Kübler, wouldn't show up for another minute and 49 seconds. Bahamontes was 4 minutes 41 seconds behind and Schaer lost 7 minutes. There could be no argument, Bobet was the best. He was now almost 13 minutes ahead of the new second place Kübler. Schaer, now third, was almost 18 minutes behind Bobet. It was a magnificent performance. The next day in the mountains had the tired riders climb the Galibier as the prelude to riding over 3 other rated climbs. Jean Dotto (France South-East) flew away for a solo victory but the main contenders were content (or cowed) to finish together.

With the major climbing done at the end of stage 19, barring misfortune, Bobet had the Tour in the bag.

1. Louison Bobet
2. Ferdy Kübler @ 12 minutes 49 seconds
3. Jean Dotto @ 17 minutes 22 seconds
4. Fritz Schaer @ 17 minutes 46 seconds
5. Jean Malléjac @ 23 minutes 15 seconds

One roadblock stood between Bobet and a Yellow Jersey in Paris and that was the stage 21b 72-kilometer individual time trial. At Nancy where the time trial ended Bobet beat even Ferdy Kübler, who had used the final time trial in 1950 to clinch his Tour win. Bobet was able to put another 2 minutes, 30 seconds between himself and the powerful Swiss rider. With 2 stages to go, that was it. Louison Bobet had won 2 tours in a row.

Final 1954 Tour de France General Classification:

1. Louison Bobet (France) 140 hours 6 minutes 5 seconds
2. Ferdy Kübler (Switzerland) @ 15 minutes 49 seconds
3. Fritz Schaer (Switzerland) @ 21 minutes 46 seconds
4. Jean Dotto (France South-East) @ 28 minutes 21 seconds
5. Jean Malléjac (France West) @ 31 minutes 38 seconds

Climber's Competition

1. Federico Bahamontes: 95 points
2. Louison Bobet: 53 points
3. Richard Van Genechten: 46 points

Points competition:

1. Ferdy Kübler: 215.5 points
2. Stan Ockers: 284.5 points
3. Fritz Schaer: 286.5 points

While the ultimate prize eluded the Swiss, they were well rewarded for their relentless aggression. They enlivened a race that, without the Italians, could have been a dull Bobet romp (instead of an exciting Bobet romp?). Kübler and Schaer taking second and third in the General Classification, along with Kübler's being the winning sprinter, was an impressive accomplishment for that small country.

Bobet went on to win the World Road Championships that year. In terrible weather against a stellar field he finished alone. Fritz Schaer must have felt frustrated to have again been beaten by the flying Frenchman, coming in second to Bobet by only 12 seconds. Showing his potential for the future, Charly Gaul was third. Only 22 riders finished that day. Scattered behind Bobet, Schaer and Gaul were Coppi, Anquetil, de Bruyne and Robic. Bobet earned a Rainbow Jersey he could wear with pride.

1955. The 1955 Tour went clockwise (Alps first) over a 4,476 kilometer course that again took in the Massif Central between the Alps and the Pyrenees. The roughly 400 kilometer reduction that imitated the length of the 1953 Tour was indicative of the general trend towards a slightly shorter Tour. Only in 1967 would it again creep up towards 4,800 kilometers. In 1971 it was 3,800 kilometers and the 2003 Centennial Tour was 3,361 kilometers. Henri Pélissier continued to win his argument that shorter races with higher speeds were superior athletic contests.

Bobet, of course, was the man to beat. He had not only won 2 Tours in a row, he was the reigning World Road Champion. His spring was impressive with a victory in one of the hardest 1-day races on the calendar, the Tour of Flanders. He was third in Paris–Roubaix. He also won the Dauphiné Libéré and came in second to André Darrigade in the French road championships. Not only was Bobet formidable, his team was impressive. His brother Jean would ride at his side as well as Jean Dotto, Antonin Rolland, Raphaël Géminiani, Jean Malléjac, Jean Forestier and André Darrigade. If Bobet did not win the Tour for an unprecedented third time in a row, it would not be because he didn't have good, experienced riders at his side.

The Belgian team had a third-year pro named Jean Brankart who had managed to get ninth the year before. Nothing in his results presaged anything remarkable beyond good, strong riding. Also on the Belgian team were Stan Ockers, second in 1952 and Alex Close, fourth in 1953. For stage wins, the greatest classics racer of the age, Rik Van Steenbergen, helped fill out a very fine team.

Federico Bahamontes did not enter the 1955 Tour so the Spanish were without a real hope for either the Yellow Jersey or the Climber's competition. The Italians returned after their 1954 absence but were without a real General Classification hope as well. The Swiss sent Ferdy Kübler to try to repeat his 1950 win. By the end of July he would be 36, the oldest man in the Tour.

Wout Wagtmans, who was so often in the fight in the hardest stages in the mountains and had worn Yellow the year before, anchored the Dutch team.

Charly Gaul was put on a team called Luxembourg-Mixte with riders from Luxembourg, Austria, Australia and Germany all "mixte" up. Gaul could not hope to have a well-oiled machine like the French team. He would be on his own.

For the first time there was a British team. Most of them were not up to the challenges of a Grand Tour. For a raft of complex social and legal reasons that go back to the very start of cycle racing in the 19th century, the British had generally not sanctioned massed-start road races on their island. Their cycling organizations had stifled the growth of professional cycling, preferring to encourage what they thought was a finer, more purely amateur sport. Of the 10 men on the team, only 2 finished, Tony Hoar and Brian Robinson. Robinson finished a respectable twenty-ninth, Hoar was the Lanterne Rouge at sixty-ninth. But, as Geoffrey Wheatcroft notes, 130 good pro riders started the 1955 Tour and only 69 finished. Hoar did better than 61 other entrants.

Starting in northern France and heading east towards Belgium, the first day of the 1955 Tour had a split stage. In the morning they rode 102 kilometers from Le Havre to Dieppe. Spanish rider Miguel Poblet entered the history books when he won the stage and became the first of his countrymen to don the Yellow Jersey. When the Dutch team won the afternoon's 12.5 km team time trial, Poblet still had the Yellow Jersey. Not surprisingly, Great Britain finished last in the team time trial, over 5 minutes behind the winners.

The next day on the road to Roubaix a 4-man break beat the main pack by 2 ¹/₂ minutes. French team rider Antonin Rolland won the sprint but Wout Wagtmans took the lead. Important for the tactics and politics of the race as it unfolded, Rolland was now in fourth place in the General Classification.

Stage 3 was a classic cobbled northern European stage going from Roubaix, France to Namur, Belgium. Bobet, who had won the Tour of Flanders that year and would win Paris–Roubaix the next, could handle the rough roads of the region. He powered a break that included the Yellow Jersey'd Wagtmans. Bobet won the stage and moved to fourth in the overall and Wagtmans extended his lead slightly with Rolland the new second place.

In modern Tours these early stages are boring promenades of controlled riding with a final furious sprint. In stage 4 there was nothing of the sort. 9 men got over 7 minutes on the peloton and there was a new Yellow Jersey. Rolland was in that break, and as a reward for his consistent heads-up riding he was the new leader with a 9 minute, 21 second lead over Wagtmans and a huge 13 minutes, 32 seconds over his team captain, Bobet. Now does Rolland, a domestique with a substantial lead in the General Classification, ride for his captain or does Bobet now ride for Rolland?

Stage 6 traveled to Zurich. Of course Ferdy Kübler wanted to win on his home turf. He escaped with 6 others but he didn't have the jump to win the sprint. André Darrigade notched another of his eventual 22 career stage wins. The next day the pack let a group of non-contenders, so they thought, leave them over 17 minutes behind. Dutchman Wim Van Est again took the Yellow Jersey with a slim 25 second lead over Rolland. In that break was a serious, capable, but unsung rider named Roger Walkowiak. He'll get himself into a good break next year. That will be very interesting stuff, indeed.

Van Est, a non-climber and non-descender, couldn't hope to keep the Yellow Jersey for long. In fact, with a monster Alpine stage the next day, he had to know his time in the lead was over almost as soon as it had started. Stage 8 had the Aravis, Télégraphe and the Galibier. The Tour would now be fought in earnest.

Charly Gaul had started both the 1953 and the 1954 Tours. He finished neither. In 1955, he blossomed. Away on the first of the 3 climbs, he was able to get as much as 15 minutes on the field before finally finishing 13 minutes, 47 seconds ahead of the chasers. Kübler led in the first chasing group of 6 men, Bobet among them. Almost 16 minutes after Gaul gave his lesson in climbing, Géminiani and Rolland finished. Rolland was back in Yellow and Gaul was now third. Bobet was sixth, over 11 minutes behind Rolland. The results of this stage were wholly unexpected. While it was still in the early days of the Tour, Gaul was an element that had not been in their calculations. He was now.

Gaul tried to smash the field in the mountains 2 days in a row and couldn't do it. He was first over the first 3 climbs but crashed on the second mountain, the Cayolle. A resuscitated Géminiani crested the 555-meter La Turbie first and came in alone. At 2 minutes were Bauvin, Bobet, Rolland, Astrua and Fornara. Gaul needed another minute and a half to arrive. A fine performance, but not one that would give him the Tour.

So, the General Classification after stage 9 and the Alpine stages finished:

1. Antonin Rolland

2. Pasquale Fornara @ 11 minutes 3 seconds

3. Louison Bobet @ 11 minutes 33 seconds

4. Charly Gaul @ 11 minutes 53 seconds

5. Vincent Vitetta @ 13 minutes 56 seconds

6. Jean Brankart @ 16 minutes 5 seconds

Bobet was now facing a problem greater than a teammate's ascendancy. The skin problem that had plagued him his entire career reasserted itself as terrible saddle sores. Ollivier writes that even in his hotel room, alone, Bobet would cry out in agony.

Stage 11 was where the temper of the race changed. So far Bobet had been observing the correct protocols and not attacking his teammate Rolland. He had to have been seething with ambition. Stage 11 was 198 kilometers from Marseille to Avignon with Mt. Ventoux between the two cities. The French set out to neutralize the small Luxembourg climber who was giving them so much trouble. Well before the foot of Mt. Ventoux Géminiani got away with Kübler and a teammate on Bauvin's France Northeast-Center regional squad, Gilbert Scodeller. Once on the slopes of the Ventoux Bobet accelerated several times and finally escaped from all the other riders. Gaul couldn't go with him. Because the young climber was so new to this highest level of racing, no one knew what his weak points and his strong points were. Charly Gaul's achilles heel was heat. He couldn't take it. Monday, July 18, 1955 was a very hot day and Gaul melted.

Bobet caught the break of 3. The plan was for Géminiani to assist him in the 60 kilometers still remaining to Avignon after Mt. Ventoux had been climbed. When Bobet caught Géminiani, "Gem" told Bobet to go on alone because he was cooked. Scodeller and Kübler were also shot and finished the day more than 20 minutes down.

Bobet didn't have much of a lead at the top of the Ventoux. Belgian surprise Jean Brankart was only a minute back. Several riders now riding with Géminiani were almost 4 minutes back. Gaul was 5 1/2 minutes behind. There were still 60 kilometers to go. Should the lone Bobet sit up and wait for help? French team manager Marcel Bidot told Bobet to press on and that if the chasers closed to within 45 seconds he would let Bobet know so that he could wait (winning a 3-week stage race requires avoiding unnecessary efforts that waste energy). With an inopportune flat the gap did get that close with just 5 kilometers to go.

Bobet rode on and won alone, 49 seconds ahead of Brankart, 5 minutes, 40 seconds ahead of Rolland and Wagtmans, and 6 minutes ahead of Gaul.

Bobet was now second to Rolland at 4 minutes, 53 seconds. Gaul was down to fifth, over 12 minutes behind Rolland. Rolland was still in Yellow but the consequences of the stage were huge. Bobet had shown his ability to deliver when it mattered. Gaul was rocked back on his heels. Kübler, Ockers, Close and Bauvin lost too much time to be considered competitive. Kübler's failure was heartbreaking. On the Ventoux he started to swerve. He stopped in a cafe for a while, got something to drink, then remounted. Like Abdel Khader Zaaf in the 1950 Tour, Ferdy at first took off in the wrong direction. He abandoned the next day.

Of all the contenders, Jean Malléjac's collapse was the most dramatic. Malléjac was 10 kilometers from the summit of Mt. Ventoux when he started weaving and then fell to the ground. He still had one foot strapped into the pedal, his leg still pumping involuntarily trying to turn the crank. The Tour race doctor, Pierre Dumas, had to pry Malléjac's mouth open to administer medicine. He was taken away in an ambulance. On the way to hospital he had another fit. He had to be strapped down both in the ambulance and later in his hospital bed. It was assumed that Malléjac had taken an overdose of amphetamines, but he always denied it. Half a dozen other riders also collapsed in the heat, but none with the drama of Jean Malléjac. Was Malléjac some rare exception and the other riders also clean? French team manager Bidot later said that he believed that three-fourths of the riders in the 1950's were doped.

Across the Massif Central, on the way to the Pyrenees, the General Classification stayed stable except for Gaul, who slipped from fifth place, at 12 minutes, to ninth at 14 minutes. By the end of stage 16 with the first Pyreneen stage the next day, the General Classification stood thus:

1. Antonin Rolland
2. Louison Bobet @ 4 minutes 53 seconds
3. Pasquale Fornara @ 6 minutes 18 seconds
4. Jean Brankart @ 10 minutes 44 seconds
5. Raphaël Géminiani @ 12 minutes 20 seconds

6. Giancarlo Astrua @ 12 minutes 44 seconds

7. Wim Van Est @ 12 minutes 50 seconds

8. Vincent Vitetta @ 13 minutes 56 seconds

9. Charly Gaul @ 14 minutes

10. Alex Close @ 18 minutes 41 seconds

Stages 17 and 18 were the pair of mountain stages that would probably settle the 1955 Tour. Stage 17 went over the Aspin and the Peyresourde on the way to St. Gaudens. As expected, Gaul attacked on the Aspin. He had no problems with the heat, it was a rainy day. Bobet went after the fleeing Luxembourger on the Peyresourde. He couldn't catch him, especially after a flat tire. But he did get close enough. Gaul won the 249-kilometer stage after 7 ¹/₂ hours of racing, with Bobet only 1 minute, 24 seconds behind. Astrua, Géminiani, Brankart, Lorono and Ockers were 3 minutes, 18 seconds back. Rolland followed in at almost 9 minutes with Bauvin and Wagtmans. Bobet was now in Yellow with Rolland 3 minutes behind. Bobet said that he had "seized the race".

Stage 18 with the Tourmalet and Aubisque allowed Bobet to put his hold on the Tour into the "barring misfortune" category. Brankart won the stage with Bobet, Gaul and Géminiani finishing with him at the same time. With the climbing done, the overall standings must have looked good to Bobet:

1. Louison Bobet

2. Antonin Rolland @ 6 minutes 4 seconds

3. Charly Gaul @ 7 minutes 43 seconds

4. Jean Brankart @ 7 minutes 45 seconds

5. Raphaël Géminiani @ 10 minutes 21 seconds

There remained the usual challenge to icing the victory, the final individual time trial. Bobet's seat was on constant fire. The inflamed boil made it so that he was barely able to sit in the saddle. The stage 21 time trial was 68.6 kilometers that must have been pure hell for Bobet. He was in no condition to win the stage, but he held the day's winner, Brankart, to only 1 minute, 52 seconds. Bobet had enough time in hand to concede that much. Now there was only the promenade to Paris. Bobet had matched and exceeded Philippe Thys: both had won 3 Tours, but only Bobet had won 3 in a row.

Final 1955 Tour de France General Classification:

1. Louison Bobet (France): 130 hours 29 minutes 26 seconds
2. Jean Brankart (Belgium) @ 4 minutes 53 seconds
3. Charly Gaul (Luxembourg) @ 11 minutes 30 seconds
4. Pasquale Fornara (Italy) @ 12 minutes 44 seconds
5. Antonin Rolland (France) @ 13 minutes 18 seconds

Climber's Competition:

1. Charly Gaul: 84 points
2. Louison Bobet: 70 points
3. Jean Brankart: 44 points

Points Competition:

1. Stan Ockers: 322 points
2. Wout Wagtmans: 399 points
3. Miguel Poblet: 409 points

This was the high point of Bobet's career, although 1954 might be considered the year in which he was at his competitive best. By 1955, Bobet had become a masterful and complete rider. He had won many of the most important races in the world. They were varied, from time trials to stage races: Milano–San Remo, Tour of Lombardy, Tour of Flanders, the World Championships, Grand Prix des Nations, Tour of Luxembourg as well as the Tour de France. He would win Paris–Roubaix the next year. Bobet's wins were attained while often suffering the debilitating effect of his brittle, dry skin that could break out into painful boils at any time. Bobet believed that the effort of winning the 1955 Tour with terrible sores left him a lesser rider for the rest of his career. Certainly he never again reached the magnificent highs of 1954 and 1955.

His fellow riders, many of whom were put off by both his touchy personality and his high social aspirations, didn't love him. Still, Louison Bobet must be considered one of the greatest riders of all time.

1956. There were no previous Tour winners at the start line of the 1956 edition. With the obvious exception of the first Tour in 1903, the only other time this had happened was in 1927. Bobet had finally agreed to have surgery to repair his boils. Kübler and Koblet were finished as far as Tour competitiveness was concerned. Robic was recovering from yet another accident. With no Tour *Patron*, the race was wide open.

While there was no *Patron*, the 1954 Tour was bright with capable talent. The French National team included Géminiani, Malléjac, Darrigade, Bauvin and Rolland. Each of these men could win the Tour. Italy had Nino Defilippis and a not yet matured Gastone Nencini. Belgium brought Raymond Impanis, Brankart and Ockers. Would this be the year for Wout Wagtmans of Holland who had worn the Yellow Jersey several times, but never in Paris? Spanish climbing wonder Federico Bahamontes would ride, but not for the overall win. The climbing competition seduced him from considering fighting for the Yellow Jersey. Charly Gaul, as usual, was on a weak team of riders from Italy, Portugal, Luxembourg and even Great Britain. That's where Brian Robinson ended up in 1955, on the Luxembourg-Mixte team. That placement was no odder than Ireland's Seamus Elliot riding for the France Ile-de-France regional team. The regional teams were also rich with talent. Remember Roger Walkowiak who got into a long break in 1955? He was on the France Northeast-Center team.

The French team made it clear that this was a Tour up for grabs: after 3 years of riding for Louison Bobet, they had no clear designated leader. They had regressed back to their pre-1953 condition, having several riders possessing great ambition, each hesitant to sacrifice for the others. If there could be a Tour favorite, it was thought to be Charly Gaul. With just 3 stages to go in the just completed Giro, Gaul, down 16 minutes, climbed the Bondone pass in freezing weather. 60 riders abandoned the Giro during that day's horrifically cold stage. But Gaul, who could not take the heat, thrived in cooler weather and spun up the mountain and into the leader's Pink Jersey. Tempering the thought that Gaul was a General Classification threat was the knowledge that both he and Bahamontes were usually willing to let themselves accumulate time losses on the flat stages because they were really interested in the climber's competition.

The 1956 Tour was counter-clockwise (Pyrenees first) with the opening day a trip from Reims in northeastern France to Liège in Belgium. At 4,527 kilometers, it was about the average length of a mid 1950's Tour. As Desgrange's harsh rules regarding bicycle repairs became ever more distant, the Tour now allowed wheel changes in the case of flats instead of requiring the repairing or replacement of the tire. With each of these steps, the element of chance and misfortune was reduced and the Tour became more of an athletic contest. Bobet's 3 successive wins is indicative of this trend. With improving roads, bicycles, training, medicine, diet and rules, an athlete could capitalize upon his physical and mental superiority. The best man could win. As the Tour moves forward there will be an ever increasing tendency of better racers winning consistently.

André Darrigade, the man Géminiani called the greatest French sprinter of all time, won the first stage, beating his 2 breakaway companions, former Yellow Jersey Fritz Schaer and Brian Robinson. 2 days later a 9-man break beat the "cracks" by 15 minutes, and Belgian rider Gilbert Desmet assumed the lead.

Gaul made it clear that he had kept his Giro-winning form when he won the 15-kilometer individual time trial in stage 4a. Given Gaul's indifference to time losses early in the Tour, it was not surprising that he was, after that time-gaining victory, still over 15 minutes behind Desmet. That afternoon a 26-man break arrived over 15 minutes ahead of the field. Making the break were the men who wanted to wear Yellow in Paris: Bauvin, Darrigade, Wagtmans, Nencini, Ockers, Rolland and that man who liked to get into hopeless breaks, Walkowiak. Since Desmet (along with Bahamontes and Gaul) wasn't in the break, Darrigade was again the Tour's leader.

On Stage 7, one of those stupid breaks that the peloton sometimes ignores got away. 31 riders came in 18 minutes, 46 seconds ahead of a Yellow Jersey'd André Darrigade. Ockers, Gaul and Bahamontes were all left behind. In the break were Wagtmans, Bauvin, Desmet, Defilippis and Roger Walkowiak. Walkowiak, by making the earlier stage 4b break and being careful not to lose time elsewhere became the Tour leader. His best-ever previous Tour performance was forty-seventh in the 1953 Tour.

Here was the new General Classification:

1. Roger Walkowiak
2. Fernand Picot @ 1 minute 22 seconds
3. Gilbert Scodeller @ 2 minutes 53 seconds
4. Gerrit Voorting @ 5 minutes 7 seconds

5. Nello Lauredi @ 7 minutes

6. Wout Wagtmans @ 10 minutes 28 seconds

7. Gilbert Desmet @ 10 minutes 38 seconds

8. André Darrigade @ 11 minutes 28 seconds

9. Gilbert Bauvin @ 12 minutes 31 seconds

10. Jan Adriaenssens @ 15 minutes 19 seconds

Walkowiak rode for the France Northeast-Center regional team. He had some good, but unspectacular riders on his team including Adolphe Deledda. The war of personalities that would erupt within the French team was not present in the squad of honest workmen on Walkowiak's team. Walkowiak was stunned by his leadership in the Tour. Like so many other journeymen who have found themselves wearing Yellow for a day, he assumed that he would defend the Jersey for a while before giving it up. The manager of his team had other ideas. He saw that the tall "Walko" had talent and ability, enough of both to win the Tour. He convinced Walkowiak that he could be the victor, and that to do so, he could not wear out himself and his team defending the lead for the next 14 stages. He had to relax a bit and let someone else do the hard work of patrolling the peloton. Meanwhile, Charly Gaul was unworried that he was so far back in the General Classification. He felt that the mountains would give him ample opportunity to make up the time he needed to win.

On the tenth stage Walkowiak let go (or missed) a break containing Voorting, Darrigade, Lauredi and Bauvin. Voorting took over the lead; Darrigade was second at 1 minute, 43 seconds. Walkowiak was now seventh, 9 minutes behind Voorting.

The next day, stage 11, the Tour arrived at the Pyrenees. First on the menu was a 255-kilometer stage from Bayonne to Pau with the Aubisque climb. Darrigade proved he was more than just a sprinter, that he had real depth, when he was able to finish in the front group that contained almost all of the best Tour riders, including Gaul, Ockers, Bahamontes and Walkowiak. Walkowiak was still seventh, but was now 7 minutes back. The next day with the Aspin and the Peyresourde was too much for both Darrigade and Wagtmans; both lost over 14 minutes. Belgian Jan Adriaenssens was the new leader and Walkowiak remained seventh, now 5 minutes, 40 seconds back.

The last Pyreneen stage didn't change things with 49 riders finishing together. Missing from this front group were the feuding Bauvin and Darrigade. The split French team gave the opportunistic Walkowiak an opening. Darrigade and Bauvin sat sixth and seventh, Bauvin 30 seconds behind Darrigade. Bauvin had lost time in a fall in the Pyrenees or he surely would have been higher in the standings. Adriaenssens retained the lead. He kept it until stage 15 when he finished almost 9 minutes behind the main field, when the entire Belgian team came down with food poisoning. Only one of their suffering team, André Vlayen, actually had to retire that day. Again Wagtmans was the leader. Walkowiak was now fifth, 4 minutes, 27 seconds behind Wagtmans.

At the end of stage 16, before the Alpine stages, the General Classification stood thus:

1. Wout Wagtmans
2. Nello Lauredi @ 1 minute 33 seconds
3. Gerrit Voorting @ 2 minutes 27 seconds
4. Fernand Picot @ 3 minutes 25 seconds
5. Roger Walkowiak @ 4 minutes 27 seconds
6. André Darrigade @ 5 minutes 58 seconds
7. Gilbert Bauvin @ 6 minutes 33 seconds

The stage 17 road from Gap to Turin went over the Izoard, the Montgenèvre and Sestriere climbs. The lead group of 17 finishers contained Bauvin, Ockers, Wagtmans, Walkowiak, Gaul, Bahamontes and Adriaenssens. But it did not have Lauredi, Voorting or Darrigade. Wagtmans was still in the lead and Walkowiak was now second at his same 4 minutes, 27 seconds. Bauvin was third, his time also unchanged at 6 minutes, 33 seconds.

Stage 18 crossed Mont Cenis, the Croix de Fer and the Luitel. The climbing specialists, down on time in the General Classification knew they had only this stage to regain any real time. So far the others had been able to neutralize the climbers' efforts to create large time gaps in the mountain stages. Now Bahamontes, Gaul and Ockers put the field under serious pressure. At the start of the final climb most of the real contenders were still together. Gaul took flight, separating himself from even Bahamontes. Walkowiak stuck with the Spaniard and managed to come in with Bahamontes and Gastone Nencini, 7 minutes, 29 seconds behind Gaul. That was good company and good enough for the Yellow Jersey.

Wagtmans came in 30th, in Raphaël Géminiani's group. They were 15 minutes, 38 seconds behind Gaul and about 8 minutes behind Walkowiak. In looking back years later, Wagtmans found his collapse that day inexplicable. He expected to find the going tough in the Alps but, excepting the specialists like Gaul, he was as fine a climber as any alive at the time. He was just without the power he needed that crucial day in order to finally cinch the Yellow Jersey. Bauvin was less than 2 minutes behind the Bahamontes group. He was now second to Walkowiak at 3 minutes, 56 seconds.

Bahamontes gave his team a scare on the Col de Luitel. Overcome by bad morale he dismounted and threw his bike down the ravine. The bike was retrieved and the brilliant but difficult Spaniard was talked into continuing. He did and, as we saw, came in fourth that day.

Going into the final time trial, stage 20, Walkowiak had a 3 minute, 26 second lead over Gilbert Bauvin. The time trial was almost his undoing. Bauvin rode an excellent crono, coming in fifth, 2 minutes, 37 seconds behind stage winner Miguel Bover. Walkowiak came in twenty-fourth, 4 minutes, 48 seconds behind Bover. His lead in the General Classification was shaved to 1 minute, 25 seconds. He kept that slim lead over the next 2 stages to Paris. When the Tour entered the *Parc des Princes* the crowds jeered with derisive whistles. They wanted one of their heroes to win the Tour, not an unknown from a regional team. To this day, there is the phrase "a la Walko" meaning a win by an undeserving or unknown rider.

Walkowiak was the second man, after Firmin Lambot in 1922, to win the Tour without winning a stage.

Many thought Walkowiak an unworthy winner. He never did anything as well again. He didn't finish the 1955 or the 1957 Tours and came in 75th in 1958. But people who denigrate Walkowiak's win fail to understand the nature of racing. We have a method of determining who is worthy of the Yellow Jersey: it uses a watch. The man with the lowest elapsed time at the end of the race is the winner. If the favorites were too interested in watching each other and let a break go, then they are the unworthy ones. As old Henri Desgrange used to say, bicycle racing is a sport of head and legs. Writers concentrate on Walkowiak's time gain in the one early break. His win was far more than that. He and his manager Ducazeaux carefully laid out a plan to win the Tour and executed it perfectly. They did it during a Tour that was terribly hard. It was the fastest Tour to date at 36.268 kilometers an hour.

Here are Bernard Hinault's words: "There are people who say that Walkowiak should not have won the Tour. They should have been on that Tour! He took the jersey, he lost it and he regained it. Then, he was there every day. No one has the right to say it was given to him. He was not a thief. The Tour is not a gift."

The Tour might not have been a blessing to Walko. He took what he thought to be a dismissal of his victory by the public very hard. The man who had dropped Bobet on the Cote de Laffrey in 1955, when Bobet was at his apogee, and then won the Tour de France the next year never did anything great on his bike again. He owned a bar after retiring from racing but felt that his patrons had nothing good to say about his racing. Unhappy, he went back to working in a factory, unwilling to even discuss his Tour win for years. Only now will he talk about it. What a shame.

A couple of final notes. Team manager Marcel Bidot thought that if André Darrigade had surrendered his ambitions and worked for Gilbert Bauvin, Bauvin would have been able to shave those 85 seconds between first and second place and Bauvin would have been the 1956 Tour winner. Maybe. And if frogs had pockets they could carry guns.

Walkowiak's bike (like Bobet's 1954 and 1955 bikes) had aluminum cotterless cranks but the small, lightweight Gaul still had the heavier steel cottered cranks.

Final 1956 Tour de France General Classification:

1. Roger Walkowiak (North-East Central): 124 hours 1 minute 16 seconds
2. Gilbert Bauvin (France) @ 1 minute 25 seconds
3. Jan Adriaenssens (Belgium) @ 3 minutes 44 seconds
4. Federico Bahamontes (Spain) @ 10 minutes 14 seconds
5. Nino Defilippis (Italy) @ 10 minutes 25 seconds
6. Wout Wagtmans (Holland) @ 10 minutes 59 seconds

Climber's Competition:

    1. Charly Gaul: 71 points

    2. Federico Bahamontes: 67 points

    3. Valentin Huot: 65 points

Points Competition:

    1. Stan Ockers: 280 points

    2. Fernand Picot: 464 points

    3. Gerrit Voorting: 465 points

Chapter 8

1957–1964. The Jacques Anquetil Years.
Perhaps the most original and interesting man
in the history of cycling becomes
the first 5-time winner

1957. With the 1957 Tour, a new era begins, the age of Jacques Anquetil. Before proceeding, it would be good to take a look at the extraordinary, yet independent, strangely selfish and wholly original man. His personality and talents will color the Tour for years to come.

From the beginning, he could turn a huge gear with a beautiful style. In fact, his smooth, effortless manner was what most writers of the age find so appealing about Anquetil. At only 19 he won his first Grand Prix des Nations—the unofficial world championship of time trialing—beating second place Roger Creton by 6 minutes, 41 seconds on a 140-kilometer course.

While Roger Walkowiak was winning the 1956 Tour, Anquetil—at the ripe old age of 22—was busy setting a new World Hour Record. He raised it to 46.159 kilometers beating Coppi's 45.798 kilometers set in 1942. Jacques Anquetil entered the Tour 8 times and was the first 5-time winner, riding the Tour in his own special, economical style.

Anquetil was a master time-trialist. His list of wins is heavily weighted towards this specialty. He won the Grand Prix des Nations 9 times, including a run of 6 in a row between 1953 and 1958. He wasn't quite the dominating presence in the Barrachi Trophy 2-man time trial.

The trading of pace in a 2-man effort doesn't involve the same sustained, perfectly controlled effort. Nonetheless, his record is enviable: 3 victories, 5 seconds and 1 third.

His ability to gain substantial time in a time trial allowed him to ride stage races with an economy denied the others. He had the privilege of riding defensively in the mountains. It was said of him that no rider could drop him, yet he could drop no rider. It comes down to the fact that he usually just did not have to attack on the climbs. He could preserve his standings in General Classification in the mountains, often just keeping it within reach. He would then pour all of his strength into the time trial where he was almost invulnerable.

He was tactically astute, always aware of the relative position of each of the danger men; he never put out any more effort than was absolutely necessary. This sort of riding lost him the love of the French who valued "*La Gloire.*" Glory, panache and élan were expected of a great French champion, not cold calculation.

The 1957 Tour was clockwise (Alps first) and at 4,664 kilometers was about 140 kilometers longer than the 1956 edition.

In the mid to late 1950's, France was brimming with talent. The 1957 national squad included last year's winner, Roger Walkowiak, André Darrigade, future world champion Jean Stablinski, Gilbert Bauvin and Jean Forestier. At the last moment Anquetil, only 23 years old, was added to the team.

Louison Bobet chose not to ride. He had fought an all-out war in the Giro just a few weeks before that left him exhausted. He had worn the leader's Pink Jersey for a total of 9 days, trading it with Gaul, Rolland, Defilippis and the eventual winner, Gastone Nencini. Bobet, unable to fend off the Italians intent upon winning their own Tour, missed winning the Giro by only 19 seconds. Raphaël Géminiani chose not to ride the Tour as well. There seem to be hints that he did not want to ride as a *domestique* on a team that would be dominated by Walkowiak, Darrigade and the young Anquetil. It was assumed that Walkowiak would be the main protected rider on the team, but he did not come to the Tour in top form.

The biggest challenge to the French machine would come either from the Italians with their Giro winner Gastone Nencini or the Luxembourg team's Charly Gaul. Spain's erratic climber Federico Bahamontes entered, but as usual, with his concentration fixed upon the climber's prize, he was an unlikely threat to the overall. The race was the French team's to lose.

The French tried to keep the Yellow Jersey a private affair. For the second year in a row André Darrigade won the first stage and the year's first Yellow Jersey. Teammate René Privat won the second stage in blisteringly hot weather and assumed the lead. It was said that until the 1957 Tour, the one run in 1947 was the hottest on record. 1957's heat crushed the riders. Beginning with the second stage, the riders started to withdraw in surprisingly large numbers. Among the second stage abandons were Belgium's Alex Close, Luxembourg's Charly Gaul and 9 others. More than one observer has remarked that amphetamines, the 1950's drug of choice, made it difficult for many riders to take the heat. We can't know if this was the main reason for the withdrawals, but with at least three quarters of the mid-1950's peloton using the stimulant, it must at least have been a contributing factor.

The French demonstrated their strength by winning the next day's team time trial.

That same day the Tour rode 134 kilometers across northern France from Caen to Anquetil's hometown, Rouen. On this stage 3b Anquetil got into a break of 14 riders that contained Bahamontes, Nencini and Walkowiak. Anquetil won the stage as the break came in 7 minutes, 24 seconds ahead of the field. Anquetil had a way to go to get to the top of General Classification, at this point led by his teammate Privat, but he was in the right place in his first Tour.

It was on the fifth stage from Roubaix to Charleroi that Anquetil showed that he had power beyond what his youth might promise. On a rainy day Anquetil was the main engine of a break that included his teammate Bauvin and 3 other riders. They held off a hard-charging chasing group that closed to within 2 minutes of them at the end of the stage. Most of the rest of the field took another quarter of an hour to finish. Notably missing from the first two groups were Walkowiak, Bahamontes, Nencini and Darrigade. The blond time-trialist from Normandy was now the leader of the Tour de France and had dealt many of his challengers a hard blow.

The General Classification after stage 5:

1. Jacques Anquetil
2. Marcel Janssens @ 1 minute 1 second

3. Jean Forestier @ 3 minutes 17 seconds

4. René Privat @ 3 minutes 29 seconds

5. Roger Walkowiak @ 3 minutes 52 seconds

6. Max Schellenberg @ 4 minutes 9 seconds

For a day the French let regional rider Nicolas Barone take the Yellow when a break of non-contenders got away on stage 7 into Colmar. That was quickly corrected the next day. Jean Forestier found himself in a break of 16 that opened a gap of over 17 minutes. Forestier (1955 Paris–Roubaix and 1956 Tour of Flanders winner) was a solid rider who was firmly in Yellow. The new General Classification:

1. Jean Forestier

2. Fernand Picot @ 5 minutes 4 seconds

3. Wim Van Est @ 11 minutes 54 seconds

4. Jacques Anquetil @ 14 minutes 28 seconds

Anquetil again showed that despite his extreme youth, his energy was not flagging under the demands of a major stage race. He won the stage 9 sprint when 10 riders left the field over 10 minutes behind. Forestier was still in Yellow but Anquetil was now in second place, only $2\,^1/_2$ minutes back. Anquetil was savvy. Often before hard climbing stages racers will try to dose their efforts in order to be fresh for the mountains. There was a rest day after stage 9, so Anquetil had a day to recover from a hard day's work before the real test began in the Alps.

Bahamontes abandoned even before the climbing began. With Coppi gone from the Tour scene, perhaps it's good to have an enigma in our drama. Bahamontes fills that requirement very well. The stories differ as to exactly why he dropped out. It was clear that at this point his morale, always fragile, was terrible. His friend Miguel Poblet had abandoned on stage 4. Bahamontes had a boil on his arm that made it hard for him to ride. He thought he should be the team's sole protected rider, not Jesus Lorono. The abandonment was probably for all these reasons. In 1956 he threw his bike down a ravine when he tried, unsuccessfully, to quit. This year, to make his feeling extra-clear, "Baha" took off his shoes and threw them down the ravine. No amount of begging from his teammates or his manager could get him to resume racing. He took the first available train back to Spain.

Stage 10 had the riders cross the Tamié and the huge Galibier.

The attacks came on the lower slopes of the Galibier. Nencini got clear with several others. It seems that the occasional lassitude that would sometimes overcome Anquetil let him become unconcerned about the break up the road containing Nencini. When the gap grew to over 5 minutes, team manger Bidot urged Anquetil to close the gap to the man who had just taken the Giro from Bobet. Anquetil did chase and nearly caught Nencini, failing by only 1 minute, 1 second. Anquetil was now firmly in the lead.

Neither of the next 2 mountain stages presented any challenge to Anquetil's lead. So, after stage 12 the Tour rolled across southern France and then to Barcelona in Spain. Before the Pyrenees, Anquetil looked to be having a wonderful first Tour:

1. Jacques Anquetil
2. Jean Forestier @ 4 minutes 2 seconds
3. Marcel Janssens @ 11 minutes 2 seconds
4. Fernand Picot @ 11 minutes 50 seconds
5. Wim Van Est @ 13 minutes 57 seconds

Again, just before a mountain stage, Anquetil took the opportunity to deliver another blow to those who had hopes to wear Yellow in Paris. Normally the Tour would have scheduled the Saturday in Barcelona as a rest day. Instead, a short 9.8-kilometer individual time trial in Montjuich was run. This was raw meat for the finest time trialist of the era, perhaps the greatest ever. Anquetil was able to put another 12 seconds between himself and Forestier in case there were any doubts as to who the strongest rider on the French team really was. Janssens, Picot and Van Est were tossed from the higher General Classification standing.

The first day in the Pyrenees took in the Puymorens mountain on the road back into France. Anquetil lost a few seconds to Forestier. The biggest occurrence of the day was the tragedy of the famous cycling reporter Alex Virot. He was sitting on the back of a motorcycle when it apparently lost control on a rocky dirt road. Both the driver, René Wagner, and Virot died after crashing at the bottom of a ravine. This was Wagner's only accident in his entire driving career.

The seventeenth stage, 236 kilometers from Ax les Thermes to St. Gaudens was a real bear of a stage, containing the Portet d'Aspet, the Portillon and the Port. For the first time Anquetil, who was a capable but not brilliant climber, came under pressure. Notably Nencini and the Belgian Jan Adriaenssens tried to see if the young Norman would fold. The French team rallied around him and in the end Anquetil finished only 5 seconds behind the winner, Nino Defilippis. Nencini crashed and finished eighteenth, right behind Walkowiak. Clearly, "Walko" didn't have whatever it was he had the year before.

The next day was another classic Pyreneen stage with both the Tourmalet and the Aubisque on the day's menu. Anquetil was clearly feeling extraordinarily good, at least at the start. He took off on the Tourmalet. He missed getting his feed bag and by the time he got on the Soulor (just next to the Aubisque) he was out of food and energy. Other riders, including the bandaged Nencini, passed Anquetil. Late in the stage he got help and managed to finish only 2 1/2 minutes behind the front group. He was still in control with a healthy lead.

After stage 19, with the climbing finished, here were the General Classification standings:

1. Jacques Anquetil
2. Marcel Janssens @ 9 minutes 14 seconds
3. Adolf Christian @ 10 minutes 17 seconds
4. Jean Forestier @ 12 minutes 59 seconds
5. Jesus Lorono @ 16 minutes 3 seconds
6. Gastone Nencini @ 18 minutes 43 seconds

Anquetil's strategic position was better than it looked. 2 days later in the 66-kilometer individual time trial, Anquetil showed no mercy. The stage results:

1. Jacques Anquetil: 1 hour 32 minutes 17 seconds
2. Nino Defilippis @ 2 minutes 11 seconds
3. Wim Van Est @ 2 minutes 56 seconds
4. Jesus Lorono @ 3 minutes 14 seconds
5. Jean Forestier @ 4 minutes 3 seconds

André Darrigade won the final 2 stages. The French team had exhibited a dominance that they had not known since the days of André Leducq and Antonin Magne in the early 1930's.

The French national team won the Yellow Jersey, 13 stages, the

Green Points Jersey and the competition for the best team. They had held the Yellow Jersey for every day of the Tour but 1. It wasn't an easy Tour: only 56 of the 120 starters made it to Paris.

Final 1957 Tour de France General Classification:

1. Jacques Anquetil (France): 135 hours 44 minutes 42 seconds
2. Marcel Janssens (Belgium) @ 14 minutes 56 seconds
3. Adolf Christian (Austria) @ 17 minutes 20 seconds
4. Jean Forestier (France) @ 18 minutes 2 seconds
5. Jesus Lorono (Spain) @ 20 minutes 17 seconds
6. Gastone Nencini (Italy) @ 26 minutes 3 seconds

Climber's competition:

1. Gastone Nencini: 44 points
2. Louis Bergaud: 43 points
3. Marcel Janssens: 32 points

Points competition:

1. Jean Forestier: 301 points
2. Wim Van Est: 317 points
3. Adolf Christian: 366 points

1958. This was one of the most emotional and dramatic Tours in history. As we've seen in past Tours, the selection of the French team can sometimes profoundly affect the Tour more by who is left off the team than who is put on. By dint of his clear superiority in the 1957 Tour, Anquetil was in a position to dictate with whom he would ride. He didn't want both Louison Bobet and Raphaël Géminiani on the team, two good friends working together, possibly threatening his supremacy. One or the other, but not both. Team manager Marcel Bidot acquiesced and chose Bobet, the man who had given him 3 Tours and had won many of the most important races in the world.

Géminiani was never afraid to speak his mind and this offense gave no exception. He was enraged. He felt that he had given his all to the French team for years, constantly sacrificing himself for others. He said he was "dismissed without a care". The man nicknamed by Bobet "*le gran fusil*"—literally, "the long rifle" but perhaps we might say "top gun"—plotted his revenge.

Géminiani was placed on the France Center-Midi regional team. This was not a band of talentless racers who were not up to the task of contesting a Tour de France. They were iron-hard pros who could really help: Antonin Rolland, Henry Anglade, Jean Dotto and Jean Graczyk, among others. Experienced Tour rider Adolphe Deledda was the director. Géminiani declared that he would ride for victory. This was war.

Anquetil's team had Bobet, of course. The rest of the team was mostly the same veterans Bidot has used in previous Tours: Bauvin, Privat, Walkowiak, Darrigade and Mahé. One should be able to expect great things from these men.

Charly Gaul was put on a Holland/Luxembourg combination team that even had an Italian added for good measure. Again, Gaul was mostly on his own. Gaul exacerbated his problem of minimal team support. Feeling that he didn't have a unified, capable team behind him he refused to share his winnings. His teammates, professionals after all who were riding for a living, responded in kind through their lack of commitment to the small climber. In addition, teammates like Wim Van Est and Gerrit Voorting had their own ambitions and had no plans to sacrifice themselves for Gaul.

The Italian threat was growing as they rebuilt after the Coppi/Bartali/Magni years of the late 1940's and early 1950's. Gastone Nencini and Vito Favero were worthy racers whom all the teams had to respect, this year more than ever.

The 1958 Tour was a bit shorter at 4,319 kilometers going counter-clockwise (Pyrenees first). It had 23 stages with no rest days, a schedule that would not be allowed under current rules. To honor the World's Fair, the first stage was scheduled to depart from Brussels. A fan had given Géminiani a donkey as a present. For his first shot in his new war Géminiani named it Marcel and at the World's Fair gave it to French team manager Bidot, making sure that the occasion was photographed to maximize the humiliation.

For the third year in a row André Darrigade won the first stage and the Yellow Jersey. As the Tour raced across northern France Gilbert Bauvin again found himself the leader, this time after the fifth stage. Nencini, Anquetil and the very motivated and angry Géminiani were tied with the same time, about 7 minutes behind Bauvin. Bobet was doing 30 seconds better than the trio.

Bobet and Géminiani riding together in stage 5.

During stage 6, from Caen to St. Brieuc in Brittany, the Long Rifle fired his first big round and hit the bulls-eye. He drove a break that had Favero and Henry Anglade in it to a huge winning margin. The main group containing Darrigade, Gaul, Nencini, Anquetil, Bahamontes and Bobet were beaten by almost 11 minutes. Gem had done himself a world of good and boosted himself to third place.

The overall standings after stage 6:

1. Gerrit Voorting

2. François Mahé @ 1 minute

3. Raphaël Géminiani @ 2 minutes 32 seconds

Neither Bobet nor Anquetil were enjoying good health. For now the domestique Mahé was the best defender of the French interests.

The next day Brian Robinson made history by being the first British rider to win a stage. He sprinted against the Italian Arrigo Padovan but Padovan, who was first across the line, was relegated to second place for irregular sprinting. Robinson was again on a hodge-podge team, this time a group called "Internations". His teammates were Irish (Seamus Elliot), Portuguese, Austrian, Danish as well as British.

Stage 8 was a 46-kilometer individual time trial at Chateaulin, near Brest in western Brittany. It was raining. A day of bad weather was perfect for Charly Gaul and terrible for the ill Anquetil. The small, almost fragile looking Gaul put in an astonishing performance by winning the undulating stage, beating the master of the discipline by 7 seconds. Gaul was clearly in fine form. He was third in the Giro that year, notably finishing 3 1/2 minutes ahead of Bobet and 4 1/2 ahead of Nencini. Gaul's effort in the time trial had lifted him to fifteenth place in the General Classification, still almost 11 minutes behind Voorting.

Since we were discussing the Giro, a story must be told because Géminiani was not the only angry rider at the Tour in 1958. Charly Gaul had developed an active dislike for Bobet. During the 1957 Giro several riders including Bobet, Gaul and Nencini stopped to urinate. Bobet and Nencini remounted and rode by Gaul, then the current leader of the Giro, who was still busy answering nature. In Géminiani's words, Gaul "made an indecent gesture with his organ of virility" at Bobet. The Giro erupted into a fury as the insulted Bobet drove the group of leaders hard and left Gaul in the dust. Gaul lost the Pink Jersey to Nencini that day. The next day Bobet set out to take the lead from Nencini. Bobet's team attacked early, taking Nencini and Gaul with them. Nencini was dropped because of a flat tire and Bobet took the opportunity to press on and gain time. Gaul sat up and waited for Nencini. He paced him up the remaining climbs preferring to sacrifice his own placing rather than let Bobet win the Giro. With Gaul's help Nencini was able to conserve enough time to save his lead. The entire effort left Bobet too exhausted to ride the 1957 Tour and deepened an already poisonous enmity.

In stage 9 André Darrigade was in a break of 7 riders that beat a compact field to the finish in St. Nazaire by close to 10 minutes. The Yellow Jersey returned to the very fleet Darrigade. Also in the winning break and having his fortunes greatly improved was the Italian Vito Favero. He was now second, 23 seconds behind Darrigade. Géminiani was sixth at 1 minute, 47 seconds and Anquetil was distant thirteenth place, over 10 minutes back. Darrigade and the others maintained these positions as the Tour made its way down southeastern France.

All the while, Géminiani kept up his infernal war on the peloton and especially the French national team. When the very dangerous Nencini was in a threatening break the French team asked Géminiani and his men for help. Gem replied, "There must be something wrong with your eyes. Can't you see the color of my jersey [light blue]? Not the same as yours [tricolor] is it? Sorry. You'll have to do your own chasing." Remember this episode, it will matter later. His non-stop aggression worried Bobet. Bobet warned that Géminiani was riding powerfully, as well as he had ever ridden in his career. Moreover he had new-found ambition to win. His team had good morale and was also riding well.

The first day in the Pyrenees involved an assault on the Aubisque. Stage 13 was 230 wet, drizzly kilometers from Dax to Pau. This was the kind of weather that let Charly Gaul excel. Bahamontes was the first of the big men to go on the Aubisque. But because it was a long way to Pau after the Aubisque and the poor descending Bahamontes would take a long time to get off the mountain, the others let him go. The main group of contenders followed at their own pace up the Aubisque for a while and then watched Gaul fly away from them. Again, like Bahamontes, he would surely be caught on the way to Pau.

It worked out that way. Géminiani, Anquetil, Gaul, Bahamontes, Bobet and Bauvin finished together, 3 minutes behind a breakaway duo of Louis Bergaud and Piet Damen. Géminiani, who had been careful to maintain a good General Classification position the entire run-in to the mountains, was now the Yellow Jersey. Favero was a very close second, only 3 seconds behind.

The next day was another day of climbing with the Aspin and Peyresourde. Bahamontes again flew away at the first opportunity. This time he made his solo effort stick, coming in 2 minutes ahead of the leading group of hopefuls. Favero led in Gaul, Géminiani, Anquetil, Nencini, Bobet and Bauvin. Favero's second place that day gave him a 30-second time bonus and the Yellow Jersey. Géminiani was now second at 27 seconds.

The final Pyreneen stage with the Portet d'Aspet changed little except that Favero again managed to get second and therefore extend his lead over Géminiani to 57 seconds.

Stage 18, a 21.5-kilometer individual time trial up Mount Ventoux upset the applecart. Gaul had, as usual, let himself bleed time on the flats, always confident that he could make the time up in the mountains. After the Pyrenees he was sitting in eighth place, 10 minutes, 41 seconds behind Favero. He unleashed a wonderful ride, beating Bahamontes by a half-minute. Anquetil finished 4 minutes behind Gaul, Géminiani and Bobet were 5 minutes back. But Géminiani had the Yellow Jersey again. And now, for the first time in his career, Gaul was a true threat to win the Tour de France. The Alps started the next day. The new General Classification:

1. Raphaël Géminiani
2. Vito Favero @ 2 minutes 1 second
3. Charly Gaul @ 3 minutes 43 seconds

The next day things again went Gem's way. He finished in the lead quartet with Nencini, Anquetil and Adriaenssens when the race went over several second and third category climbs. Gaul had mechanical problems and was forced to chase in the heat, which he detested, and lost 11 minutes. Favero's loss of 46 seconds meant that Géminiani now had over 3 minutes on the Italian. Gaul was a distant eighth at over 15 minutes.

Stage 20 out of the year's 24 arrived and still Géminiani seemed to be having the ride of his life. Like Kübler in 1950, Géminiani abandoned his emotional, intuitive style and became a careful, calculating rider. Already possessing a superb tactical mind, he had no intention of letting this chance of a lifetime slip away. From Gap the race went over the Vars and the Izoard to Briançon. Unsurprisingly, Bahamontes was the first man to finish. Géminiani beat Gaul by 21 seconds and Favero by 30. Gaul had been saving everything for these Alpine stages yet seemed to be shooting blanks at the Top Gun. Now there were only 4 stages left. The next stage, number 21, went over the mountainous Chartreuse Massif in the southeastern corner of France. Géminiani had only a time trial and then Paris. Victory and revenge, both of which seemed likely at this point, would be sweet.

The first of the remaining obstacles was that brutal 219-kilometer, 5-mountain stage 21 from Briançon to Aix les Bains. Gaul knew that this was his last chance. The first climb, the Lautaret, didn't break things up, the front men remained together. On the way down the first mountain the weather turned nasty with cold rain. This was Charly Gaul weather. The next climb was the Luitel. Gaul was gone in a flash. He had planned his attack and made no secret of what he intended to do. He used this stage to get revenge on Louison Bobet for whom, as you remember, Gaul had a flaming hatred. Before the start of the stage, Gaul told Bobet that he would attack on this second climb of the day. He even told him which switchback. Gaul knew that Bobet could be subject to complex self-doubts and played upon them to magnify his revenge.

Géminiani, like all experienced Grand Tour riders, knew that the fastest way to failure can be to let an opponent dictate the pace of the race on his own best turf. Gem knew he could not match the dancing, small-gear twirling Gaul as he raced up the mountain in the cold weather he preferred. Géminiani, an excellent climber in his own right, set out to limit the damage. Anquetil tried to lead the chase, but ran out of gas. Bobet tried to help but he was physically and mentally broken that day. On rode the little Luxembourger in shorts and short sleeves, his cloth cap turned backwards, his hands on the tops grasping the levers.

Tired, wet and cold, Géminiani's judgment, usually his best weapon, failed him. He called on the now shattered French team to help him chase. They were of no use and probably wouldn't have helped him anyway. He passed by the feed station without taking on food, forgetting that on a cold mountain stage energy stores get used up very quickly. He had a needless repair done to his bike. He lost time and then energy as his glycogen stores ran out. On he slogged in the horrible weather, mostly alone, realizing the terrible nature of his situation.

At the end of the stage second-place Favero came in 10 minutes after Gaul finished, Géminiani was down 14 minutes, Nencini 19. Most of the riders death-marched solo or in groups of 2 or 3. Darrigade lost 47 minutes. Gaul had enough time to change into clean clothes before the others arrived.

And Géminiani whose morale had been so high and looked to be the year's winner? He collapsed into the arms of his handlers shouting, "Judas!" at Bobet and the French team. Somehow, in his fury, he

Charly Gaul on the way to a monumental stage victory.

expected the formerly disdained French team to come to his rescue. Even if they wanted to, no one was going to catch Charly Gaul that day. The conditions were considered so extraordinary management didn't enforce the time limits for elimination of riders. Géminiani lost the Yellow Jersey. The new General Classification was tight, indeed:

1. Vito Favero
2. Raphaël Géminiani @ 39 seconds
3. Charly Gaul @ 1 minute 7 seconds

It all came down to the 23rd stage, the penultimate day of the 1958 Tour de France. Anquetil, very ill with pulmonary congestion, didn't start the day's 74-kilometer individual time trial. Gaul had already shown that he was the 1958 Tour's fastest man against the clock by winning the 2 previous time trials. He didn't disappoint. He was able to beat both Favero and Géminiani by over 3 minutes and therefore take the lead. The best-placed French team rider was Bobet at eighth place, over a half-hour behind Gaul. With only the final stage into Paris left, Charly Gaul, the man most experts think the greatest climber of all time, had finally won the Tour de France.

The final day's run in to Paris was marred by a terrible accident. As the sprinters wound it up on the *Parc des Princes* velodrome, Darrigade ran into the boss of the velodrome who stepped onto the track. Darrigade was able to finish the stage and needed only a few stitches. The unlucky official, Constans Wouters, died 11 days later.

Final 1958 Tour de France General Classification:

1. Charly Gaul (Holland-Luxembourg): 116 hours 59 minutes 5 seconds
2. Vito Favero (Italy) @ 3 minutes 10 seconds
3. Raphaël Géminiani (Center-Midi) @ 3 minutes 41 seconds
4. Jan Adriaenssens (Belgium) @ 7 minutes 16 seconds
5. Gastone Nencini (Italy) @ 13 minutes 33 seconds
6. Jozef Planckaert (Belgium) @ 28 minutes 1 second
7. Louison Bobet (France) @ 31 minutes 39 seconds
8. Federico Bahamontes (Spain) @ 40 minutes 44 seconds

Climber's Competition:

1. Federico Bahamontes: 79 points
2. Charly Gaul: 64 points
3. Jean Dotto: 34 points

Points Competition:

1. Jean Graczyk: 347 points
2. Jozef Planckaert: 406 points
3. André Darrigade: 553 points

This would be a good time to look at what might be the most important change to racing that occurred in the 1950's: the introduction of "*extra-sportif*" sponsors. Until the 1950s bicycle and bicycle component manufacturers sponsored racers. This severely limited the income of racers, as these were generally smaller companies. Sometimes a racer would get only a bike, clothes and his room and board paid. For income he often depended upon race prizes. Even successful racers had to keep turning the pedals in lots of races in order to gain a decent income. Lance Armstrong's limited racing schedule would have been an impossible luxury to a pre-war rider. In the post-war years the bicycle factories found themselves competing more and more with motorcycle and car companies as Europe grew increasingly prosperous. As the fortunes of the bike industry started to head downhill racers were offered contracts that were sometimes almost a third lower than what they had been making in the early 1950's. In 1954 Fiorenzo Magni's bike sponsor could no longer meet the expenses of the team. Magni approached the Nivea cosmetics company. It seemed an odd combination, the rugged-looking, balding Magni selling face cream, but it worked. While there had been a small team in Britain with a non-cycling sponsor, Magni was a 3-time Giro winner, 3-time Tour of Flanders victor in consecutive years, and had worn Yellow. Magni had brought extra-sportif money into mainstream cycling. This was a dramatic change and the cycling establishment fought it, wanting to preserve their monopoly on racing sponsorship. *Extra-sportif* sponsors would only make racing publicity more expensive.

Géminiani completed the change. He had been riding "Géminiani" bikes made for him by Mercier and other firms. After he retired from racing in 1960 he continued to equip pro teams to promote his bikes. In 1962 he acquired the backing of the "St. Raphaël" aperitif company for his own team which at that time had Jacques Anquetil on its roster. That 1962 St. Raphaël team is considered the first professional team that was mainly financed by a firm outside the cycling industry. The St. Raphaël team paradoxically didn't ride Géminiani's bikes. Instead they rode Halyett cycles, the bikes that Anquetil rode to his first 3 Tour victories. Before long Ford and a host of other large firms would join in sponsoring professional racing teams.

1959. Oh, this one is interesting. In 1958 the French had been vexed with both the consequences of their team selection and the poor health of their protected riders, Anquetil and Bobet. This year the French would ride poorly, even displaying a willingness to lose rather than let the wrong Frenchman win.

The 1959 Tour, at 4,358 kilometers and 22 stages was about the usual length for a Tour of that era. It was counter-clockwise, Pyrenees first, Central Massif, then Alps.

Let's look at the important teams because in this Tour personalities reign supreme.

France: Jacques Anquetil, Louison Bobet, Robert Cazala, Raphaël Géminiani (impossible to leave off the team after his 1958 performance), André Darrigade, René Privat and Roger Rivière were the backbone of the 12-man French effort.

A month before the start of the Tour Anquetil had suffered a crushing loss in the Giro. He had been trading the leader's Pink Jersey with Charly Gaul throughout much of the Giro and was in the lead going into the penultimate stage. That day included the Grand St. Bernard, the Forclaz and the Petit St. Bernard climbs. As in the 1956 Giro and the 1958 Tour, Gaul unleashed a magnificent 1-stage effort that put the race in his hands. This time Gaul's superb climbing over a stage that took 9 $1/_2$ hours to complete left Anquetil almost 10 minutes behind. Gaul won the Giro with a 6 minute, 12 second final lead over Anquetil.

Roger Rivière was a second year pro who had no prestigious stage race wins. He was, however, 2-time World Professional Pursuit Champion and had, that previous September, eclipsed Anquetil's World Hour Record. Team manager Marcel Bidot faced the same problem that had confounded Alfredo Binda almost a decade before. How to get 2 strong, ambitious personalities to work together for a common goal? Or, as Binda had put it, put a dog and a cat in a sack? Anquetil announced that he was riding for his own victory. How they came to work together reflects badly on both Anquetil and Rivière. And Louison Bobet? He had designs, however unrealistic, on being the first man to win the Tour 4 times.

Spain: Federico Bahamontes had, like his countrymen, been concerned almost entirely with the King of the Mountains (KOM) competition. We've seen that he was, after Gaul, the finest climber alive. Yet his performances were crippled because he was a terrible descender. Bahamontes's obsession with the KOM meant that he was be willing to lose time the whole Tour as long as he was the first to the top of each rated climb. He didn't worry about being caught on the descent or time losses in general throughout a Tour.

In 1959, Bahamontes was signed to ride on the Ticofilina-Coppi team. The great *campionissimo* convinced Bahamontes to consider himself a contender for General Classification victory rather than just going for the King of the Mountains. Somehow, Coppi got through to the erratic Bahamontes. For the first time in 5 attempts this new Bahamontes approached the Tour with an eye towards the Yellow Jersey in Paris.

Holland-Luxembourg: As usual Charly Gaul was placed on a mixed team of Dutchmen and Luxembourgers that ensured that he was on his own and would get little support. Gaul was the reigning Giro winner and had to be considered an extremely formidable challenger. He was a bomb that could go off on any mountain and when he was on form, there was no defense against him.

Italy: 1958's standout Italians Nencini and Favero didn't come. Ercole Baldini, winner of the 1958 Giro was the best of a middling Italian team. Baldini's questionable climbing in a race that would surely feature a shootout between Gaul, Bahamontes and Anquetil made a win for the Italians unlikely.

Belgium: A solid team with proven Tour hard-men: Jan Adriaenssens, Jean Brankart, Jos Hoevenaers, Eddy Pauwels and Jozef Planckaert. Adriaenssens had worn Yellow and placed fourth the year before.

The devil in the details of the lineups was the selection of the regional French teams. Henry Anglade was a capable but not terribly well liked racer. He was easy to leave off the national team. This was to his liking because of the probable instability of a French team that had so many stars and so many egos. It had been years since Manager Bidot had been able to bind (by written contract!) his team to ride for a Bobet who was at one time the finest living stage racer. Prophetically, Anglade was on the Center-Midi team as Géminiani had been the year before.

The Tour started off well enough for the French (by this I mean the national team). For the fourth year in a row André Darrigade won the first stage and the first Yellow Jersey. Things kept going very well for them in the third stage, 217 kilometers from Namur in Belgium to Roubaix. A 10-man break finished with a lead of almost 11 minutes. French team rider Robert Cazala won the sprint and the overall lead. He had a slim 27-second margin over Center-Midi rider Bernard Gauthier.

Rivière fired the first shot in the battle for dominance of the French team in the stage 6 time trial. Rivière won the 43.5-kilometer test that went from Blain to Nantes on France's west coast. Baldini finished 21 seconds behind and Anquetil was almost an entire minute slower. Cazala did well enough in the time trial to enlarge his lead over Gauthier to 1 minute, 27 seconds. Marguerite Lazell writes that Cazala and Bobet were roommates and that Bobet was pleased and untroubled that for now Cazala was keeping the Yellow Jersey in French hands pending Bobet's taking it at an opportune time.

The next day Anglade was in a 12-man break that beat the peloton by almost 5 minutes. It was early days, but Anglade was now the best-placed rider who was not in the stage 3 break, but he was still 6 minutes, 45 seconds behind Cazala.

Stage 9, 207 kilometers from Bordeaux to Bayonne, scrambled the eggs. The Belgians dropped the hammer and the chase was on. Most of the French team went after them but Cazala didn't make it into this important move and finished 74th. Belgian Eddy Pauwels was the new leader. The Tour was now at the foot of the Pyrenees.

The General Classification stood thus:

1. Eddy Pauwels
2. Robert Cazala @ 1 minute 46 seconds
3. Henry Anglade @ 2 minutes 22 seconds
4. Bernard Gauthier @ 3 minutes 13 seconds
5. Jan Adriaenssens @ 3 minutes 22 seconds
6. Jos Hoevenaers @ 3 minutes 32 seconds
7. Roger Rivière @ 3 minutes 38 seconds

With the exception of Cazala, Belgians and regional riders were dominating, occupying the top 6 places.

Pauwels couldn't hope to keep the lead. The next day's trip over the Tourmalet stripped him of the Yellow Jersey when he finished twenty-eighth, almost 15 minutes behind the lead group of 4. A regional rider in the break, Michel Vermeulin, was now the new leader.

The next day, stage 11, went over the Aspin and the Peyresourde. The top riders stayed together leaving the basic standings in place. The race then had a transitional day before the hilly country of the Central Massif.

Stage 13 changed the race. Anglade won the stage (beating Anquetil by a half-wheel) in a break that was initiated by Baldini. Anquetil, Bahamontes, Robinson, Adriaenssens and Mahé were in this very important move. A look at the new General Classification shows how serious this particular escape had been.

1. Jos Hoevenaers
2. Henry Anglade @ 3 minutes 43 seconds
3. François Mahé @ 5 minutes 15 seconds
4. Ercole Baldini @ 7 minutes
5. Federico Bahamontes @ 7 minutes 4 seconds
6. Jacques Anquetil @ 7 minutes 27 seconds
7. Jan Adriaenssens @ 7 minutes 58 seconds
8. Roger Rivière @ 9 minutes 51 seconds

It was becoming clear that Anglade was far more than pack fill. He had almost always been in the right place at the right time. Again, a regional rider was a real threat to win the Tour. In addition, Bahamontes had not let himself bleed big chunks of time during the stages leading to the mountains. He was actually ahead of the two French big men, Anquetil and Rivière. By making it into the stage 13 break Anquetil was $2\,^1/_2$ minutes ahead of his rival Rivière. This stage was tough enough and ridden fast enough that 8 riders were eliminated for finishing outside the time limit. And what about our time bomb, Charly Gaul? This was a very hot day. At the descent of the day's major climb, the Montsalvy, Gaul stopped to put his head in a fountain. He and Bobet both lost 20 minutes that day.

Again the 1959 Tour was turned upside down. This time it was the Puy de Dôme 12.5-kilometer hill-climb time trial. This time Bahamontes was the best climber, beating Gaul by 1 minute, 26 seconds and Anglade by 3 minutes. Hoevenaers kept the lead but things were close:

1. Jos Hoevenaers
2. Federico Bahamontes @ 4 seconds
3. Eddy Pauwels @ 40 seconds

4. Henry Anglade @ 43 seconds

5. François Mahé @ 3 minutes 50 seconds

6. Jacques Anquetil @ 5 minutes 8 seconds

By getting into a break the day before, Pauwels had again lifted himself to a very high placing. Gaul was in a distant fifteenth place, over 23 minutes behind Hoevenaers. In the sixteenth stage Pauwels did it again. He slipped into the winning break and was again in Yellow by 6 seconds.

The final showdown of the race would be in the Alps. Stage 17, from St. Etienne to Grenoble had a pair of category 2 climbs. Bahamontes and Gaul separated themselves from the pack and won by 3 ¹/₂ minutes. Gaul got the stage win, Bahamontes got the Yellow Jersey.

The next day determined the outcome of the Tour. The famous stage 18 of the 1959 Tour was 243 kilometers long, going from Le Lautaret to St. Vincent d'Aosta in Italy. The climbing was brutal: the Galibier was at almost the start of the stage (kilometer 7). Then came the Iseran at kilometer 114 and finally the Petit Saint-Bernard at kilometer 186. The Spanish team was very tired and vulnerable, having expended a lot of energy defending and helping Bahamontes the day before. It was expected that the French team would attack that day, using its very great collective strength.

The accounts of the exact chronology of this important stage differ, but there is agreement on the major points in the action. Almost from the gun Gaul attacked and was first over the Galibier. The old warhorses Jean Robic and Bobet were almost immediately dropped. On the descent of the Galibier Anglade crashed twice. Before the beginning of the Iseran climb, two riders escaped, Michele Gismondi and Adolf Christian. They got to the top of the Iseran over 5 minutes ahead of Gaul and Bahamontes. Bobet, in great distress, abandoned the Tour having made it a point of honor to make it to the top of the Iseran. Both Bahamontes and Gaul had mechanical trouble on the way down the Iseran and lost contact with the Anquetil/Rivière group they had been in.

At this point it could have been expected that such fine, powerful riders as Anquetil and Rivière would really take advantage of the situation and redouble their efforts, making it difficult if not impossible for Bahamontes and Gaul to regain contact. But, because each was afraid of assisting the other, they let Bahamontes and Gaul get back on.

The main contenders then negotiated the climb of the Petit St. Bernard together. On the descent, now wet and dangerous, several riders including Anglade, Baldini and and Gaul detached themselves from the leaders. Bahamontes, who had been part of the Baldini/Gaul/Anglade group let them go ahead and was caught by the Anquetil/Rivière chasers. This chase group now started to work hard to catch the leaders. Why did they suddenly find the energy and motivation to work together and shut down the gap when they now had the Yellow Jersey with them, a Yellow Jersey from Spain? The consensus is that Rivière and Anquetil could not tolerate the idea of a regional rider winning the Tour. They would prefer the Spaniard Bahamontes win the Tour, rather than the difficult upstart Anglade.

Stage 18 results:

First, Ercole Baldini, followed at the same time by Gaul, Gérard Saint, Anglade, Michele Gismondi, Adolf Christian.

Then, at 47 seconds: Brian Robinson, Anquetil, Brankart, Rivière, Adriaenssens, Mahé, Michel Van Aerde, Bahamontes, José Gomez Moral.

This stage needs a bit more explanation. Anquetil was always aware of the relative value of French riders on the post-Tour Criterium circuit. Back then this is where famous riders made their real income by earning appearance money for these local races. Another Frenchman stealing their glory would lessen their own worth in this marketplace.

The 1959 Tour had a further complication that created loyalties and alliances that were not visible on the surface. There were two major agents representing the riders involved here. Daniel Dousset represented Anquetil, Rivière and Bahamontes while Piel Poulidor represented Anglade. Each agent wanted to have the most popular, capable and desirable riders. The better the riders in the agent's stable, the more leverage he had and therefore the higher prices he could charge for all of his riders. It was to the advantage of Anquetil and Rivière to advance Bahamontes and give their agent Dousset more power, and deny Piel Poulidor the advantage of representing Anglade as a Tour winner. In effect a given agent's riders formed a quiet, hidden team within the race. This system withered in the 1980s as rider's salaries as well as their individual power rose within cycling.

In future Tours we will again see an out-of-contention Anquetil work to deprive a fellow countryman of a Tour win to preserve his own position as the finest active French rider. Anquetil never understood why he was never loved by his fellow countrymen. It was more than his passionless riding: he was the original dog in a manger. The great Tour writer Pierre Chany angrily called this stage a "giant turnip".

The General Classification after stage 18:

1. Federico Bahamontes
2. Henry Anglade @ 4 minutes 4 seconds
3. François Mahé @ 7 minutes 58 seconds
4. Jacques Anquetil @ 9 minutes 16 seconds
5. Ercole Baldini @ 9 minutes 40 seconds
6. Jos Hoevenaers @ 10 minutes 30 seconds
7. Jan Adriaenssens @ 10 minutes 46 seconds
8. Roger Rivière @ 11 minutes 36 seconds

The next day, the last one in the Alps, cost Anglade another minute, making it even more difficult for him to use his final opportunity to win the Tour, the stage 21 time trial. During stage 20, another chapter writ large on Tour history came to a close. Jean Robic, "Old Leatherhead" was eliminated for failing to make the time cutoff. The colorful, talented Robic, winner of the first post-war Tour had failed to finish the Tour in his last 4 attempts (1953, '54, '55, '59). I would have liked the tough bird to have a nicer end to his career. After retiring from racing he couldn't find a comfortable place in the world. A lonely, divorced man, he died in 1980 in a car crash.

The era's great men of the clock, Rivière and Anquetil handily beat the rest of the field in the stage 21 time trial. Rivière bested Anquetil over the 69.2-kilometer course by 1 minute, 38 seconds. More importantly, Anglade could not come close to beating Bahamontes by the 5 minutes, 40 seconds he needed. Bahamontes's lead was safe, and he became the first Spaniard to win the Tour de France. When the Tour arrived in the *Parc des Princes* velodrome in Paris for the Tour's final meters the riders were greeted by derisive whistles. They knew exactly what Rivière and Anquetil had done and unlike 1956, the heckling was well deserved. Later, Anquetil showed his contempt for the fans by naming his new boat "Whistles 59".

Final 1959 Tour de France General Classification:

1. Federico Bahamontes (Spain): 123 hours 46 minutes 45 seconds
2. Henry Anglade (France Center-Midi) @ 4 minutes 1 second
3. Jacques Anquetil (France) @ 5 minutes 5 seconds
4. Roger Rivière (France) @ 5 minutes 17 seconds
5. Francois Mahé (France West-South-West) @ 8 minutes 22 seconds

and the erratic Charly Gaul, twelfth @ 23 minutes 59 seconds

Climber's Competition:

1. Federico Bahamontes: 73 points
2. Charly Gaul: 68 points
3. Gérard Saint: 65 points

Points Competition:

1. André Darrigade: 613 points
2. Gérard Saint: 524 points
3. Jacques Anquetil: 503 points

1960. Jacques Anquetil won the Giro in May, beating Gastone Nencini by only 28 seconds. Anquetil not surprisingly took the lead in the Giro for good in the stage 14 68-kilometer time trial. Charly Gaul had tried to find his usual rabbit in the hat when he won the penultimate stage that took the race over the Gavia pass. But for the master climber of his age, it was too little too late. He finished the Giro in third place, almost 4 minutes behind Master Jacques. Neither Gaul nor Anquetil chose to ride the Tour that year. It's thought that Anquetil didn't want a repeat of 1959 with the loyalties of the team split between Roger Rivière and himself. The rivalry between the 2 had ended in disgrace for Rivière and Anquetil when they let Bahamontes win the Tour.

That left Roger Rivière the leader of the French team. Still, although Rivière had notable accomplishments on the track and he had won prestigious time trials, he had yet to notch a major stage race win. With riders like André Darrigade, Jean Dotto, Jean Graczyk and Henry

Anglade on their team, if the French didn't win the Tour in 1960 it was-n't because their team lacked power. It would be because some other failing of theirs let another rider win.

The major challenge to the French would have to come from the Italians. Nencini was now at the apogee of his career. Nino Defilippis, Ercole Baldini, and Arnaldo Pambianco were great riders in their own right and as part of a team they were doubly formidable.

The British again had a team in the Tour. Most notably, this was the first Tour start for Tom Simpson (the year before Simpson had moved from England, where road racing was almost unknown, to France). The move worked well for the ambitious Englishman. He won 7 minor races and came in fourth in the World Road Champi-onships held in Zandvoort, Holland that year. Simpson was a man on the way up.

The Belgians had no shortage of horsepower. Jan Adriaenssens was third in 1956, wearing the Yellow Jersey for 3 days that year. In 1959 he had slipped to seventh, but was only 10 minutes behind the winner, Bahamontes.

The 1960 Tour went counter-clockwise, Pyrenees first. Contin-uing a long, although somewhat unsteady trend that began after the mammoth 5,745 kilometer 1926 Tour, the 1960 Tour was about 200 kilometers shorter than the year before. The 4,173 kilometers were divided into 22 stages (opening day was a split stage) giving an average stage length of 189 kilometers. This was roughly 20 kilometers longer than those of today but about 30 kilometers shorter than an average stage in 1950.

Belgian Julien Schepens won the first stage's 14-man sprint into Brussels. Nencini and Anglade, the alert veterans, were in this lead bunch while Rivière was in the first chase group, over 2 minutes back. It was the 27.8-kilometer individual time trial that afternoon that was really interesting. Rivière won, beating Nencini by 32 seconds and Anglade by 48. Because Nencini was one of the heads-up riders in the first stage, he donned the Yellow Jersey with Anglade second, 31 sec-onds back. Rivière was sitting in seventh place, 92 seconds behind. Riv-ière had the power to win races but he lacked the tactical know-how and brains to win. As Desgrange had said over a half-century before, cycle racing is a head and legs sport.

The next day 1959 winner Federico Bahamontes became ill and had to abandon.

The problems with the French team started on stage 4, but it would take a few days for the effects to become manifest. 6 riders including 2 French team members, Anglade and Graczyk along with Baldini and old Wim Van Est made a successful break and beat a compact field to the finish by 6 minutes, 19 seconds. After coming so close in 1959, for the first time in his career Anglade was in Yellow. Rivière was in tenth place now, almost 8 minutes behind his teammate. Having come in second the year before and now in Yellow, one should have assumed that Anglade would at least be accorded a high level of protection within his own team.

It all came apart for the French on the sixth stage, 191 kilometers from St. Malo to Lorient in Brittany. Rivière attacked (one account says the move was initiated by Nencini) and took Nencini and the extremely capable Jan Adriaenssens with him. Alarmed, Anglade talked to team manager Marcel Bidot and asked Bidot to have Rivière stop his attack which was taking along 2 powerful riders who were fully capable of winning the Tour. Rivière ignored Bidot's pleas and powered on. He hated the easy-to-dislike Anglade (Anglade's nickname was "Napoleon") and had no intention of doing him any favors. The carnage from the effort was complete. The main pack containing Anglade finished 14 minutes, 40 seconds behind the Rivière group. Adriaenssens was now the Yellow Jersey with Nencini at 72 seconds and Rivière at 2 minutes, 14 seconds.

Anglade's reaction to the day's events dripped with contempt for Rivière's stage-racing abilities. Speaking about the French team's chances, he prophesied "we've just lost the Tour." Anglade knew Rivière would ride defensively in the mountains, trying to stay with Nencini, and he further predicted that Rivière would come to grief trying to descend while holding Nencini's wheel. Anglade and the other professional riders with deep road experience knew exactly how dangerous Nencini was going downhill. Raphaël Géminiani had said "the only reason to follow Nencini downhill is if you have a death wish." After the 1960 Giro Anquetil also gained a deep respect for Nencini's bike handling and passed on a warning to the other members of the French team.

Anglade himself was an excellent descender. He and Nencini had a personal race, man-to-man, down a mountain in Italy in 1959 to settle the question of who was the best living descender. Anglade beat the dangerous Italian but he had the measure of the man and had seen Rivière descend—and come close to disaster the previous year—as well. Anglade knew what he was talking about.

As the Tour traveled south down the western face of France Adriaenssens kept his lead. After stage 9 and at the foot of the Pyrenees, the standings stood thus:

1. Jean Adriaenssens

2. Gastone Nencini @ 1 minute 12 seconds

3. Roger Rivière @ 2 minutes 14 seconds

4. Jean Graczyk @ 2 minutes 15 seconds

Stage 10 had the Soulor and the Aubisque climbs. Nencini decided that this would be a good time to dispatch Rivière but the young Frenchman hung on grimly. When he was dropped on the first climb Rivière regained contact on of all places, the descent of the Aubisque. Rivière won the stage with Nencini second, the 2 riders finishing with the same time. Nencini was now the Yellow Jersey with Rivière at 32 seconds and Adriaenssens at 79 seconds. Fourth place Jozef Planckaert was at a distant 7 minutes, 8 seconds. It looked like a 3-way race from here on.

Rivière's plan was exactly as Anglade had described. He would stick like glue to Nencini through the road stages and beat him in the stage 19 time trial. At that point he was a 3-time world pursuit champion, had set the world hour record in 1957, and bettered it again in 1958. His Hour Record was so good that it stood for a decade. Rivière could be forgiven if he thought that he could easily take back a few seconds in an 83-kilometer time trial.

The next day, stage 11, had the Tourmalet, Aspin and the Peyresourde. On the final climb Nencini attacked and increased his lead over Rivière by a minute.

The fourteenth stage took the Tour through the Cevannes, the mountains just south of the Massif Central. On the first of the day's 3 rated climbs, Nencini was the fourth man over the Col du Perjuret with Rivière glued to his wheel. Nencini dropped like a rock down the very technical descent. Rivière was unable to stay with Nencini and went off the side of the mountain and into a ravine. His back was broken from the fall. Rivière was never to ride a bike again. At first he blamed his mechanics but it turned out that Rivière was so doped with painkillers that he couldn't manage his downhill speed. By the early 1960s many riders were using a horrible cocktail of drugs: amphetamines as a stimulant, Palfium to kill the pain in their legs and then sleeping pills at night to counteract the amphetamines. It is generally thought that the Palfium caused his crash by making it impossible for Rivière to feel his brake levers.

After the tragic events of stage 14, here were the standings:

1. Gastone Nencini
2. Jan Adriaenssens @ 2 minutes 25 seconds
3. Graziano Battistini @ 6 minutes
4. Jozef Planckaert @ 8 minutes 14 seconds

Through the Alps the relative positions stayed stable. Anglade tried to shake things up but Nencini never faltered. In fact, the Italians improved their position when Battistini won stage 16 which went over the Vars and Izoard. He was now within about a minute of Adriaenssens and could probably smell second place.

Battistini secured second place the next day when he got into the winning group (which included Nencini and Anglade) of the seventeenth stage that went over the Lautaret, the Luitel and the Granier.

All that was left to overcome was the stage 19 time trial. Run from Pontarlier to Besançon it was almost as if someone had designed the 83-kilometer downhill course just for Nencini. He didn't win and he didn't need to. He had a solid 4 minutes on his teammate Battistini and almost 6 on Adriaenssens going into the time trial. His performance that day increased his lead over both.

From there, it was an easy 2 stages to Paris. All that Anglade had predicted after stage 6 had come to pass. Rivière, through his amateurish, grudge-driven riding had ended up handing the Tour to Nencini. That was 2 years in a row that Rivière's selfish riding had probably cost his team the victory. Nencini was a gracious winner. He gave the bouquet of flowers he earned for winning the Tour to the French team manager, Marcel Bidot to give to Rivière. It was a nice gesture to the man who had done the most, however inadvertently, to give Nencini his victory. The highest placed Frenchman was Raymond Mastrotto, sixth place at 16 minutes, 12 seconds. *Ma foi!*

1960 Tour de France final General Classification:

1. Gastone Nencini (Italy): 112 hours 8 minutes 42 seconds

2. Graziano Battistini (Italy) @ 5 minutes 2 seconds

3. Jan Adriaenssens (Belgium) @ 10 minutes 24 seconds

4. Hans Junkermann (Germany) @ 11 minutes 21 seconds

5. Jozef Planckaert (Belgium) @ 13 minutes 2 seconds

6. Raymond Mastrotto (France) @ 16 minutes 12 seconds

7. Arnaldo Pambianco (Italy) @ 17 minutes 58 seconds

8. Henry Anglade (France) @ 19 minutes 17 seconds

Climber's competition:

1. Imerio Massignan: 56 points

2. Marcel Rohrbach: 52 points

3. Graziano Battistini: 44 points

Points Competition:

1. Jean Graczyk: 74 points

2. Graziano Battistini: 40 points

3. Gastone Nencini: 35 points

1961. Anquetil had made a smooth win of his 1957 Tour. Illness and deep divisions within the French team had prevented a repetition of his impressive freshman victory. He wanted to ride the 1961 Tour but wanted no part of the stupidity (even if he had contributed to it) that had ruined previous French chances. He wanted a team that would ride for him and him alone. Team manager Bidot acceded to Anquetil's demands and recruited the riders Anquetil wanted. Henry Anglade, André Darrigade, François Mahé, Jean Forestier and Jean Stablinski gave the French team and Anquetil a loyal backbone. To make his intentions crystal clear Anquetil announced that he would take the Yellow Jersey the first day and hold it all the way to Paris. This was big talk from a man who had come in second in the Giro to Arnaldo Pambianco by almost 4 minutes just 2 weeks before, but he meant it.

Nencini wasn't entered but the Italian team had last year's Tour runner up, Graziano Battistini along with Guido Carlesi and Vito Favero. This was a team unlikely to defeat an Anquetil-led French team that didn't splinter but if the French faltered, the Italians would be able to step in. The Spanish sent 2 riders of note, José Perez-Frances and Fernando Manzaneque. Manzaneque was probably the most solid, consistent Iberian rider of the era, often earning very high placings. But big wins were rare for him.

And there was Charly Gaul. He rode for a Swiss/Luxembourg composite team but he disdained his teams as ineffectual. He rode on his own for himself. He depended upon delivering a blockbuster punch on a hard mountain day, preferably in cold weather. He was fourth in the 1961 Giro. He won the Giro's penultimate stage that took in the giant Stelvio climb but he could only gain 2 minutes on Pambianco. Sometimes Gaul could destroy the field in just a few kilometers, other times he seemed to have no power and would allow the gap to the leader to grow beyond repair. No one could predict when he would fly away but everyone knew that he was always capable of stealing a Grand Tour in a single day if the opportunity presented itself.

The 1961 Tour was clockwise starting at Rouen in Normandy, up to Belgium, then south through the Vosges and Chartreuse Mountains, followed by the Alps, Pyrenees and then north to Paris.

André Darrigade started the Tour about where he left off the year before. For the fifth time he won the opening stage and the first Yellow Jersey when he was the quickest of the 15 riders who successfully broke away. Joining Darrigade were Anquetil and Carlesi. Almost 5 minutes back with the peloton: Gaul, Battistini and Adriaenssens who were now already in a deep hole. Anquetil easily won that afternoon's 28.5-kilometer time-trial at Versailles. He beat Battistini by 2 minutes, 39 seconds, Gaul by almost 3 minutes and Adriaenssens by 3 minutes, 24 seconds. Anquetil had not only taken the Yellow Jersey on the first day and fulfilled his prediction, he had demonstrated his superb form and outstanding tactical sense.

The GC after the first day stood thus:

1. Jacques Anquetil
2. Joseph Groussard (teammate of Anquetil) @ 4 minutes 46 seconds
3. Guido Carlesi @ 5 minutes 25 seconds

Through the Vosges Mountains Carlesi maintained his time gap behind Anquetil. Spanish climber Fernando Manzaneque and French (now) regional rider Jean Dotto managed to insert themselves between Anquetil and Carlesi. Gaul was in twelfth place, 8 minutes, 13 seconds behind Anquetil. The French team patrolled the race, keeping everything under control. By the time the Tour reached stage 9, the first Alpine stage, the French team had won a total of 5 stages, Darrigade 2 of them. This was a very different French effort from the last 4 years.

Stage 9 had 4 big climbs, finishing with the Col de Porte. Gaul took off on the second climb, the Granier. He crashed on the descent of the third climb, the Cucheron, but pressed on to win alone. It was a wonderful stage win but he could only take 100 seconds out of Anquetil who finished with Manzaneque, Junkermann and the Italian climber Imerio Massignan. Carlesi came in almost 2 minutes behind the Anquetil group. The second Alpine day with the Croix de Fer and Mount Cenis changed nothing in the important standings. Anquetil still had 5 minutes on second place although now that runner-up was Manzaneque. Even after the Maritime Alps there were no significant tactical moves or changes to the times. After stage 12 with the Alpine stages finished, the General Classification stood thus:

1. Jacques Anquetil
2. Fernando Manzaneque @ 5 minutes 37 seconds
3. Charly Gaul @ 6 minutes 33 seconds
4. Guido Carlesi @ 7 minutes 43 seconds
5. José Perez-Frances @ 8 minutes 14 seconds

There were 2 massive climbing stages in the Pyrenees left. So far Anquetil had been able to contain Gaul. The first of these hard stages was the sixteenth, 208 kilometers from Toulouse to a new summit, Superbagnères. With the Ares, Portillon and the 1,800-meter high climb to Superbagnères, Gaul should have been able to deal the French a hard blow. But nothing happened. Gaul finished with Anquetil. Why? Who knows? Gaul didn't always attack when his opposition thought he would. Perhaps he was still hurting from his crash. His performances were erratic and unpredictable and by now his best years were behind him. And so now it was down to 1 mountain stage.

Stage 17 was again Charly Gaul territory with the Peyresourde, Aspin, Tourmalet and the Aubisque climbs. Again Gaul held his fire. 24 of the best riders (including Anquetil, Manzaneque and Gaul) finished together, 4 minutes behind Eddy Pauwels, André Foucher, and Marcel Queheille. With 4 stages left and only a time trial left between the riders and Paris, Anquetil had the Tour about sewn up.

As expected Anquetil did win the stage 19 time trial, beating Charly Gaul by almost 3 minutes over the 74.5-kilometer course. While Gaul hadn't excelled in the mountains, his time trial skills, unusual in a specialist climber, were still intact and allowed him to get second in the stage and move up to second place in the General Classification. So going to Paris with 2 stages to go, here were the standings:

1. Jacques Anquetil

2. Charly Gaul @ 10 minutes 2 seconds

3. Guido Carlesi @ 10 minutes 6 seconds

With the standings between Gaul and Carlesi that tight Gaul should have been alert for trouble. Sure enough, the plucky Italian detached himself from the main group on the way to the finish at the *Parc des Princes* velodrome in Paris and took over second place.

Final 1961 Tour de France General Classification:

1. Jacques Anquetil (France): 122 hours 1 minute 33 seconds

2. Guido Carlesi (Italy) @ 12 minutes 14 seconds

3. Charly Gaul (Luxembourg) @ 12 minutes 16 seconds

4. Imerio Massignan (Italy) @ 15 minutes 59 seconds

5. Hans Junkermann (Germany) @ 16 minutes 9 seconds

6. Fernando Manzaneque (Spain) @ 16 minutes 27 seconds

Anquetil had fulfilled his prediction. He acquired the Yellow Jersey on the first day and kept it the rest of the Tour. While a wonderful accomplishment, it's not the same as winning the first stage and then holding the lead to the finish. This has only been done by Garin (1903, and 1904 before being relegated), Thys (1914), Bottecchia (1924), Frantz (1928) and Romain Maes (1935). Taking the lead on the second stage and holding it to the end has been done 5 times: Pottier (1906), Faber (1909), Thys (1920), Scieur (1921), Magne (1934), Anquetil (1961). Note that the great Philippe Thys is on both of these lists. Today the Prologue time trial is often won by a short-distance power specialist who cannot compete in the mountains, making a start-to-finish Tour win unlikely to occur in the foreseeable future.

Climber's competition:

1. Imerio Massignan: 95 points
2. Charly Gaul: 61 points
3. Hans Junkermann: 48 points

Points competition:

1. André Darrigade: 174 points
2. Jean Gainche: 169 points
3. Guido Carlesi: 148 points

1962. The Tour abandoned the national team format and went back to trade teams. Both professional cycling and the bicycle industry itself were at a low ebb. For years the bicycle manufacturers had been begging the Tour to allow the reintroduction of trade teams, arguing that that the industry's very survival was at stake. The Tour was the most watched event in cycling and the sponsors badly needed the publicity. The Tour's national team format was cruel to the sponsors in another way: they still had to pay their riders' salaries during this publicity blackout. Feeling that the national teams made for a more honest race as well as lending dignity and stature to the competition the Tour organization was reluctant to make the change. Born out of the rational belief that the trade teams had colluded to fix the 1929 edition, Tour founder Henri Desgrange had adopted the national team format in 1930. For decades it was extremely successful even though there were times when it was obvious that riders often respected their trade team affiliation more than their national team allegiance. Bending to necessity Tour boss Goddet abandoned the national teams. They would be used again only in 1967 and 1968.

The organization of the Tour was altered when Émilien Amaury who owned *Le Parisien Libéré* became financially involved with the Tour. It was Amaury who had influenced the decision of the French Cycling Federation to award the Tour to Jacques Goddet after the end of World War Two. Félix Levitan, who had been been a writer in Amaury's paper, became the co-organizer of the Tour. Eventually it was worked out that Goddet would run the sporting side and Levitan concerned himself with the Tour's finances. The 2 did not like each other but they were able to make the relationship work until 1987 when Levitan was sacked.

Under the trade team system Anquetil would be riding the Tour for his St. Raphaël-Halyett team with teammate Rudi Altig. Among others on his team were his super-loyal friend Jean Stablinski and Jean Graczyk, the latter 2 having ridden with Anquetil in earlier Tours on the national team. Observers wondered about the Altig-Anquetil chemistry. Anquetil entered the Vuelta a España (then held in the spring) hoping to add the third Grand Tour to his palmares. His powerful team suffocated the competition. But Altig, who had been granted some freedom, became the leader. Anquetil felt that this would all be fixed at the stage 15 individual time trial and that he would emerge the Vuelta's leader. But no, Altig was on form and even beat the crono master himself, Anquetil, by a second, retaining the leadership. This was no surprise as Altig was twice world professional pursuit champion. Anquetil did not start the final stage, complaining of gastric troubles. It's generally assumed that he quit rather than finish behind his German teammate. Other than this adventure, Anquetil's spring was unremarkable except for one piece of chutzpah. He wanted his director sportif and former rival and teammate, Raphaël Géminiani, replaced for the Tour. The sponsors refused.

This was the first Tour for one of the race's great legends, Raymond Poulidor. Inexplicably left off the French team in 1961 at the advice of Antonin Magne, Poulidor had enjoyed a spectacular 1961, his second year as a pro. That year he won Milan–San Remo and the French road championships, was second in the 4 Days of Dunkirk and third in the Midi Libéré and the World Road Championships. With national politics unable to block him in 1962 Poulidor was entered riding for Mercier with Magne as his director. As a metaphor of Poulidor's "almost" career, he started his first Tour with a cast on his recently broken wrist.

The 1962 Tour was counter-clockwise, starting in Nancy and heading straight up to Belgium for 3 stages. At 4,274 kilometers, it was about the usual length for a Tour of the time. With 24 stages (2 days had split stages), the average stage length was 178 kilometers, around 10 kilometers longer than the current standard.

Altig showed he had kept his Vuelta-winning form by winning

the first stage and the first Yellow Jersey. While Anquetil, Carlesi, Simpson, Nencini and Anglade had finished up front, the peloton had badly fractured. Bahamontes and Poulidor ended the day about 8 minutes back. Half the field lost 10 to 30 minutes on the road that day. Without the guiding voice of Fausto Coppi, Bahamontes had slid back to his old way of riding for the climber's prize rather than for the overall victory.

The reigning world champion, Rik van Looy, was nicknamed the "Emperor of Herentals" for both his hometown in Belgium and the authoritative way he treated the other riders. He took a wrong turn at the end of the second stage when the Tour finished in the city of his birth and missed a chance to win the second stage. André Darrigade won the stage and took the lead. Van Looy's Flandria squad avenged the embarrassment by winning that afternoon's team time trial which was also held in Herentals. This team time trial didn't affect the individual rider's standings as it was only used to calculate the competition for the Tour's best team.

The next day Altig won the 41-man sprint at Amiens and retook the Yellow Jersey when the Tour returned to France. Anquetil, staying out of trouble, was the last man in the front group. No one seemed to be able to keep the lead for long. When a big group rolled off the front of the peloton in stage 6 that finished in Brest, Altig and Anquetil's Dutch *domestique* Albertus Geldermans were sent up to the break to keep an eye on things and protect the team's interests. When the break crossed the line 5 minutes ahead of the peloton Geldermans became the new Yellow Jersey.

Geldermans could only stay in the lead for 2 days. A successful 30-man break in stage 8a put Darrigade in Yellow. Tom Simpson had been staying close to the action so far and had been sharp enough to be in that Darrigade break. He was now sitting in second place, more than 2 minutes behind.

That afternoon Anquetil began his serious assault on the Tour when he won the 43-kilometer individual time trial. Baldini was second at 22 seconds and Altig third, 46 seconds behind. Notable for later in the Tour, Jozef Planckaert was fourth, a little over a minute slower than Anquetil.

After stage 8b, the first of the 3 individual time trials and still a few days before the Pyrenees, the General Classification stood thus:

1. André Darrigade
2. Tom Simpson @ 51 seconds
3. Albertus Geldermans @ 1 minutes 21 seconds
4. Gilbert Desmet @ 1 minute 59 seconds
5. Henry Anglade @ 2 minutes
6. Luis Otano @ 2 minutes 16 seconds
7. Rudy Altig @ 3 minutes 20 seconds
12. Jacques Anquetil @ 4 minutes 11 seconds

The day after the time trial Darrigade had to relinquish the lead when another break was able to stick it out to the end of the stage. Flandria's Willy Schroeders was the new unlikely (or so it seemed) leader. Schroeders kept the Yellow Jersey for 3 days, even through the first of the relatively minor climbing in the Pyrenees in stage 11. During that stage 11 one of the Tour's following motorcycles crashed and caused about 30 riders to fall. Most notably, Rik Van Looy, the only rider in cycling history to win all the classics, was forced to abandon. Van Looy might not have been accruing high placings, but had been racing aggressively, keeping the others on their toes.

Stage 12, from Pau to St. Gaudens, promised a reordering of the standing with 3 big mountains on the menu: the Tourmalet, the Aspin and the Peyresourde. It was too much for Schroeders who finished over 8 minutes back as the major contenders completed the stage together in a group of 18. Bahamontes, gathering all possible King of the Mountains points was careful to be the first to the top of each climb. That day Tom Simpson made history by being the first British rider to wear yellow. Geldermans was second now, at 30 seconds. Anquetil had moved up to sixth at 3 minutes, 20 seconds.

The next day's mountain stage was an 18.5-kilometer uphill time trial to Superbagnères. 34-year-old Bahamontes was first but the real news was that Jozef Planckaert came in second beating third-place Anquetil by 3 seconds and Charly Gaul by 4. Planckaert was now the leader. Anquetil was sitting at fourth, 1 minute, 8 seconds back. Planckaert was a complete rider. He was the reigning Belgian Road Champion and had won Paris–Nice and Liege–Bastogne–Liege that spring. The Yellow Jersey was resting on very strong shoulders.

Stage 14 was supposed to be a hard day with the Ares and the

Portet d'Aspet mountains and then a final climb to the fortified city of Carcassonne, but it was made harder for some by what has now come to be known as the "Wiel's Affair". Hans Junkermann, riding for the Wiel's team, had been ill the night before the stage started. He asked for and was granted a delay to the start of the stage. After the Superbagnères time trial the day before, Junkermann was sitting in seventh place, only 4 minutes down on Planckaert. Given Junkermann's high placing and status as the Wiel's team captain, the delay seemed reasonable. The pack rolled off and pretty soon Junkermann was off the back and then off his bike, unable to continue. Junkermann claimed that he had been sickened by bad fish served at the hotel the evening before. 14 of the Tour's entrants, including Nencini, Schroeders and 3 of Junkermann's teammates, also had to withdraw during the stage. In all, 8 teams were affected. "Foul," cried the hotel, "we didn't serve any fish." This was a hot day and it is now believed that doping gone wrong was at the root of the rider's troubles. A cartoonist drew a picture of the riders at the dinner table with syringes for the fish bones. The riders were furious at the way the newspapers handled the affair and threatened to strike. Louison Bobet's brother, Jean, talked them out of making a bad situation worse. Note for future events in Tour history that the riders were incensed at being ridiculed for an obvious lie. They believed that they had the right to dope and no one could call them on it.

With the climbing in the Pyrenees over and the peloton a bit lighter by 14 riders, the General Classification stood thus:

1. Jozef Planckaert
2. Gilbert Desmet @ 50 seconds
3. Albertus Geldermans @ 1 minute 5 seconds
4. Jacques Anquetil @ 1 minute 8 seconds
5. Tom Simpson @ 2 minutes

As the Tour traveled across southern France the standings changed little. The eighteenth stage should have been brilliant with climbing fireworks: climbers Massignan, Gaul and newcomer Poulidor were sitting 7 to 9 minutes behind Planckaert, and were running out of time to take the Tour. With a 68-kilometer time trial coming up at the twentieth stage, Anquetil was in a marvelous position. The others should have been expected to attack him on a day that had the Col de la Bonette (a climb new to the Tour that year), the Vars and the Izoard. Instead it was a strange day. The first 100 kilometers took 4 hours to cover. Then the attacks came but flat tires and a neutralizing tendency among the better riders ended up letting a pure sprinter, Emile Daems, win the day. Planckaert had adopted the suicidal strategy of staying with Anquetil no matter where he went, no matter how fast or slow he rode. While this made Anquetil nervous and angry, the tactic left Planckaert open for destruction when the time trial came. At the end of the stage with Poulidor, Planckaert, Anquetil, Gaul and Massignan finishing almost at the same time, the standings were unaffected. Anquetil remained 1 minute, 8 seconds behind Planckaert although he was now in second place, Desmet and Geldermans having lost time that day.

Stage 19 gave the adventurous climbers a chance to repeat history. It followed the same route as the legendary twenty-first stage of the 1958 Tour where Charly Gaul had single-handedly destroyed the entire field and crushed Géminiani's quest for Tour victory. The manager of Raymond Poulidor's Mercier team was the great rider of the 1930's, Antonin Magne. Magne told Poulidor that he should not aspire to be the best injured rider in the Tour. Now that the cast had been taken from his hand he should shoot for greatness and this stage with its hilly roads in the Chartreuse Mountains would be perfect. Sitting in ninth place in the General Classification and almost 10 minutes behind Planckaert, he wasn't considered a threat and therefore could count on being allowed some freedom. At the top of the third major climb of the day, the Porte, Poulidor was a full minute clear of his nearest chaser, Henry Anglade. On the next climb, the Cucheron, he was still clear of Bahamontes by a minute, with Anquetil and Planckaert 2 minutes, 40 seconds further back. By the end of the stage in Aix-les-Bains Bahamontes and Anglade had come together but they lost ground while Poulidor pressed his advantage. Poulidor won the stage with a 2 minute, 30 second lead over Bahamontes and Anglade. Anquetil, Planckaert, Gaul and 16 others were 3 minutes, 16 seconds in arrears. This fantastic ride lifted Poulidor to third place.

With the climbing done and the riders facing the final individual time trial, the standings were thus:

1. Jozef Planckaert
2. Jacques Anquetil @ 1 minute 8 seconds

3. Raymond Poulidor @ 5 minutes 43 seconds

4. Gilbert Desmet @ 7 minutes 15 seconds

5. Albertus Geldermans @ 7 minutes 23 seconds

6. Tom Simpson @ 7 minutes 30 seconds

The twentieth stage was a 68-kilometer time trial from Bourgoin to Lyon. Planckaert was only going to win the Tour if something dreadful kept Anquetil from doing well that day. No such luck for the Belgian. Anquetil was stunning, riding at 43.6 kilometers an hour. He caught his 3-minute man Poulidor at the halfway mark, beating the accomplished Baldini by 3 minutes, Poulidor by 5 minutes and Planckaert by 5 minutes, 19 seconds. In the 1 hour, 33 minutes Anquetil needed to ride the time trial, he had clinched his third Tour win. He was now tied with Thys and Bobet, although Bobet was the only member of the trio who had won 3 years in a row. The 1962 Tour set a new record, being raced at an average speed of 37.306 kilometers an hour.

Final 1962 Tour de France General Classification:

1. Jacques Anquetil (St. Raphaël-Halyett): 114 hours 31 minutes 54 seconds

2. Jozef Planckaert (Faema-Flandria) @ 4 minutes 59 seconds

3. Raymond Poulidor (Mercier) @ 10 minutes 24 seconds

4. Gilbert Desmet (Carpano) @ 13 minutes 1 second

5. Albertus Geldermans (St. Raphaël-Halyett) @ 14 minutes 4 seconds

6. Tom Simpson (Leroux-Gitane) @ 17 minutes 9 seconds

Climber's competition:

1. Federico Bahamontes: 137 points

2. Imerio Massignan: 77 points

3. Raymond Poulidor: 70 points

Points competition:

1. Rudi Altig: 173 points

2. Emile Daems: 144 points

3. Jean Graczyk: 140 points

1963. Anquetil had a terrific spring winning Paris–Nice, the Dauphiné Libéré, the Critérium National and the Vuelta. He particularly redeemed himself in the Spanish Tour (after his questionable exit the year before) by winning the race just as he had won the 1961 Tour, gaining the leadership in the stage 1b time trial on the first day and holding it all the way to the end.

The Tour organization wasn't looking forward to another edition suffocated by Anquetil's superb, albeit conservative riding. To reduce his advantage in the time trials, they did just as they had done in 1953 to counter the Swiss mastery of the discipline, they reduced the total distance to be ridden against the clock. In 1962 Anquetil had 129.5 kilometers at his disposal. In 1963 he had only 79 kilometers. Because his climbing was considered inferior to some of the mountain specialists, the finish lines for some mountain stages were moved closer to the final summits. This helped the mountain goats who could gain time on a mountain but were often unable to stay away for the remaining distance along rolling or flat terrain.

Yet, for all of his springtime racing brilliance, Anquetil's start was in doubt. He had been infected with a tapeworm and his doctors advised him not to start. It was only a couple of days before the June 23 start date that Anquetil decided to try for his fourth Tour victory.

After his brilliant stage 19 ride through the Chartreuse the previous year, it was widely thought that 1963 would be Poulidor's year to be a major Tour contender. His spring was auspicious. He won the Belgian semi-classic Fleche Wallonne. Tellingly, he came in second to Anquetil in the Critérium National. The rivalry between the 2 had not yet matured so Poulidor couldn't have known how prophetic that second place was. Anquetil was dismissive of Poulidor's capabilities, feeling that the slow-talking man from Limousin presented no threat.

Federico Bahamontes did the unexpected by getting into the 4-man winning break on the first stage. Belgian Eddy Pauwels won the sprint and the year's first Yellow Jersey. Maybe that eccentric climber from Spain, now 35 years old, had some power left in those incredibly defined legs and some real ambition in his heart to match. With the race designed with climbers in mind, perhaps Bahamontes thought it was worth a go. He had an 88-second lead on Anquetil long before the first ascent.

Seamus Elliot, an Irishman riding on Anquetil's St. Raphaël team, led a 10-man break to the finish in Roubaix to win the third stage and become the first rider from the Emerald Isle to wear the Yellow Jersey. Erin Go Bragh! Henry Anglade was also in the break and was now sitting in second place, 1 minute, 14 seconds behind Elliot.

The relative positions did not change much as the Tour headed southwest through Normandy and Brittany. The first time trial, stage 6b, was a 24.5-kilometer affair at Angers in Anjou. Showing that he was throwing off the ill effects of his tapeworm, Anquetil won the stage. Poulidor didn't suffer the humiliation he had endured in the final time trial the year before where he was caught at the midway point. He was second, only 45 seconds behind Anquetil. Was this indicative of Poulidor's improvement or Anquetil's weakness? With the 1-minute time bonus for winning the stage Anquetil had brought himself up to seventh place, 6 minutes, 14 seconds behind the new leader, Gilbert Desmet.

The next 3 stages took the Tour almost due south for its rendezvous with the Pyrenees. They were without major incident and left the General Classification thus on the eve of the start of the major climbing:

1. Gilbert Desmet
2. Henry Anglade @ 6 seconds
3. Seamus Elliott @ 1 minute 2 seconds
8. Jacques Anquetil @ 6 minutes 14 seconds
12. Federico Bahamontes @ 7 minutes 33 seconds
13. Raymond Poulidor @ 7 minutes 44 seconds

Stage 10 was a 148.5-kilometer ride that went over the Aubisque and the Tourmalet. Bahamontes was first over both climbs but the revelation was that Anquetil was able to go with him. A 5-man group of Esteban Martin, Poulidor, Anquetil and José Perez-Frances had a 1 minute, 17 second gap on the first major group of chasers with the rest of the field anywhere from 4 to 28 minutes behind them. Anquetil, a competent sprinter, achieved his first-ever mountain stage win. The exploit moved him up to third, 3 minutes, 46 second behind the surprisingly capable Desmet. The stage results left the world gap-jawed. This was a new Anquetil who could trade pedal-strokes with the specialist climbers on their own turf and then beat them in the sprint. He had attained a level of ability that few racers in the history of the sport had achieved. Poulidor had also done well, but this was expected of a man whose strength was his climbing.

The next day's trip over the Aspin, the Peyresourde and the Portillon let Anquetil gnaw a bit more on Desmet's lead. Anquetil was now second, 3 minutes, 3 seconds behind. Poulidor was only able to gain 11 seconds on Anquetil that day. Not enough, he was still 2 minutes, 19 seconds behind his Norman rival and any gap at all was too much with another time trial facing them after the Alps.

Stage 12 was the last day in the Pyrenees but changed nothing. Almost the entire field finished together even after climbing the Ares and the Portet d'Aspet. The riders got little respite from the climbing on the way to the Alps. There were 2 days through the Massif Central, with a rest day in between. Anquetil used these stages to further his cause, bringing Desmet's lead to only 2 minutes, 33 seconds.

The Alpine stages commenced with stage 15, 174 kilometers that went over the Grand Bois and the Porte. This was the day for Bahamontes to shine. He won the stage, the time bonus and second place overall. After the first day in the Alps, Bahamontes and Anquetil were almost tied:

1. Gilbert Desmet
2. Federico Bahamontes @ 2 minutes 30 seconds
3. Jacques Anquetil @ 2 minutes 33 seconds
6. Raymond Poulidor @ 5 minutes 22 seconds

Stage 16, Grenoble to Val d'Isère should have been the day for Bahamontes to ice the cake with the Croix de Fer and the Iseran climbs. But it was not to be. Fernando Manzaneque won the stage, leaving the main group of contenders almost 8 minutes back. Bahamontes finished with Anquetil and Poulidor in a group of 12. Bahamontes had the lead, but riders in the past have had bigger leads on Anquetil when there was still a time trial to ride and they all suffered the same fate.

1. Federico Bahamontes
2. Jacques Anquetil @ 3 seconds
3. Henry Anglade @ 2 minutes 43 seconds
4. Raymond Poulidor @ 2 minutes 52 seconds

The next day's climbing gave the Spaniard another bite of the apple with the Petit and Grand St. Bernard passes, the Forclaz and finally the third category Montets. The day is famous not for the racing but for the clever way Anquetil's director Raphaël Géminiani circumvented the rules. Poulidor had planned to attack early. The very experienced Géminiani told Anquetil that this would be a tough attack to sustain because of the winds that the riders would encounter after the summit of the Grand St. Bernard. So Anquetil held his fire when Poulidor went. After the Grand St. Bernard and before the Forclaz, Anquetil did hook up with Bahamontes and Poulidor. Eventually their group became 10 riders strong. But Géminiani wanted to give his man a little more help before the start of the unpaved Forclaz with its section of 25% gradient. He had Anquetil signal for a new bike. Géminiani, while swearing loudly at Anquetil's bike, deftly used a bit of slight of hand and cut a derailleur cable. This ruse was necessary since the only way the Tour rules allowed a bike change was for a mechanical problem and Anquetil now had one. Géminiani gave Anquetil a special light climbing bike with lower gears to allow him to negotiate the steep, difficult road of the Forclaz. He was able to stay with the soaring Spaniard who did everything in his power to lose the sticky Anquetil. Poulidor and the others were resoundingly dropped but this new climbing Anquetil stuck to Bahamontes. At the top Géminiani gave Anquetil his now repaired regular racing bike with which Anquetil was able to ride to the finish together with Bahamontes and win the stage. Anquetil was now the leader with Bahamontes second, 28 seconds back. Poulidor lost 8 minutes, 23 seconds that day.

2 days later Anquetil was able to deal the *coup de grace* over the 54.5 kilometers of the final time trial. He won it handsomely and thereby earned what no racer had ever attained, 4 Tour de France victories. This was the 50th Tour and it was appropriate that it be won in some auspicious way. Poulidor deeply disappointed those who had hoped he would mount a serious challenge. His eighth place, 16 minutes, 46 seconds behind Anquetil earned him contemptuous whistles from the crowds at the Parc des Princes where the Tour finished. Anquetil had a rare moment where the crowd had more affection for him than for Poulidor. I hope he enjoyed it while he could.

Final 1963 Tour de France General Classification:

1. Jacques Anquetil (St. Raphaël-Gitane): 113 hours 30 minutes 5 seconds

2. Federico Bahamontes (Margnat-Paloma) @ 3 minutes 35 seconds

3. José Perez-Frances (Ferrys) @ 10 minutes 14 seconds

4. Jean-Claude Lebaube (St. Raphaël-Gitane) @ 11 minutes 55 seconds

5. Armand Desmet (Faema-Flandria) @ 15 minutes

6. Angelino Soler (Faema-Flandria) @ 15 minutes 4 seconds

7. Renzo Fontona (Ibac) @ 15 minutes 27 seconds

8. Raymond Poulidor (Mercier-BP) @ 16 minutes 46 seconds

Climber's competition:

1. Federico Bahamontes: 147 points

2. Raymond Poulidor: 70 points

3. Guy Ignolin: 68 points

Points competition:

1. Rik Van Looy: 275 points

2. Jacques Anquetil: 138 points

3. Federico Bahamontes: 123 points

1964. Anquetil started the 1964 season well. He won Ghent–Wevelgem and then the Giro d'Italia. If he won the 1964 Tour he would achieve the Giro-Tour double, a feat previously accomplished in the same year only by Fausto Coppi. He would also perform the then-unequaled feat of winning the Tour de France for a fifth time.

He had taken the 1964 Giro lead in the stage 5 time trial and had held the leader's Pink Jersey for the rest of the race. Subjected to relentless attacks, he was forced to work especially hard to defend his lead in the Giro. The effort left him exhausted. Many wondered if Anquetil could ride an effective Tour that started just 2 weeks after this brutal Giro ended. Anquetil was aiming for the stars. While his 4 Tour wins were the record, a fifth win while doing a Giro-Tour double would make him one of the greatest racers in history.

There were no new challengers on the Tour scene so the main contenders for the 1964 Tour were the same as the year before, Bahamontes and Poulidor.

Poulidor brought excellent form to the 1964 Tour. He won the 1964 Vuelta a España, which was then run early in the year, as well as the Critérium National. He was second at Milan–San Remo and the Dauphiné Libéré and fourth in Paris-Nice. He had every right to expect that he would do well and possibly even win the Tour.

Let's stop a minute and take a look at Raymond Poulidor.

The battles between Poulidor and Anquetil enlivened racing (and arguments between racing fans) as much in France as the Bartali-Coppi contests fired up the Italians a generation before. Poulidor was the superior climber and Anquetil was the better time trialist. Poulidor was never able to gain enough of an advantage in the mountains to make up for his losses against the clock. Anquetil was also the superior tactician and psychologist. When his physical limits threatened his chances he could call upon his superior intellect and salvage a race. This was a gift denied Poulidor.

Here is Pouildor's Tour Record:

14 participations

7 stage victories

No overall victories and never a single day in Yellow, not one.

By the years:

1962: 3rd overall, 1 stage victory

1963: 8th overall

1964: 2nd overall, 1 stage victory

1965: 2nd overall, 2 stage victories

1966: 3rd overall, 1 stage victory

1967: 9th overall, 1 stage victory

1968: Did not finish

1969: 3rd overall

1970: 7th overall

1972: 3rd overall

1973: Did not finish

1974: 2nd overall, 1 stage victory

1975: 19th overall

1976: 3rd overall

Here's a selection of other Poulidor wins: Milan–San Remo, Fleche Wallonne, Grand Prix des Nations (even though he wasn't a time trialist of Anquetil's caliber, he was still very, very good against the clock), Vuelta a España, Critérium National, Dauphiné Libéré, Catalonian Week and Paris–Nice.

In 1974, at the Montreal World Road Championships, only 39-year old Raymond Poulidor could stay with Eddy Merckx when he attacked on the last time up Mount Royal, finishing just 2 seconds behind the great man. If anyone could paraphrase Raphaël Géminiani this time, it was Poulidor. He was first because he was the first human across the line. No normal person was going to beat Merckx that day.

This was an extraordinary career by any measure.

In the wars for the affection of the French people, Poulidor won hands down. It baffled and angered Anquetil that even though Anquetil could beat Poulidor over and over again, "Pou-Pou", the "Eternal Second" was first in the French hearts and remains there today. I have often thought that Poulidor tapped into a piece of the French psyche that made Crecy and Agincourt possible. It was at Crecy, France that the English, with their technically superior longbows, slaughtered the French armored knights. Later, at Agincourt, the French knights jostled for position to be first to hurl themselves against the English longbowmen only to be slaughtered again. *Le Gloire* (glorious renown) isn't necessarily gained by victory.

To continue:

The 1964 Tour was 4,504 kilometers divided into 25 stages going clockwise, Alps first then the Pyrenees. To increase the drama the Tour would head into the Massif Central and climb the Puy de Dôme, an extinct volcano whose final 5 kilometers have a gradient that approaches 13%.

For the first part of the Tour as the race sped east from Rennes in Brittany, Anquetil was unremarkable. He knew he had a finite supply of energy and had announced in advance his plans to let others do the racing in the first week. He didn't even place in the top 10 of a stage until stage 8.

His teammate Rudi Altig, however, did have early ambitions. After passing through Brittany and Normandy, the Tour headed into Belgium and then southeast into Germany. Altig wanted to be wearing the leader's jersey while the Tour went through his home country. By winning the fourth stage into Metz he was in an excellent position to realize his ambition. He had the Green Points Jersey and was only 31 seconds behind the current leader, Bernard Van de Kerckhove.

The next stage traveled through the Vosges, hilly country in eastern France that encouraged breakaways. Altig powered a 5-man break 4 minutes clear of the field into Fribourg and secured the overall lead. Rudi Altig the German rider was in Yellow in Germany. Anquetil was not entirely pleased that his teammate had been so successful. In that break was a rider on the Pelforth team, Georges Groussard, who was now in second place, only a minute behind Altig. Groussard was an excellent rider with fine climbing skills and Altig had given him a 4-minute boost. Anquetil did not relish the prospect of overcoming that time gain just so that Altig could enjoy a little bit of German glory.

Stage 7 went through the Jura, mountains on the northeastern edge of the Alps. Tongues wagged when Poulidor got into a 15-man break that included Groussard and left the rest of the peloton (with Anquetil) a half-minute behind. Altig was still in Yellow but Poulidor had stolen a march on a very obviously tired Anquetil.

Stage 8 was the first full-blown Alpine stage with both the Télégraphe and the Galibier. Bahamontes was first over both summits. Poulidor went after him on the Galibier and came close to making contact with the flying Spaniard. Meanwhile, Anquetil was suffering, losing time on the climb. Once over the top he used his considerable descending skills to try to close the gap. Even with a flat tire he was still able to limit his losses to Poulidor to only 17 seconds. Bahamontes won the stage, Poulidor came in second and thereby gained a 3 second time bonus. Anquetil's worries about Groussard turned out to be completely justified. The Pelforth rider was now in Yellow.

So, after the first day of hard climbing here were the standings:

1. Georges Groussard
2. Federico Bahamontes @ 3 minutes 35 seconds
3. Raymond Poulidor @ 4 minutes 7 seconds

4. André Foucher @ 4 minutes 8 seconds

5. Henry Anglade @ 4 minutes 23 seconds

6. Rudy Altig @ 4 minutes 38 seconds

7. Hans Junkermann @ 4 minutes 47 seconds

8. Jacques Anquetil @ 5 minutes 22 seconds

Anquetil showed he was up for the race the next day in the Briançon–Monaco stage which took in 3 major climbs. None of the contenders was able to get away from the others, and 22 riders came into Monaco, driven hard by an Anquetil who had miraculously found incredible stores of energy. It was a track finish and Poulidor should have won, but he sprinted too early, not realizing that there was another lap to ride. Anquetil beat Tom Simpson for the stage. Poulidor's missing (and Anquetil's winning) the time bonus for winning the stage would loom very large at the end of the Tour. Anquetil was now in fifth place, 4 minutes, 22 seconds behind Groussard.

Stage 10b was a 20.8-kilometer time trial and Anquetil won it with Poulidor just 36 seconds behind.

Anquetil was relentlessly hunting Groussard and getting closer by the day. The General Classification after the 10b time trial:

1. Georges Groussard

2. Jacques Anquetil @ 1 minute 11 seconds

3. Raymond Poulidor @ 1 minute 42 seconds

4. Federico Bahamontes @ 3 minutes 4 seconds

By the time the Tour came to its rest day in Andorra in the Pyrenees, the only significant change in General Classification was that Bahamontes had dropped to fifth. Good Grand Tour riders always go for a ride on the rest day. The body has become habituated to cycling and a day completely off the bike makes it very difficult to start the next day, the rider's legs are "blocky" and devoid of power. Poulidor and the others dutifully gave their bodies the exercise they needed. Everyone but Anquetil, that is. Jacques liked to enjoy life. He went to a picnic and enjoyed himself on big portions of barbecued lamb and as usual, drank heartily. His director, Raphaël Géminiani, was there and apparently encouraged the drinking.

At the start of the Tour a psychic had predicted that Anquetil would abandon on the fourteenth stage after suffering an accident. Anquetil could be a coolly rational man but he took this prediction seriously. It's thought that he behaved in this self-destructive way at the barbecue because he believed he would probably not finish the stage the following day.

The next day, stage 14, Party Boy didn't even bother to warm up. Poulidor's manager, Antonin Magne, knew that Anquetil would be vulnerable after his day of excess and instructed Poulidor to drop the hammer on the first climb. The other contenders, including Federico Bahamontes, Julio Jimenez and Henry Anglade, also sensed Anquetil's weakness and poor preparation and attacked furiously. The climbing out of Andorra up the Port d'Envalira, a climb new to the Tour that year, started almost immediately. Anquetil was quickly put out the back door. The hard profile of the day's early kilometers gave Anquetil no chance to warm up. At the top, Anquetil was about 4 minutes behind the leaders and was contemplating quitting. He had even loosened his toe-straps.

One of his *domestiques*, Louis Rostollan, who had stuck with him on the climb shouted at him, "Have you forgotten that your name is Anquetil? You have no right to quit without a fight!" Team director Géminiani came up to Anquetil and bellowed his rage, screaming at him to chase the leaders, to give it all he had in the descent. The story goes that Géminiani gave Anquetil a bottle with champagne in it. With this restorative circulating in the bon vivant's system, he could now effectively compete.

Anquetil was by now warmed up. He could use his superb descending skill to catch the leaders through the dense fog on the descent.

Into that fog Anquetil went, riding like a man possessed, taking risks no man should take. He used the headlights and brake lights of the following cars to let him know when to slow for corners. He caught the group with Henry Anglade and Georges Groussard and made common cause with them. From the crest of the Envalira it was 150 kilometers to the finish. Given good fortune he had enough time and distance to salvage his Tour. Using his time trialing skills he made it up to the Poulidor/Bahamontes lead group.

With just a few kilometers to go Poulidor flatted and got a new wheel. His mechanic, in a zeal to make sure he didn't lose any more time, pushed Poulidor before he was ready and caused him to crash. By the time Poulidor was up again and riding Anquetil's group was gone. Poulidor came in with the second group, 2 minutes, 36 seconds behind Anquetil.

Here were the standings after that hair-raising adventure:

1. Georges Groussard

2. Jacques Anquetil @ 1 minutes 26 seconds

3. Henry Anglade @ 3 minutes 5 seconds

4. Federico Bahamontes @ 3 minutes 11 seconds

5. André Foucher @ 4 minutes 16 seconds

6. Raymond Poulidor @ 4 minutes 28 seconds

The story of Anquetil's Tour being saved with a bidon of champagne is romantic, but Anquetil's wife Jeanine insisted that it wasn't true.

Poulidor hadn't given up yet. Stage 15 was a ride over the Portet d'Aspet, the Ares and the Portillon. Poulidor won it and gained 1 minute, 43 seconds back from Anquetil.

There was still 1 monumental, monstrous day of climbing left. 1 day remained for the pure climbers to try to reclaim the Tour. There were still 2 time trials left to ride, totaling 70 kilometers where Anquetil could easily wipe out his 86 second deficit. He had only to ride defensively and not lose more time, the usual Anquetil formula. Stage 16 was 197 kilometers long and had the Peyresourde, the Aspin, the Tourmalet and the Aubisque climbs. The road turned upward almost immediately with the slopes of the Peyresourde coming at the fourteenth kilometer. Bahamontes took off after only 4 kilometers, quickly followed by his compatriot Julio Jimenez. When they reached the crest of the Peyresourde, Bahamontes let Jimenez take the lead and the climber's points. Bahamontes was looking for bigger fish than the King of the Mountains. He smelled Yellow. Over the Aspin Bahamontes again let Jimenez take the lead over the top. The Anquetil group was 3 minutes back at this point. At the top of the Tourmalet the Anquetil group was over 5 minutes back. But Bahamontes could not descend well and his lead was halved. On the Aubisque Jimenez could no longer stay with Bahamontes. Alone, Bahamontes soared to a lead of over 6 minutes at the top. Back in the field the Pelforth domestiques were rallying and chasing, trying to defend Groussard's Yellow Jersey. On the run-in to Pau Bahamontes's lead was slowly eroded until it was 1 minute, 54 seconds at the end. Bahamontes had been away for 194 kilometers. It was a wonderful ride, but he hadn't gained enough time to hold off Anquetil in the time trials. With 1 of the time trials the very next day, he was surely toast. And Poulidor? He sat in the entire day, recovering from his stage win the day before. Anquetil noted that if Poulidor should win the Tour that year, he should thank Anquetil for the work he did that day holding Bahamontes in check.

The new General Classification:

1. George Groussard
2. Federico Bahamontes @ 35 seconds
3. Jacques Anquetil @ 1 minute 26 seconds
4. Raymond Poulidor @ 1 minute 35 seconds

And then, what must have seemed to be the inevitable happened. Anquetil won the 42.6-kilometer time trial, beating the day's second place Poulidor by 37 seconds. Bahamontes was twelfth, 4 minutes back. Anquetil was now the leader, ahead of Poulidor by 56 seconds. Bahamontes was third at 3 minutes, 31 seconds. Groussard paid the price defending the Yellow for 10 days, and lost 6 minutes. It was now a 2-man race.

Stage 20, with its finish at the top of the Puy de Dôme, was the scene of the 1964 Tour's most dramatic showdown. The Puy de Dôme is an extinct volcano in the center of France. It has an elevation gain of 515 meters in only 6 kilometers. It averages 9%, but gets steeper as the road approaches the summit. The tenth kilometer is almost 13% before it backs off a bit to between 11 and 12%. The final kilometer is still a tough 10%. With such a hard incline, its total 14 kilometers could transform the Tour. Poulidor was the better climber and a tired Anquetil knew it.

Probably 500,000 spectators lined the roads of the old volcano, sure that there would be fireworks that day. Upon reaching the Puy, Julio Jimenez and Federico Bahamontes took off up the mountain. This was as Anquetil wanted. This break took the time bonuses out of play. Poulidor would be riding for just the time gain he might acquire by beating Anquetil if he were so lucky. Poulidor and Anquetil were otherwise unconcerned about the Spanish escape because neither Jimenez nor Bahamontes would be likely to take the Yellow. They were worried about each other. Instead of sitting on Poulidor's wheel, Anquetil rode next to him trying to gain the psychological edge. Neither felt very well. "I never felt again as bad on a bike," Poulidor said later. Anquetil felt worse.

Anquetil and Poulidor, mano a mano on Puy de Dôme.

As they closed in on the summit, Poulidor attacked and Anquetil stayed with him. "All I cared was that I was directly next to Raymond. I needed to make him think I was as strong as he, to bluff him into not trying harder."

Poulidor attacked again. Anquetil stayed with him. There is a famous picture of Anquetil and Poulidor bumping into each other while climbing the volcano, neither giving in the slightest bit; each trying to cow the other; each riding at his limit.

Passing under the Flamme Rouge (1 kilometer to go flag), Anquetil's attention lapsed for just a moment and he let Poulidor go. There was nothing Anquetil could do. He was spent. Poulidor poured on the gas, racing for the finish line and hoping to erase the 56-second deficit and finally don the Yellow Jersey. He waited at the finish, counting off the seconds.

Anquetil crossed the line, limp with exhaustion, 42 seconds later. He had saved his lead by 14 seconds. Magne, Poulidor's manager, believes that Poulidor could have won the Tour that day if he had used a 42 x 26 as Bahamontes used instead of the 25 that he led Magne to believe was the right choice.

There was the formality of the final time trial in which Anquetil put another 21 seconds between himself and Poulidor. With the time bonus, Anquetil won his astounding fifth Tour de France by 55 seconds over Poulidor.

Poulidor said, "I know now that I can win the Tour."

Final 1964 Tour de France General Classification:

1. Jacques Anquetil (St. Raphaël-Gitane): 127 hours 9 minutes 44 seconds
2. Raymond Poulidor (Mercier-BP) @ 55 seconds
3. Federico Bahamontes (Margnat-Paloma) @ 4 minutes 44 seconds
4. Henry Anglade (Pelforth) @ 6 minutes 42 seconds
5. Georges Groussard (Pelforth) @ 10 minutes 34 seconds
6. André Foucher (Pelforth) @ 10 minutes 36 seconds

Climber's Competition:

1. Federico Bahamontes: 173 points
2. Julio Jimenez: 167 points
3. Raymond Poulidor: 90 points

Points Competition:

1. Jan Janssen: 208 points
2. Edward Sels: 199 points
3. Rudi Altig: 165 points

Glossary

@: In English language race results an ampersand is used to denote the amount of time or number of points behind the winner. In the example below Luis Ocana won the race, taking 6 hours, 51 minutes, 15 seconds to complete the course. Joop Zoetemelk was behind him and crossed the finish line 15 seconds later. Pollentier was still further behind and crossed the line 3 minutes and 34 seconds after Ocana. Van Impe and Thévenet were with Pollentier but slightly behind him. The "s.t." means that they were given the same time as Pollentier. If a rider finishes close enough to a rider who is in front of him so that there is no real gap, he will be given the same time as the first rider of that group. French or Spanish results will use often use "m.t." to denote same time. If no time is given, same time is assumed.

1. Luis Ocana: 6 hr 51 min 50 sec
2. Joop Zoetemelk @ 15 sec
3. Michael Pollentier @ 3 min 34 sec
4. Lucien van Impe s.t.
5. Bernard Thévenet s.t.

Abandon: To quit a race. See also Broom Wagon

Arc-en-ciel: French for rainbow. See Rainbow Jersey

Arrivée: French for the finish line

Arrivée en altitude: French for hilltop finish.

Attack: Generally a sudden acceleration in an attempt to break free of the peloton. On flat roads it is usually done by riding up along the side of the pack so that by the time the attacker passes the peloton's front rider he is traveling too fast for the pack to easily react. In the mountains it is usually enough to accelerate from the front.

Autobus: French. In the mountains the riders with poor climbing skills ride together hoping to finish in time to beat the time limit cutoff. By staying together in a group they hope that if they don't finish in time they can persuade the officials to let them stay in the race because so many riders would otherwise be eliminated. It doesn't always work. Often the group lets a particular experienced racer who knows how to pace the Autobus lead them in order to just get in under the wire. This risky strategy minimizes the energy the riders have to expend. Synonyms include Grupetto (Italian) and Laughing Group. See Time Limit.

Bell Lap: If the riders are racing the final meters of a race on a velodrome or on a circuit in a town, a bell is rung at the start of the final lap.

Bidon: Water bottle. Now made of plastic, early ones were metal with cork stoppers. Until 1950 they were carried on the handlebars, sometimes in pairs. Around 1950 riders started mounting bottle cages on the downtube. The trend to dispensing with the bar-mount cages started in the early 1960s and by 1970 they were a thing of the past. In the early 1980s, as a result of the sport of Triathlon, builders started brazing bosses on the seat tube allowing mechanics to attach a second cage so that riders could again carry 2 bottles.

Bonification: Time bonus (actually time subtracted) awarded to a rider. Stage races vary and the Tour is always tinkering with its rules. Bonifications can be earned several ways: winning or placing in a stage, winning or placing in an intermediate sprint, being among the first riders over a rated climb. The rules have changed over the years. At one time in the early 1930s the Tour awarded a 4-minute time bonus for winning a stage. In 2005 the bonification was 20 seconds.

Bonk: To completely run out of energy. Sometimes a rider will forget to eat or think he has enough food to make it to the finish without stopping to get food. The result can be catastrophic as the rider's body runs out of glycogen, the stored chemical the muscles burn for energy. Famously José-Manuel Fuente didn't eat during the long stage 14 in the 1974 Giro. He slowed to a near halt as his body's ability to produce energy came to a crashing halt. Merckx sped on and took the

Pink Jersey from the Spaniard who had shown such terrible judgment. It's happened to many great riders including Indurain and Armstrong but not always with such catastrophic results. The French term is défaillance but that term can also mean exhaustion or mental failure, such as when Gaul attacked in the Cevannes in the 1958 Tour. Bobet was unable to respond, mostly because he suffered a loss of confidence. This also would be a défaillance.

Break: Short for breakaway.

Breakaway: One or more riders escaping from the front of peloton, usually as the result of a sudden acceleration called an "attack". Riders will work together sharing the effort of breaking the wind hoping to improve their chances of winning by arriving at the finish in a smaller group. This can also be called a "break". Some riders do not possess the necessary speed to contest mass sprints and therefore try very hard to escape the clutches of the peloton well before the end of the race. Franco Bitossi was a master of the lone break even though he possessed a fearsome sprint. Hennie Kuiper won many famous victories this way as well. Sometimes a break will escape during a Tour stage and no team will take responsibility to chase it down. Sometimes the gap results in an unexpected winner as in the case of Roger Walkowiak in 1956. See Chapatte's Law.

Bridge: Short for bridge a gap. To go from one group of cyclists to a break up the road.

Broom Wagon: When Desgrange added high Pyreneen climbs to his 1910 Tour he thought it would be necessary to have a rescue wagon follow the riders in case the mountain roads were beyond their ability to ascend, hence the Broom Wagon to sweep up the exhausted racers. It is still in use, following the last rider in a stage. Today when a rider abandons he usually prefers to get into one of his team cars. Years ago the Broom Wagon had an actual broom bolted to it but today this wonderful bit of symbolism is gone. In the 1910 Tour if a rider could not finish a mountain stage he could restart the next day and compete for stage wins but he was out of the General Classification competition. Today an abandonment sticks. The rider is out of the Tour for that year. Before a rider enters the broom wagon an official removes the dossard or back number on the rider's jersey. In French the Broom Wagon is called the Voiture Balai.

Bunch: When preceded by "the", usually the peloton. Far less often a group of riders can be "a bunch"

Cadence: The speed at which the rider turns the pedals.

Caravan: The long line of vehicles that precede and follow the racers.

Caravan publicitaire: The line of cars and trucks that precedes the race, promoting various companies' goods and services. When Henri Desgrange switched the Tour to using National instead of trade teams, he became responsible for the racers' transport, food and lodging. By charging companies money for the privilege of advertising their goods to the millions of Tour spectators along the route he was able to help pay the new expenses. When the Tour reverted to trade teams the publicity caravan remained.

Category: In Euopean stage racing it is a desgination of the difficulty of a mountain climb. This is a subjective judgment of the difficulty of the ascent, based upon its length, gradient and how late in the stage the climb is to be ridden. A medium difficulty climb that comes after several hard ascents will get a higher rating because the riders will already be tired. The numbering system starts with "4" for the easiest that still rate being called a climb and then with increasing severity they are 3, 2, 1. The most challenging are above categorization, or in the Tour nomenclature, "Hors catégorie", HC. In the Giro the hardest climbs are rated a Category 1.

Chairman Bill McGann: A man mad about bikes. A harmless drudge.

Chapatte's Law: Formulated by former racer and Tour commentator Robert Chapatte, it states that in the closing stages of a race a determined peloton will chase down a break and close in at the rate of 1 minute per 10 kilometers traveled. If a break is 3 minutes up the road the peloton will need to work hard for 30 kilometers to catch it. TV race commentator Paul Sherwen regularly uses Chapatte's Law to come up with his often surprisingly accurate predictions of when a break will be caught.

Circle of Death: In 1910 Desgrange introduced high mountains into the Tour. The big stage with the Peyresourde, Aspin, Tourmalet and Aubisque was called the "Circle of Death" by the press who doubted that the riders could perform the inhuman task that was asked of them. Now the hardest mountain Tour stage is still occasionally called the Circle of Death.

Classic: One of 7 one-day races whose history and prestige will make the career of its winner. They are: Milan–San Remo, Tour of Flanders, Gent–Wevelgem, Paris–Roubaix, Flèche Wallone, Liège–Bastogne– Liège and the Tour of Lombardy. Gent–Wevelgem is traditionally held mid-week between Flanders and Paris–Roubaix. Only Rik Van Looy has won them all. Some writers include a few other races in their list of Classics: Omloop Het Volk, Amstel Gold Race, Rund um den Hernniger Turm, San Sebastian Classic, Championship of Zurich (also called "Züri Metzgete"), Paris–Brussels and Paris–Tours.

Col: French for mountain pass.

Combine: The Tour has had a competiton that uses an aggregate of General Classification, Mountains and Points competitions to arrive at the winner of the Combine category.

Commissaire: A race official with the authority to impose penalties on the riders for infractions of the rules. A common problem is dangerous or irregular sprinting. The commissaire will usually relegate the offending rider to a lower placing.

Contre-la-montre: French for time trial

C.L.M.: French abbreviation for contre-la-montre or time trial.

CLM par équipes: French for team time trial.

Criterium: A bike race around and around a short road road course, often a city block. Good criterium riders have excellent bike handling skills and usually possess lots of power to enable them to constantly accelerate out of the corners. The Dutch and the Belgians are the masters of the event.

Crono: Short for time-trial. See Cronometro, Time Trial.

Cronometro: Italian for time trial. Cronometro individuale is individual time trial and Cronometro a squadre is team time trial.

Cyclamen Jersey: The purple jersey of the points leader in the Giro.

Départ: French for the start line of a race.

Défaillance: French for a total mental or body collapse. See Bonk for more.

Directeur Sportif: The manager of a bike team. Although French, it is the term used in English as well.

DNF: Did not finish. Used in results to denote that the racer started but did not complete the race.

DNS: Did not start. Used in results to denote a racer who was entered in a race but failed to start. Often seen in results in stage races where the rider abandons after the completion of a stage.

Domestique: French. Because bicycle racing is a sport contested by teams and won by individuals a man designated to be the team leader has his teammates work for him. These men have been called domestiques since Tour founder Henri Desgrange used it as a term of contempt for Maurice Brocco whom he believed was selling his services to aid other riders in the 1911 Tour. Today the term has lost its bad connotation and serves as an acknowledgement of the true nature of racing tactics. Domestiques will chase down competitors and try to neutralize their efforts, they will protect their team leader from the wind by surrounding him. When a leader has to get a repair or stop to answer nature his domestiques will stay with him and pace him back up to the peloton. They are sometimes called "water carriers" because they are the ones designated to go back to the team car and pick up water bottles and bring them back up to the leader. In Italian the term is "gregario".

Dossard: French for the rider's race number on the back of his jersey.

Drafting: At racing speed a rider who is only a few inches behind another bike does about 30% less work. Riding behind another rider in his aerodynamic slipstream is called drafting. This is the basic fact of bike racing tactics and why a rider will not just leave the peloton and ride away from the others, no matter how strong he is. Only in the rarest of cases can a racer escape a determined chasing peloton. To make an escape work he needs the pack to be disinterested in chasing for some length of time so that he can gain a large enough time gap. Then, when the sleeping pack is aroused they do not have enough time to catch him no matter how fast they chase. Hugo Koblet's wonderful solo escape in the 1951 Tour is one of the rare instances when a solo rider outdid a determined group of elite chasers. A rider who drafts others and refuses to go to the front and do his share of the work is said to be "sitting on." There are a number of pejorative terms for a rider who does this, the best known is "wheelsucker".

Drop: When a rider cannot keep up with his fellow riders and comes out of their aerodynamic slipstream, whether in a break or in the peloton, he is said to be dropped.

Échappée: French for breakaway

Echelon: When the riders are hit with a side wind they must ride slightly to the right or left of the rider in front in order to remain in that rider's slipstream, instead of riding nose to tail in a straight line. This staggered line puts those riders further back in the pace line in the gutter. Because they can't edge further to the side, they have to take more of the brunt of both the wind and the wind drag of their forward motion. Good riders then form a series of echelons so that all the racers can contribute and receive shelter.

Équipe: French for team

Escape: When used as a noun it is a breakaway. When used as a verb it is the act of breaking away.

Ètape: French for stage.

Feed zone: The specific point along a race route where the riders pick up food and drink. Racing etiquette generally keeps racers from attacking at this point, but there have been some famous initiatives that have started while the riders were having musettes (bags) of food handed up. In 1987 a carefully crafted plot to attack Jean-Francois Bernard who was then in Yellow was executed by Charly Mottet and his Systeme U team. They informed Stephen Roche and Pedro Delgado of their plans so that there would be enough horsepower to carry it through, which they did.

Field: See Peloton

Field Sprint: The race at the finish for the best placing among those in the peloton. The term is usually used when a breakaway has successfully escaped and won the stage and the peloton is reduced to fighting for the remaining lesser places.

Fixed gear: A direct drive between the rear wheel and the cranks. The rear cog is locked onto the rear hub so that the rider cannot coast. When the rear wheel turns, the crank turns. Because this is the most efficient of all possible drive trains riders in the early days of cycle racing preferred fixed gears to freewheels. When the Tour added mountains in 1905 the riders had to mount freewheels so that they could coast down the descents; otherwise their velocity was limited by their leg speed. Track bikes use fixed gears.

Flamme Rouge: French. A red banner placed at the beginning of the final kilometer of a race.

Flyer: Usually a solo breakaway near the end of a race.

Fugue: French for breakaway

GC: General Classification

General Classification: The ranking of the accumulated time or placings, whichever basis the race uses to determine its winner. The Tour (since 1913) and the Giro use time. Lance Armstrong was the winner in the General Classification for all Tours between 1999 and 2005. See Stage Race.

Giro d'Italia: A 3-week stage race, like the Tour de France. It is held in Italy, traditionally in May. It was first run in 1909.

Grand Tour: There are three Grand Tours, all lasting 3 weeks: the Tour de France, the Giro d'Italia and the Vuelta a España.

Green Jersey: In the Tour, awarded to the leader of the Points Competition (except 1968 when the Points Jersey was red). In the Giro, the leading climber wears a green jersey.

Grimpeur: French for a rider who climbs well. Italian is scalatore.

Gruppo: Italian, literally, "group". In road racing it is the peloton. When they are all together without any active breakaways, it is "gruppo compatto". When referring to the bicycle "gruppo" means the core set of components made by a single manufacturer, such as a Campagnolo Gruppo.

HD: 1. The intials of Henri Desgrange, the father of the Tour de France. For years the Yellow Jersey had a stylized "HD" to commemorate Desgrange's memory. Sadly, to make room for commercial sponsors Desgrange's intitals were removed from the Yellow Jersey. 2. Hors délais or finishing outside the time limit. See time limit.

Hilltop finish: When a race ends at the top of a mountain, the rider with the greater climbing skills has the advantage. It used to be that the finish line was far from the last climb, allowing the bigger, more powerful riders to use their weight and strength to close the gap to the climbers on the descents and flats. The Tour introduced hilltop finishes in 1952 and did it with a vengeance ending stages at the top of L'Alpe d'Huez, Sestrières and Puy de Dôme. In order to reduce Anquetil's advantage in the time trials and flatter stages the 1963 Tour moved the finish lines closer to the last climbs of the day, further helping the purer climbers.

Hook: To extend an elbow or thigh in the way of another rider, usually during a sprint, to impede his progress while he is attempting to pass. Often it is said that a rider "threw a hook". Means the same thing.

Hors-délais: French. See time limit

Hot Spot: See intermediate sprint

Individuel: French. Independent rider in the Tour. See Touriste-Routier

Intermediate sprint: To keep the race active there may be points along the race course where the riders will sprint for time bonuses or other prizes (premiums, or "preems"). Sometimes called "Hot Spots".

Isolés: A class of independent rider in the Tour. See Touriste-Routier

ITT: Individual time trial

Jump: A rider with the ability to quickly accelerate his bike is said to have a good "jump".

Kermesse: A lap road race much like a criterium but the course is longer, as long as 10 kilometers.

King of the Mountains: Winner of the Grand Prix de la Montagne. In 1933 the Tour de France started awarding points for the first riders over certain hard climbs, the winner of the competition being the King of the Mountains. In 1975 the Tour started awarding the distinctive polka-dot jersey or maillot a pois to the leader of the classification. The first rider to wear the dots was the Dutch racer Joop

Zoetemelk. The classification has lost some of its magic in recent years because of the tactics riders use to win it. Today a rider wishing to win the KOM intentionally loses a large amount of time in the General Classification. Then when the high mountains are climbed the aspiring King can take off on long breakaways to be first over the mountains without triggering a panicked chase by the Tour GC contenders.

KOM: King of the Mountains

Lanterne Rouge: French for the last man in the General Classification. Some years riders will actually compete to be the Lanterne Rouge because of the fame it brings and therefore better appearance fees at races.

Laughing Group: See Autobus

Loi Chapatte: See Chapatte's Law.

Maglia Rosa: Italian, see Pink Jersey.

Maillot a Pois: French for Polka Dot jersey awarded to the King of the Mountains.

Maillot Blanc: White Jersey. Currently worn by the best rider under 25. In the 1970s white was worn by the Combine leader.

Maillot Jaune: See Yellow Jersey.

Maillot Vert: French for Green Jersey. In the Tour de France it is worn by the leader of the points competition.

Massed Start Road Race: All the riders start at the same time This is different from a time trial where the riders are set off individually at specific time intervals.

Mechanical: A problem with the function of a racer's bicycle, usually not a flat tire. Because rules have sometimes been in place that prevent rider's changing bikes unless a mechanical problem is present mechanics have manufactured mechanicals. In the 1963 Tour de France Anquetil's manager Géminiani cut one of Anquetil's gear cables so that he could give him a lighter bike to ascend the Forclaz.

Minute Man: In a time trial the rider who starts a minute ahead. It's always a goal in a time trial to try to catch one's minute-man.

Musette: A cloth bag containing food and drinks handed up to the rider in the feed zone. It has a long strap so the rider can slip his arm through it easily on the fly, then put the strap over his shoulder to carry it while he transfers the food to his jersey pockets.

M.T.: French for même temps or same time; Spanish for mismo tiempo. See "@"

National Team: From 1930 to 1961, and 1967 and 1968 the Tour was organized under a National Team format. The riders rode for their country or region. See Trade Teams.

Natural or nature break: Because races can take over 7 hours the riders must occasionally dismount to urinate. If the riders are flagrant and take no care to be discreet while they answer the call of nature they can be penalized. Charly Gaul lost the 1957 Giro when he was attacked while taking such a break so he later learned to urinate on the fly.

Off the back: To be dropped.

Paceline: Riders riding nose to tail saving energy by riding in each others slipstream. Usually the front rider does the hard work for a short while, breaking the wind for the others, and then peels off to go to the back so that another rider can take a short stint at the front. The faster the riders go the greater the energy saving gained by riding in the slipstream of the rider in front. When the action is hot and the group wants to move fast the front man will take a short, high-speed "pull" at the front before dropping off. At lower speeds the time at the front is usually longer. See echelon

Palmarès: French for an athlete's list of accomplishments.

Parcours: The race course.

Pavé: French for a cobblestone road. Riding the pavé requires skill and power. Some riders such as the legendary Roger de Vlaeminck can seem to almost glide over the stones knowing exactly what line to take to avoid trouble. De Vlaeminck, who won the Paris–Roubaix 4 times, rarely flatted in this race famous for its terrible cobbles because of his extraordinary ability to pick his way over the tough course while riding at high speed.

Peloton: The main group of riders traveling together in a race. Breaks leave the front of it, dropped riders exit its rear. Synonyms: bunch, group, field, pack.

Pink Jersey: Worn by the rider who is currently leading in the General Classification in the Giro d'Italia. It was chosen because the sponsoring newspaper La Gazzetta dello Sport is printed on pink paper.

Podium: The top three places, first, second and third. Many racers know that they cannot win a race and thus their ambition is limited to getting on the podium. In major races such as the Tour and the Giro, attaining the podium is such a high accomplishment that it almost makes a racer's career.

Poinçonnées: Riders in early Tours who had their bikes hallmarked or stamped so that the officials could know that the competitors started and finished with the same bike.

Point Chaud: French for Hot Spot. See intermediate sprint.

Points: The usual meaning is the accumulation of placings in each stage. Today the Tour gives more points to the flatter stages so the the winner of the points competition is a more likely to be sprinter. See General Classification. In the Tour the Points leader wears a green jersey, in the Giro he dons a purple jersey.

Polka-Dot Jersey: Awarded to the King of the Mountains

Prologue: French. An introductory stage in a stage race that is usually a short individual time trial, normally under 10 kilometers. The Tour has also used a team time trial format in the Prologue.

Pull: A stint at the front of a paceline.

Purple Jersey: In the Giro a purple, or more specificlly cyclamen, jersey is awarded to the leader of the points competition.

Rainbow Jersey: The reigning world champion in a particular cycling event gets to wear a white jersey with rainbow stripes. The championships for most important events are held in the Fall. A former World Champion gets to wear a jersey with rainbow trim on his sleeves and collar. If a World Champion becomes the leader of the Tour, Giro or Vuelta he will trade his Rainbow Jersey for the Leader's Jersey. In the 1975 Tour after Thevenet defeated Merckx on the climb to Pra Loup, Merckx gave up his Yellow Jersey to Thevenet and wore his Rainbow Jersey the rest of the Tour.

Revitaillement: French for taking on food and drink, usually in the feed zone. Contrôl de revitaillement is French for the Feed Zone.

Rouleur: French for a rider who can turn a big gear with ease over flat roads. Rouleurs are usually bigger riders who suffer in the mountains.

Routier: French for road racer.

Same time: See "@"

Soigneur: Today a job with many duties involving the care of the riders: massage, preparing food, handing up musettes in the feed zone and sadly, doping. Usually when a doping scandal erupts the soigneurs are deeply involved.

Souvenir Henri Desgrange: A prize to the first rider of the highest summit of the Tour. In 2005 the Tour awarded Alexandre Vinokourov a 5,000 Euro purse when he was first over that year's highest point, the 2,645-meter high Galibier. In 1974 it was also the Galibier and the prize of 2,000 Francs was won by Spanish climbing ace Vicente Lopez-Carril.

Sprint: At the end of a race the speeds get ever higher until in the last couple of hundred meters the fastest riders jump out from the peloton in an all-out scramble for the finish line. Teams with very fine sprinting specialists will employ a "lead-out train". With about 5 kilometers to go these teams will try to take control of the race by going to the front and stepping up the speed of the race in order to discourage last-minute flyers. Sometimes 2 or 3 competing teams will set up parallel pace lines. Usually the team's train will be a pace line organized in ascending speed of the riders. As the team's riders take a pull and peel off the next remaining rider will be a quicker rider who can keep increasing the speed. Usually the last man before the team's designated sprinter is a fine sprinter who will end up with a good placing by virtue of being at the front of the race in the final meters and having a good turn of speed himself.

S.T.: Same time. See "@"

Stage race: A cycling competition involving 2 or more separate races involving the same riders with the results added up to determine the winner. Today the victor is usually determined by adding up the accumulated time each rider took to complete each race, called a "stage". The one with the lowest aggregate time is the winner. Alternatively the winner can be selected by adding up the rider's placings, giving 1 point for first, 2 points for second, etc. The rider with the lowest total is the winner. The Tour de France used a points system between 1905 and 1912 because the judging was simpler and cheating could be reduced. Because points systems tend to cause dull racing during most of the stage with a furious sprint at the end they are rarely used in determining the overall winner. Because points systems favor sprinters most important stage races have a points competition along with the elapsed time category. In the Tour de France the leader in time wears the Yellow Jersey and the Points leader wears green. In the Giro the time leader wears pink and the man ahead in points wear purple or more accurately "cyclamen". The race's ranking of its leaders for the overall prize is called the General Classification, or GC. It is possible, though rare, for a rider to win the overall race without ever winning an individual stage.

Stayer: A rouleur

Switchback: In order to reduce the gradient of a mountain ascent the road engineer has the road go back and forth up or down the hill. The Stelvio climb is famous for its 48 switchbacks as is L'Alpe d'Huez for its 21. In Italian the term is Tornante.

Team time trial: See time trial. Instead of an individual rider, whole teams set off along a specific distance at intervals. It is a spectacular event because the teams go all out on the most advanced aerodynamic equipment and clothing available. To maximize the slipstream advantage the riders ride nose to tail as close to each other as possible. Sometimes a smaller front wheel is used on the bikes to get the riders a few valuable centimeters closer together. With the riders so close together, going so fast and at their physical limits, crashes are common. Some teams targeting an overall win practice this event with rigor and the result is a beautifully precise fast-moving team that operates almost as if they were 1 rider. Sometimes a team with a very powerful leader who is overly ambitious will shatter his team by making his turns at the front too fast for the others. Skilled experienced leaders take longer rather than faster pulls so that their teammates can rest.

Technical: Usually refers to a difficult mountain descent or time trial course on winding city streets, meaning that the road will challenge the rider's bike handling skills.

Tempo: Usually means riding at a fast but not all-out pace. Teams defending a leader in a stage race will often go to the front of the peloton and ride tempo for days on end in order to discourage break-aways. It is very tiring work and usually leaves the domestiques of a winning team exhausted at the end of a Grand Tour.

Tifosi: Italian sports fans, sometimes fanatical in their devotion to an athlete or team. The term is said to be derived from the delirium of Typhus patients.

Time Bonus: see Bonification

Time Limit: To encourage vigorous riding the Tour imposes a cutoff time limit. If a racer does not finish a stage by that time limit, he is eliminated from the race. This prevents a racer's resting by riding leisurely one day and winning the next. The time limit is a percentage of the stage winner's time. Because it is the intention of the Tour to be fair, the rules are complex. On flat stages where the riders have less trouble staying with the peloton and the time gaps are smaller, the percentage added to the winners' time is smaller. On a flat stage it can be as little as 105% of the winner's time if the speed is less than 34 kilometers an hour. In the mountain stages it can be as high as 117% of the winner's time. The faster the race is run, the higher the percentage of the winner's time allowed the slower riders. The Tour has 6 sets of percentage time limits, each a sliding scale according to the type of stage (flat, rolling, mountain, time trial, etc.) and the stage's speed. If 20% of the peloton fails to finish within the time limit the rule can be suspended. Also riders who have unusual trouble can appeal to the commissaires for clemency. More than once Paul Sherwen, now a television racing commentator, was given special dispensation for riding courageously when he had suffered misfortune but bravely continued and yet finished outside the time limit.

Time trial: A race in which either an individual or team rides over a specific distance against the clock. It is intended to be an unpaced ride in which either the individual or team is not allowed to draft a competitor. The riders are started at specific intervals, usually 2 minutes.

In the Tour the riders are started in reverse order of their standing in the General Classification, the leader going last. Usually the last 20 riders are set off at 3-minute intervals. If a rider catches a racer who started ahead of him the rules say that he must not get into his slipstream but must instead pass well to the slower rider's side. This is one of the more often ignored rules in cycling. The Tour's first time trial was in 1934.

Touriste-Routier: A class of riders in early Tours who did not ride on a team and were entirely responsible for their own lodging, food and equipment. Various classes of independent or "individuel" and "isolé" riders persisted through 1937. As with all aspects of the Tour, the rules and designations regarding the riders constantly changed. Generally the best riders rode on teams. The best independent performance was Mario Vicini's second place in the 1937 Tour.

Track: See Velodrome

Trade team: A team sponsored by a commercial entity. Until the mid-1950's, cycle team sponsorship was limited to companies within the bicycle industry. That changed in 1954 when Fiorenzo Magni's bicycle manufacturer fell into financial difficulty. Magni was able to supplement the shortfall by getting the Nivea cosmetic company to sponsor his team. The move was initially resisted but it is now the standard. Bicycle companies do not have the monetary resources to finance big-time racing teams. Because the Tour organization suspected collusion between the various trade teams the Tour banished them from 1930 to 1961, and 1967 and 1968. During those years the teams were organized under a national and regional team format. Riders rode for their country, such as France or Italy, or if need be to fill out the race's roster, regions such as Ile de France.

TTT: Team time trial

Transfer: Usually a Tour stage will end in a city one afternoon and start the next morning from the same city. When a stage ends in one city and the next stage starts in another, the riders must be transferred by bus, plane or train to the next day's starting city. This schedule is normally done so that both the finish and start city can pay the Tour organization for the privilege of hosting the Tour. The racers loathe transfers because this delays their massages, eating and resting.

UCI: The governing world body of cycling, the Union Cycliste Internationale.

Velodrome: A oval bicycle racing track with banked curves. They can be sited either indoors or outdoors. Olympic tracks are usually 333 1/3 meters around but indoor ones are smaller and have correspondingly steeper banking. Some road races like Paris–Roubaix have the riders ride onto the velodrome and finish after a couple of laps on the track. In the past the Tour would regularly do this, often with the rider's time being clocked as he entered the velodrome. With a 200-man field in modern Tours this is impractical.

Virtual Yellow Jersey: Not the leader of the Tour in fact. When a rider has a large enough lead on the Tour leader, so that if the race were to be ended at that very moment he would assume the leadership, he then is called the Virtual Yellow Jersey.

Virtuel Maillot Jaune: French for Virtual Yellow Jersey

Voiture Balai: French. See Broom Wagon.

Washboard: A rough riding surface with small bumps or irregularities. Like the pavé, riding on washboard requires a lot of power and puts the smaller riders with less absolute power at their disposal at a disadvantage.

White Jersey: See Maillot Blanc

Yellow Jersey: Worn by the rider who is leading in the General Classification in the Tour de France. Traditional history says that Eugène Christophe was awarded the first Yellow Jersey on the rest day between stages 10 and 11 during the 1919. It is further believed that Yellow was chosen because the pages of the sponsoring newspaper *L'Auto* was printed on yellow paper. Both may not be true. Philippe Thys says that he was given a Yellow Jersey by Tour founder Desgrange during the 1913 Tour. And Yellow may have been chosen because jerseys of that color were unpopular and therefore cheap and easy to get.

Bibliography

Books marked * are highly recommended.

*Lance Armstrong: *It's Not About the Bike: My Journey Back to Life*. New York, Berkley Books, 2000

Lance Armstrong: *Every Second Counts*. New York, Broadway Books, 2003

Samuel Abt: *Breakaway, On the Road with the Tour de France*. New York, Random House, 1985

David Armstrong: *Merckx: Man and Myth*. Silsden, England, Kennedy Brothers Publishing, undated

Don Alexander and Jim Ochowicz: *Tour de France '86 The American Invasion*. South Pasadena, Alexander and Alexander Publishers. 1985

Philippe Brunel: *An Intimate Portrait of the Tour de France, Masters and Slaves of the Road*. Denver, Colorado, Buonpane Publications. 1995

Daniel Coyle: *Lance Armstrong's War*. New York, Harper Collins, 2004

Martin Dugard: *Chasing Lance*. New York, Little, Brown and Company, 2005

Jacques Duniecq: *1972 Tour de France*. Silsden, England, Kennedy Brothers Publishing, Ltd. 1972

Peter Duker: *Tour de France 1978*. Silsden, England, Kennedy Brothers Publishing, Ltd. 1978

Graeme Fife: *Tour de France. The History, the Legend, the Riders*. Edinburgh, Mainstream Publishing Company. 1999.

William Fotheringham: *A Century of Cycling*. St. Paul, MN. MBI Publishing. 2003

Godaert, Janssens, Cammaert: *Tour Encyclopedie* (7 volumes) Gent, Belgium, Uitgeverij Worldstrips. 1997

*L'Equipe: *The Official Tour de France Centennial 1903–2003*. London, UK. Weidenfeld & Nicolson. 2004

N.G. Henderson: *Fabulous Fifties*. Silsden, England. Kennedy Brothers Publishing, Ltd. Undated

N.G. Henderson: *Yellow Jersey*. Silsden, England. Kennedy Brothers Publishing, Ltd. Undated

*Marguerite Lazell: *The Tour de France, An Illustrated History*. Buffalo, NY. Firefly Books. 2003

Eddy Merckx: *The Fabulous World of Cycling*. Belgium, Editions Andre Grisard. 1982

Pierre Martin: *The Bernard Hinault Story*. Keighley, UK, Kennedy Brothers Publishing, Ltd. 1982

*Owen Mulholland: *Uphill Battle*. Boulder, Colorado, Velopress. 2003

Owen Mulholland: Various essays published over the years

Sven Novrup: *A Moustache, Poison and Blue Glasses!* London, UK. Bromley Books. 1999

*Peter Nye: *Hearts of Lions*. New York. W.W. Norton Company. 1988

*Jean-Paul Ollivier: *Maillot Jaune*. Boulder, Colorado, Velopress. 2001

Bob Roll: *The Tour de France Companion*. New York, Workman Publishing. 2004

Jacques Seray: *1904, the Tour de France Which Was to Be the Last*. Boulder, Colorado, Buonpane Publications. 1994.

James Staart: *Tour de France—Tour de Force*. San Francisco, Chronicle Books. 2003.

David Saunders: *1973 Tour de France*. Silsden, England, Kennedy Brothers Publishing, Ltd. 1973

David Saunders: *Tour de France 1974*. Silsden, England, Kennedy Brothers Publishing, Ltd. 1974

Pascal Sergent: *100 Anni di Storia del Tour de France*. Milan, Italy, SEP Editrice, 2003

Pascal Sergent: *Paris–Roubaix*. London, UK. Bromley Books. 1997

JB Wadley: *Eddy Merckx and the 1970 Tour de France*. Silsden, England, Kennedy Brothers Publishing. Undated

Geoffrey Wheatcroft: *Le Tour. A History of the Tour de France*. London, UK. Simon & Schuster. 2003

*John Wilcockson: *23 Days in July*. Cambridge, MA, Da Capo Press, 2004

*Les Woodland: *The Crooked Path to Victory*. San Francisco, Cycle Publishing, 2003

*Les Woodland: *The Unknown Tour de France*. San Francisco, Van der Plas Publications, 2000

*Les Woodland: *The Yellow Jersey Companion to the Tour de France*. London, Yellow Jersey Press, 2003

Les Woodland: *This Island Race*. Norwich, UK, Mousehold Press, 2005

Magazines: Various issues of *Velonews*, *Pro Cycling*, *Cycle Sport*, *Bicisport*, *Bicyclist*

Websites

www.memoire-du-cyclisme.net

http://homepage.ntlworld.com/veloarchive/races/tour/index.htm

www.dailypeloton.com

www.letour.fr

www.torelli.com

www.cyclingnews.com

www.radsport-news.com

www.gazzetta.it (the website of La Gazzetta dello Sport)

Conversations, letters and e-mails over the years with the following generous people, not in any particular order: Owen Mulholland, Les Woodland, Fiorenzo Magni, Giorgio Albani, Marcel Tinazzi, Felice Gimondi, Frankie Andreu, Joe Lindsey, Steve Lubanski, Celestino Vercelli, Paolo Guerciotti, Valeria Paoletti, Antonio and Mauro Mondonico, Faliero Masi, Rene Moser, Derek Roberts, Franco Bitossi, Ferdy Kübler. Thank you all so much.

Memories of stories told to me over the years of my career by the many people in the bike industry whom I have had the good fortune to meet.

Index